MW00983836

BEHIND THE LINES

BEHIND THE LINES

A Critical Survey of
Special Operations
in World War II

MICHAEL F. DILLEY

CASEMATE
Philadelphia & Oxford

Published in the United States of America and Great Britain in 2013 by
CASEMATE PUBLISHERS
908 Darby Road, Havertown, PA 19083
and
10 Hythe Bridge Street, Oxford, OX1 2EW

Copyright 2013 © Michael F. Dilley

ISBN 978-1-61200-183-8
Digital Edition: ISBN 978-1-61200-184-5

Cataloging-in-publication data is available from the Library of Congress and
the British Library.

All rights reserved. No part of this book may be reproduced or transmitted in
any form or by any means, electronic or mechanical including photocopying,
recording or by any information storage and retrieval system, without permission
from the Publisher in writing.

10 9 8 7 6 5 4 3 2 1

Printed and bound in the United States of America.

For a complete list of Casemate titles please contact:

CASEMATE PUBLISHERS (US)
Telephone (610) 853-9131, Fax (610) 853-9146
E-mail: casemate@casematepublishing.com

CASEMATE PUBLISHERS (UK)
Telephone (01865) 241249, Fax (01865) 794449
E-mail: casemate-uk@casematepublishing.co.uk

CONTENTS

Dedicated to the Scouts, Raiders, Rangers,
Paratroopers, and Special Operators
of the United States—
Past, Present, and Future—
with great respect

It is not the critic who counts, not the one who points out how the strong man stumbled or how the doer of deeds might have done them better. The credit belongs to the man who is actually in the arena; whose face is marred with sweat and dust and blood; who strives valiantly; who errs and comes short again and again; who knows the great enthusiasm, the great devotions, and spends himself in a worthy cause; who, if he wins, knows the triumph of high achievement; and who, if he fails, at least fails while daring greatly, so that his place shall never be with those cold and timid souls who know neither victory nor defeat.

—THEODORE ROOSEVELT

...I heard the voice of the Lord saying, *"Who shall I send and who will go for us?"* Then I said, "Here am I, send me."

—ISAIAH, 6:8

Acknowledgments

No book is ever written in a vacuum or by one person exclusively. Someone always helps. In my case, the list is long and it goes back a few years. Although many chapters here appeared in other publications, I first conceived of the idea for this book in 1997. Obviously, some of the people I am thanking here may not have the same positions they had when they helped me. Nonetheless, I will list them as they were when I contacted them. If I have forgotten anyone, I apologize—my intent is to include everyone who helped with this book.

I owe my first big thanks to Gary and Mike Linderer, the founders and publishers of *Behind The Lines* magazine, who gave my writing a big boost by publishing my articles and book reviews in that excellent, but now gone, magazine. During the years the magazine was published, Gary raised my status from contributor to staff writer and senior editor. Gary even agreed to let me steal my title from the magazine, after I described the project.

Any writer's biggest resources are the wonderful people who work in libraries, archives, and museums. One of the earliest guys to help me in my research was Rich Boylen, then an Archive Research Specialist, U.S. National Archives, Suitland, Maryland. He showed me how to find things in the archives, made suggestions on some items that I later used for research, and spent a lot of time just talking with me about my projects; his knowledge of the archives material at Suitland was remarkable. Two guys who were helpful in making suggestions for research sources or for providing me with copies of items are Kevin Mahoney and Peter Wells.

Several members of the staff of *Infantry* magazine were helpful in finding and providing me with copies of articles or research papers from the library of The Infantry School, Fort Benning, Georgia. Terry Van Meter, then Chief of the Museum Division at Fort Riley, Kansas and Herbert Garcia, then Chief of the Museum for Sixth Army and the Presidio of San Francisco, San Francisco, California provided several suggestions for where I could locate material. Pat Tugwell, then with the Pentagon Library in Washington, DC helped me with obtaining copies of items I was trying to find and also offered suggestions for material.

Beverly McMaster, then in the Research Division, Donovan Technical Library, Fort Benning, and Karla Norman, then in the Research Department, Fort Leavenworth, Kansas went out of their way to make copies of material available to me on loan and even made suggestions about where I might find some items. Roxanne Merritt, then a Research Specialist for the John F. Kennedy Special Warfare Museum, Fort Bragg, North Carolina found copies of articles and research papers, made them available to me on loan, and even arranged a photo shoot so I could have a photograph of a modern Special Forces soldier rigged for rough terrain jumping. Delores E. Oplinger, then with the U.S. Army Signal Corps Museum, Fort Gordon, Georgia was extremely helpful in providing me with information concerning Army radios used in World War II.

Dr. John Partin, then Command Historian, U.S. Special Operations Command, MacDill Air Force Base, Florida and Dr. Richard Thomas, Command Historian, U.S. Army Special Operations Command, Fort Bragg helped me locate some people to interview, provided suggestions and copies of taped interviews I conducted with their assistance, and made available articles and video tapes for my temporary use. Dr. John P. Finnegan, then Command Historian, U.S. Army Intelligence and Security Command, Fort Belvoir, Virginia was instrumental in locating photographic material for me.

Two people I worked with while I was still a Federal Government employee, Mike Jensen and Kathy Hewitt, were very helpful with suggestions on organizing some of my material and even made suggestions about the appendices. Photographs are credited individually in their captions and I thank everyone who assisted me by providing pictures from their personal collections or who helped me obtain them from official sources, especially the U.S. National Archives. In addition, where military insignia are shown, the insignia is from my personal collection and, unless credited otherwise, I took the photos of them. My sister-in-law, Kathy Domenoski, helped me with a problem I was having with the Index.

Peter de Lotz in London is a bookseller extraordinaire. He sold me at least half of the books in my bibliography over the years. He also introduced me, in letters, to some of the survivors of the Tragino Aqueduct raid (Chapter 1). Because I was able to use his name with them by way of introduction, those survivors were then willing to let me interview them by letter.

Several people in the publishing world provided assistance and support for my work. George Wheeler, formerly with Pathfinder Publishing, made helpful suggestions on some of my material. Mark Gatlin, formerly with the Naval Institute Press, suggested that I look at including material beyond just telling what happened on each operation; this turned me to considering adding material of a critical nature. Sam Southworth, formerly with Sarpedon Publishing, was supportive of my writing and made suggestions about some operations I had not considered as well as comments on organization.

Several other writers over the years have helped me with my writing and with other ideas. I have already mentioned Gary Linderer, who helped in many other ways over the years, encouraging my writing and then promoting it. Two very excellent military history writers, George Cholewczynski and John Dwyer, made suggestions on my material that were very helpful. George also helped with organizational suggestions and very valuable editing assistance. Lance Zedric, my partner in writing on *Elite Warriors* and several military history articles, has continued to be supportive of me over the years, as has Russ Blaise at the Alamo Scouts Historical Foundation. Russ was also instrumental in loaning me some photographic material for my use. Other senior editors and staff writers at *Behind The Lines* were very supportive of my writing and I want to single out four of them for thanks: Kenn Miller, Kregg Jorgenson, Rob Krott, and Larry Chambers. Les Hughes, who I consider to be an authority on military insignia of special units, was helpful with suggestions, reference material, photographs, and encouragement, as was Harry Pugh, the driving force and publisher of the Chute & Dagger newsletter, who is another authority on the military insignia of special units. Dan Cragg, a writer of both military history and science fiction (with a military twist), was always available to bounce ideas off while we worked together at Phoenix Consulting Group. Dan also asked Lee Lanning to write the Foreword to this book, and I am grateful to both of them. Finally, Jack Schafer, former FBI Special Agent, writer, lecturer, and university professor, who was also a co-worker of mine at Phoenix Consulting, has been incredibly supportive of my work, helping me with ideas and editing what I thought was my final product.

At Casemate Publishers, I want to thank David Farnsworth, the publisher, and Steven Smith, head of the editorial office. In the editorial office,

I want to thank Tara Lichterman for her administrative support, and especially Libby Braden for all of her hard work and editing support. Finally, thanks to everyone else at Casemate whose names I don't know who helped work on this book. Steven Smith, by the way, was the publisher and guiding light at Sarpedon Publishers, who published the anthology *Great Raids in History*, which contained an article I wrote.

Thanks to my family and all my friends who have encouraged and supported all of my writing efforts.

I have saved the best for last although she is never last in my thoughts. My wife, Sue, has supported my writing over the years with ideas and suggestions, and what I am sure was mind-numbing editorial work. She always made what I had better, sometimes just by asking a question.

To each and all of you, I owe more than just what a simple thanks can adequately express.

— MICHAEL F. DILLEY

Foreword

A rmies of all times have recognized the need for "elite" or "special" troops. By simple definition, *elites* has come to refer to carefully screened individuals, usually volunteers, who undergo grueling physical and mental rites of passage to advance from ordinary servicemen into specialized operatives. These individuals receive sophisticated instruction and access to the latest weaponry far beyond the standard levels for traditional infantrymen. As both individuals and units, they earn and wear special uniforms, insignia, headgear, or footwear—all of which add to the mystique of the elite warriors and makes them instantly recognizable.

As a young second lieutenant, I was privileged to attend the U. S. Army Infantry Center's Ranger School and then later, as a captain, to serve as an instructor in the Ranger Department where training is as close to combat as any soldier can experience outside a war zone. As both student and teacher, I learned that select men with intense training and good equipment can accomplish all but impossible goals.

I found this observation to be accurate throughout the next twenty years that I spent in uniform, just as it had since men first divided into opposing sides. As early as 1000 AD, the Chinese military observer Ho Yen-Hsi wrote about elite units, stating, "Nothing is more important in the tactics of winning battles than to employ them." Ho Yen-Hsi then recorded the names of some of the elites such as "Gallants," "Sword Friends," "Fate Deciders," "Leapers and Agitators," and—my personal favorite—"Dissolvers of Difficult."

Famed French Marshal Maurice de Saxe included in his thought on military affairs, written in 1732, that discipline and training are as important as will and purpose. According to Saxe, "It is better to have a small number of well-kept and well disciplined troops than to have a great number who are

13

neglected in these matters. It is not big armies that win battles, it is good ones."

After completing my first two military history books about my personal experiences in combat—*The Only War We Had: A Platoon Leader's Journal* and *Vietnam 1969–1970: A Company Commander's Journal*—I turned my attention to the men of special units who earn the respect of friends and fear from foes as they risk all for cause, country, and their fellow soldiers. I wrote *Inside the LRRPs: Rangers in Vietnam* and *Inside Force Recon: Recon Marines in Vietnam* to record the feats of these elite units in Southeast Asia. I later expanded my study of U. S. special operations to include Delta Force, SEALs, paratroopers, and others in *Blood Warriors: American Military Elites.*

I am especially honored to write a foreword to this book about the "good ones"—a work that further broadens the study of special purpose and special mission organizations during the timeframe of World War II. Michael F. Dilley combines the stories of both Allies and Axis special units in the major theatres, including North Africa, Europe, the CBI, and the Pacific. More importantly he shows that special men willing to perform extraordinary deeds are not limited to a single army or country. Dilley covers experiences of elites from the United States, Great Britain, the Soviet Union, Australia, Japan, Germany, India, France, and Holland. He not only provides details of special units who operated behind enemy lines, but also includes soldiers who served behind friendly lines during World War II, including the 555th Parachute Infantry Battalion—the only African American airborne unit formed during the war—who fought forest fires in the Pacific Northwest and defused Japanese balloon bombs transported across the Pacific Ocean by the jet stream.

Michael Dilley makes a significant contribution to the history of special operations. His own experience in uniform is abundantly evident in his writing about these men who could be called the "Greatest" of the "Greatest Generation."

Michael Lee Lanning
LTC (Ret.), USA
Phoenix, Arizona

Introduction

This book consists of discussions and critiques of the employment of various special purpose, special mission units during World War II. These special purpose, special mission units were used by Allied and Axis countries and operated in various theaters of the war including Europe, North Africa, Southeast Asia, the Pacific islands, and the continental United States. The forces discussed in this book represent Britain, Japan, Russia, the United States, Australia, France, Holland, Belgium, Germany, and India. The operations run the gamut of missions assigned to special purpose, special mission units. The operations include raids, intelligence gathering missions, support to partisan/guerrilla groups, prisoner rescues, direct action missions, and two where the object was to steal something. The sponsorship of at least one of these operations would have been officially denied if the operators had been caught. Just as the missions are varied, so are the units that performed the missions. The units in this book represent many of those of special purpose, special mission organizations, from commando units that attack from the sea to parachute units that attack from the air; from reconnaissance units to sabotage units; and from partisan/guerrilla training units to those units that combine more than one of these characteristics.

In a book that I co-wrote with Lance Q. Zedric (*Elite Warriors—300 Years of America's Best Fighting Troops*, Pathfinder Publishing, 1996) we developed a broad definition of what we thought constitutes a special purpose, special mission organization. I am repeating it here because it applies to the units in this book. A special purpose, special mission organization is one that:

- Conducts missions atypical of units in its branch of service;
- Is formed to conduct a particular mission;

- Receives special training for a mission;
- Uses specialized or prototype equipment or standard equipment in a non-standard role;
- Performs scouting, ranging, raiding, or reconnaissance missions;
- Conducts or trains indigenous people in guerrilla type or unconventional warfare operations;
- Results from separate recruiting efforts, either in-service or off-the-street.

What Lance and I said then applies here as well: "[T]he reader will find many of the units discussed in this book meet more than one of the criteria." As used in this book, the terms "special purpose, special mission organizations [or units]," "special operations forces [or units]," and "special units" are considered to be interchangeable. For the sake of simplicity I will use the term "special operations forces" or the acronym SOF throughout this book.

This book is a critical examination of the missions of some of the special operations forces employed during World War II. The critique will rely on criteria from three sources.

The first criteria is based on my judgment and includes an examination of the necessity of the mission, how well such a mission fits into the overall theater plan, as well as the necessity for special operations forces to execute them. Whenever appropriate, the missions discussed here will be examined from the perspective of the larger campaign in which they were conducted. In addition to the questions regarding the operations' necessity, the missions will be examined from the point of view of what impact they had on the larger campaign. If there is no impact or, worse, if the impact is negative, we are back at the first question proposed—whether the mission was even necessary. In some cases a political consideration or decision was made that drove the necessity of the operation but such a case should be rare. For example, such political decisions definitely played a role in the defense of Moscow by Russian parachute forces, by the Skorzeny operation to rescue Mussolini, and perhaps to some extent in the decision to employ parachute troops, specifically the 555th Parachute Infantry Battalion, against balloon bombs.

If the mission had no impact on the overall campaign, this may, in some cases, point to a misuse of special operations forces, something which has occurred many times in U.S. military operations and not just in World War II. A critical mistake made by some commanders is to use special operations forces on any type of mission because they are available rather than using them for missions that fit their operational capabilities. Sometimes this works but when it does it perpetuates the mistake of misusing special operations forces rather than justifying their use. In such cases the commander(s) involved could have made better use of conventional forces available to them rather than relying on the few special operations forces. In other words, absent the existence of a special operations unit, would the operation have been conducted? If the answer is "yes," then it is almost certain that a conventional unit would have and should have conducted it.

The second examination will be of the success of these missions and will be based on criteria established by two prominent military writers. These writers are: Lucien S. Vandenbroucke, who described recurrent problems that characterize failed special operations in his book *Perilous Options—Special Operations as an Instrument of U.S. Foreign Policy* (Oxford University Press, 1993); and William H. McRaven, who articulated the principles of successful special operations in his book *Spec Ops—Case Studies in Special Operations: Theory and Practice* (Presidio Press, 1995). I have chosen these two military writers and their criteria for a variety of reasons but principally because I believe that their systems have the most merit for the kind of critical examination which this book entails.

In as many of their words as practical, I am including a description of the methods outlined by each of these authors.

Vandenbroucke examined special operations that he characterized as having failed in order to determine if they may have shared common features and what, if any, those common features might be. He determined that the commonalities were these:

- *Inadequate intelligence,* including of the objective and enemy forces defending it.
- *Poor coordination,* including lack of compatible equipment; getting one agency or service to be fully alert and responsive to the needs of another; difficulties by planners in understanding one another's standard operating procedures; and outright confusion and mutual mistrust.
- *Provision of faulty information to the national leadership,* including deliberately misleading information or one-sided information.
- *Wishful thinking,* including missions designed or evaluated on assumptions that had a limited basis in fact; rejecting information that runs counter to the hopes for success by the planners or decision makers; and the blind desire to see a proposed mission proceed and succeed.

• *Inappropriate intervention in mission execution,* including by higher military headquarters or the national leadership. This is a factor that I label as "the President as squad leader."

McRaven, on the other hand, has described a successful special operation as one that is characterized by a simple plan, one that is carefully concealed, repeatedly and realistically rehearsed, and executed with surprise, speed, and purpose. McRaven's description examines the three phases of an operation: planning, preparation, and execution. Specifically, he defines his terms as follows.

Planning phase:
• *Simplicity:* limiting the number of objectives; good intelligence; and innovation.

Preparation phase:
• *Security:* preventing the enemy from gaining an advantage through foreknowledge of the mission by concealing the timing and means of insertion.
• *Repetition:* honing routine skills to a degree that allows quick reaction to a threat, provided that threat fits within the standard scenario the unit has developed and practiced. Because special operations vary enough from the standard, new equipment and tactics must often be employed. This necessitates at least one (but preferably two) full dress rehearsals prior to insertion.

Execution phase:
• *Surprise:* catching the enemy off guard through deception, timing, and taking advantage of his vulnerabilities.
• *Speed:* getting to the objective as fast as possible to prevent expanding ones area of vulnerability and decreasing ones opportunity to achieve relative superiority.
• *Purpose:* understanding and executing the prime objective of a mission regardless of emerging obstacles or opportunities.

In the mission critiques which follow the discussions of each operation, I will examine the mission using my own criteria as well as those of Vandenbroucke and McRaven. My examination will focus mostly on negative aspects. If there are positive comments to make concerning the various individual criteria I will either make a general statement to that effect or not make any comment. This is done mostly to avoid unnecessary repetition but also to focus the comments on those aspects/criteria of the mission that had problems.

At the outset I want to say that these conclusions are my own. I am fully aware of the position of the critic and have even begun this introduction with the words of Theodore Roosevelt which put me in my place. None of my negative comments in these critiques is directed personally at any of the participants in the various missions discussed. I have only the highest professional respect and personal admiration for the special operators discussed in this book. To paraphrase David Stirling, they truly dared and, by so doing, won regardless of the mission outcome.

The selection of the operations discussed in this book was entirely my own. I am aware that several deserving units are not included here (including but not limited to the First Special Service Force and its operation at la Difensa in Italy and the British Special Boat Service, which operated in the eastern Mediterranean). My decision was not capricious or haphazard. I decided to establish a specific length and wanted to include units from several different countries. My final selection is not meant to slight any unit.

World War II saw an explosion of the formation of special operations forces world-wide. At the end of the war, virtually all of these units (with the possible exception of parachute units) were disbanded or dismantled only to be reactivated in one form or another within a few years when a new crisis arose (for example, the insurrection in Greece, the Malayan emergency, and the wars in Korea and Indochina). Of course, these reactivations brought with them their own ramp up period of organization, training, and deployment. In the early and mid 1980s the creation of major commands in the U.S. military to oversee and lead special operations forces as well as to insure better tactical and strategic use of such forces in a way that supports the campaign bodes well for the future. Perhaps the dissolution of special units at the end of a crisis is a thing of the past.

I have divided the book into two sections: Behind Enemy Lines and Behind Friendly Lines because that is where special operations forces have been employed. I believe this division also serves to demonstrate that special purpose, special mission units can be, and have been, employed wherever needed, even in areas controlled by military units of their own or allied countries. I have included discussions of single missions as well as general unit "histories," for lack of a better term, that discuss some or all of the missions of a particular unit. These histories are important to a thorough discussion of special operations forces in order to demonstrate the operational flexibility and mission-oriented training and capabilities of special operating forces.

My intention in assembling the framework for these mission discussions is to examine the historical use of special operations forces to encourage similar critical examinations of special operations in the future *while the missions are still in the planning phase.* I believe that by incorporating special operations into the objectives of the larger campaign the special operations forces will be more effectively and appropriately used. This should lead to less misuse and further encourage the need for and existence of such special operations forces. I also believe that the critical examination I use here can achieve the same purpose (more effective and appropriate use) for those conventional forces executing a campaign. Such an examination should use similar criteria incorporated into the basic principles of war: simplicity, objective, surprise, security, mass, unity of command, economy of force, offensive, and maneuver.

SOURCES

Cohen, Eliot A.; *Commandos and Politicians—Elite Military Units in Modern Democracies;* Harvard University (Harvard Studies in International Affairs, Number 40); 1978

McRaven, William H.; *Spec Ops—Case Studies in Special Operations Warfare: Theory and Practice;* Novato, CA; Presidio Press; 1995

Vandenbroucke, Lucien S.; *Perilous Options—Special Operations as an Instrument of U.S. Foreign Policy;* New York; Oxford University Press; 1993

Zedric, Lance Q. and Michael F. Dilley; *Elite Warriors—300 Years of America's Best Fighting Troops;* Ventura, CA; Pathfinder Publishing; 1996

PART 1

BEHIND ENEMY LINES

PART ONE: **BEHIND ENEMY LINES**

OVERVIEW

Behind enemy lines is where you typically expect to find special operations forces employed. This should not be a great leap of logic—certainly all special purpose, special mission organizations were organized to conduct one or more of the kinds of missions represented in this book. These missions include raids, intelligence gathering, support to guerrilla/partisan groups, prisoner rescues, and direct action missions.

Operating in enemy-controlled territory includes many of the same dangers found in operations in direct contact with enemy forces (so-called front line areas), especially the potential to be captured or killed. Added dangers increase the risk of operating in enemy territory. One of the best examples of added risk is the infamous Hitler-issued "commando order."

Irritated by the success of early operations, by mostly British commandos and paratroopers, Hitler issued an order, termed the *Fuehrerbefehl,* on 18 October 1942. This order had as its basis an accusation that Germany's enemies were employing tactics that did not conform to the various Geneva accords. Hitler accused commandos of being "especially brutal and cunning." The order said that such forces "are to be exterminated to the last man" and that it was "strictly forbidden to hold them in military custody ... even as a temporary measure." In a cover letter for high level commanders Hitler added, in the last paragraph, "Should it prove advisable to spare one or two men in the first instance for interrogation purposes, they are to be shot immediately after their interrogation."

On the other hand, employing special purpose, special mission organizations behind enemy lines added a dimension to the forces facing the enemy. This dimension is what is sometimes referred to as a force multiplier. In this case the force multiplier derives from the time, effort, and units needed by the enemy to hunt for and protect against special purpose, special mission operations in its rear area. In essence, the first part of this book attempts to determine if such efforts at force multiplication achieve this goal.

Of course, a force multiplier of this nature is only valuable if it adds to friendly forces *and* makes the enemy take action because of it. Taking action by the enemy, in this case, usually requires using forces that would otherwise have been used in direct contact. This is the ideal and sometimes, especially in the case of the Japanese parachute attack on the airfield and oil refineries at Palembang, the employment of special operations forces is such a surprise that it was not anticipated by the adversary—although, as will be seen, at Palembang the forces on the ground still had time to damage the refinery equipment.

Surprise is probably the one factor that all special operations forces desire—in addition, naturally, to success. Many of the operations discussed here involve forces arriving at a target via a route or method that the adversary had deemed unusable or unsuitable for attack and, therefore, did not even guard against. Surprise, in and of itself, is not always necessary. If the adversary force is aware of the special operations capability, its problems then become questions of where, when, in what force, and how will this capability be employed against them. This is not a new problem. In 1784, soon after he first saw a balloon demonstration, Benjamin Franklin recognized the position such a capability could put an adversary into when he said, "Where is the Prince who can afford so to cover his country with troops for its defense as then ten thousand men descending from the clouds, might not, in many places, do an infinite amount of mischief before a force could be brought together to repel them?"

Another way in which special operations forces become a force multiplier is in their partisan/guerrilla role, whether they are acting as these forces or instructing and training others to be guerrillas. In this capacity the special operations forces have the potential to both tie down adversarial forces to hunt for or protect against them as well as actually conducting operations behind enemy lines that support or supplement the major theater plan. As mentioned in the introduction, if the missions of special operations forces do not do that (i.e., support or supplement the major theater plan) then they are not of real value to the friendly commander to whom they belong.

Force multiplication is only one reason for the creation or employment of special purpose, special mission organizations, and probably not even the most important of the reasons. The capability that such organizations bring with them, whether it is a special skill or a delivery technique or a weapons system or even just access to intelligence not otherwise available, is usually a powerful justification for their creation or use. This is, however, a two-edged sword. As I have mentioned, it is often their unique capability that special operations forces bring to the battlefield that causes or permits commanders to misuse them. The basic fact though is that this capability represents another, usually different, tool or weapon available to the commander, one that enables the commander to execute his battle plan in different avenues. And that, after all, is what teamwork, the essence of victory, is all about.

One final comment. Several of the discussions that follow (including one in Part 2) are in the form of unit histories rather than operational histories. In those cases, I will attempt to address my analysis of the units and their missions as a whole—but still taking into account some of their individual missions.

SOURCES

Huston, James A.; *Out of the Blue—U.S. Army Airborne Operations in World War II;* West Lafayette, IN; Purdue University Studies; 1972

Wiggan, Richard; *Operation Freshman—The Rjukan Heavy Water Raid 1942;* London; William Kimber; 1986

CHAPTER ONE

THE TRAGINO AQUEDUCT MISSION

In June 1940, Britain had withdrawn its army out of the jaws of death from Dunkirk. In just under 50 days, the German *Wehrmacht* had overrun Norway, Denmark, Holland, and Belgium. France was on the verge of defeat. Despite these developments, Lieutenant Colonel Dudley Clarke envisioned only offensive strategies. Clarke, a Royal Artillery officer, was the Military Assistant to the Chief, Imperial General Staff. After Dunkirk, he studied what other countries in the past had done in circumstances similar to those in which Britain now found itself. He recalled the tactics used by the Spanish guerrillas during the Peninsula War; the South African Boers during their war with Britain; and, in his own experience, the role of the irregulars in Palestine in the mid-1930s. Based on this study, Clarke devised a strategy to employ small but hard-hitting units that would mount attacks from the sea striking at German targets from Narvik to the Pyrenees, then quickly withdraw back to the sea. He submitted the idea to the Imperial General Staff, which eventually adopted it. The Imperial General Staff called the units Commandos, after the mounted Boer units of the South African War.

Before the end of June 1940 Prime Minister Winston Churchill prodded the Army to raise a force of paratroopers, in a note that said: "We ought to have a corps of at least five thousand parachute troops. I hear something is being done already to form such a corps but only, I believe, on a very small scale. Advantage must be taken of the summer to train these troops who can nonetheless play their part meanwhile as shock troops in home defence." Within two days Major John F. Rock, Royal Engineers, was charged with organizing the prime minister's airborne force. Soon after, Rock was promoted to lieutenant colonel.

The recruiting process used for candidates for the Commandos also served as the basis for obtaining Commandos who would jump. Those being screened were told that Commandos would be in two categories, seaborne and airborne, and they were asked to state a preference. Early volunteers were a mix of those who had enlisted in the Regular Army and those in the Territorial Army (or T.A., which were locally raised units similar to the U.S. Army Reserve). No. 2 Special Service Company was the initial designation for the first parachute unit; this was later changed to No. 2 Commando. As with the other Commando units, it was subordinate to the Chief of Combined Operations, Admiral Sir Roger Keyes. Keyes had gained fame late in World War I for planning and executing a Commando-style raid on the port of Zeebruge. His son, Geoffrey, would later be killed on a Commando raid whose objective was to kill or capture Rommel.

Parachute training was conducted at Ringway RAF Station. Ringway was initially known as the Central Landing School for security reasons. Later, the name was changed to Central Landing Establishment, in part because incoming mail was being received addressed to "Central Laundry School" and (worse) "Central Sunday School." The name change also confirmed that Ringway would serve as the focal point for "the co-ordination and direction of all work required in the development and training of an airborne force." Since there was no previous military application of British soldiers being delivered to the battlefield by parachute, the training literally started on the ground floor. Physical training NCOs were designated as the first instructors. One of the instructor sergeants was nicknamed "Bags o' guts" because of his fondness for yelling at the students while trying to get them "into the most horrible contortions."

The instructors at Ringway had to literally start from scratch. They first constructed a series of physical training devices designed to toughen muscle groups needed in parachute jumping. Next, after studying intelligence reports about German training methods, they put together a rough training outline. This outline was subject to many changes often dictated by innovations in training techniques, tactical studies, and progression in general knowledge. The initial airborne equipment they had available consisted of a captured German parachute and jump helmet. With this humble beginning, Britain's parachute program began to take form.

Obviously, equipment was the first prerequisite—more parachutes and airplanes were required. The RAF was extremely reluctant to give up any of its planes, saying that all the bombers were needed for bombing raids on Europe. After some higher-level arm-twisting, four Whitley bombers were allocated to Ringway and immediately dubbed "flying coffins" by the parachute students. Several different methods of exiting the Whitley were tried. The instructors, who were learning their trade only about a step or two ahead of their students, decided that the most reliable method was for jumpers to drop through a hole in the belly of the plane. At about the same time that the Whitleys were delivered, the school also obtained a Bombay transport plane; this had a side door for jumping. Both types of aircraft came to be used in the early days of training at Ringway.

The first airborne jump was on 13 July 1940, using the pull-off method. In this method, the jumper stood at the rear of the plane on a platform built especially for this purpose. He faced the front of the plane and, on command, pulled his rip cord. The force of the parachute opening and catching the wind jerked him out of the plane. Needless to say, only one man jumped at a time. The early classes were organized into 50-man units and these included officers. The men came from various regiments. Corporal Philip D. Julian, a sapper from the Royal Engineers, was in K Troop. He had volunteered for special service after being successfully evacuated from Dunkirk.

When their jump training was completed, the new airborne troopers were sent to Scotland. There they underwent about six weeks of basic Commando training at the hands of Lord Lovat and his Lovat Scouts at their School of Irregular Warfare. Here they went on "wee walks" up nearby Ben Nevis, a massive fog-shrouded peak and the highest point in Scotland. Days off from training usually meant "a wee *run*" to the top of Ben Nevis.

In the course of their training, two men, introduced only as Sykes and Fairburn (both former police officers in Shanghai), taught the paratroopers the basics of unarmed combat and how to kill by fair means or foul. "Remember, gentlemen," the instructors told them, "go for the eyes, ears, or testicles." One month later, in early September, the students had completed the Commando phase of their training. Now, while they waited for an operation, the best among them began to fill out the ranks of trainers and instructors needed on staff at Ringway.

This new cadre of instructors did not stop their own training. Soon they were conducting night jumps. The first of these jumps included putting lights on the descending jumpers. As air crews and paratroopers gained experience and confidence, the lights were no longer used. On one of the night jumps, R.D. "Jock" Davidson was dragged below the plane. He remembers that "my static line got twisted round my wrist." Soon thereafter, the static line became untwisted and "no one would have been happier than when I heard the canopy of the chute snap open and knew that all was well."

In November, a demonstration jump was conducted for visiting dignitaries. At the same time, work began on the selection of a target for an operational jump. An unspecified area in Italy was chosen and it was given the codename Operation Colossus.

At about the time that Italy was designated to be the site of the first airborne operation, an engineering firm in London suggested that the RAF might consider bombing a huge aqueduct near Monte Vulture, 30 miles inland from Salerno, in the "ankle" of the Italian boot. The engineering firm had originally built the aqueduct over the Tragino River and was able to supply a copy of the construction plans. The aqueduct was the main water supply source for most provinces in southern Italy, including the towns of Brindisi, Bari, and Foggia. These all had military factories and dockyards that depended on the water. Eventually, a decision was made to use the new paratroopers instead of RAF bombers against the aqueduct.

As planning for the operation began, the unit was again redesignated; this time to 11th Special Air Service Battalion. Lieutenant Colonel Charles Jackson, commander of the unit, told his assembled troops that a "top secret" mission was being planned and asked for 40 volunteers. Almost in perfect unison every officer and man took one step forward. "Very well," Jackson said. "I thank you all, but I'm afraid this means the men who are to take part will have to be selected." The first one selected was Major Trevor A.G. Pritchard, Jackson's second-in-command and leader of K Troop. Pritchard was told to pick five other officers and then each officer was to pick five men. The team was designated "X Troop," 11th Special Air Service Battalion. The six officers were told only that they would have to train X Troop to blow up a bridge somewhere in enemy territory. Later, one officer and two men were added to X Troop as reserves.

A separate area was assigned to X Troop at Ringway. Mornings were devoted to runs and forced marches with full equipment. During the afternoons, the paratroopers rehearsed on a bridge mock-up in Tatton Park, located about five miles away from Ringway. At about the same time, eight Whitley bombers were set aside for use by X Troop. Pritchard planned to put six men into each of six planes. Sling containers, with weapons and explosives, were to be located in the bomb-bays and rigged for parachute drop. The other two planes, if they were still available, were to be used for a diversionary bomb run in Foggia, near the target area. He hoped that this maneuver would allay suspicion as to their true nature and mission.

Prior to the mission dress rehearsal, two additional men were added to X Troop. One was a civilian whose real name was Fortunato Picchi but rostered as Trooper "Pierre Dupont." The other was forty-year-old Flight-Lieutenant Ralph Lucky, who wore ribbons denoting service in the World War. Both were introduced as interpreters. The dress rehearsal went terribly, with some of the men suffering minor injuries. "Jock" Davidson called the jump "a bit of a fiasco. The wind was far too strong," he added, "and normally we would never have jumped in it, but it was our last chance before leaving so off we went." Not one of those injured allowed himself to be taken off the mission. Philip Julian injured his knee but X-rays taken at a hospital showed "all was OK" and he returned to X Troop. Most of the men thought the bad dress rehearsal was a good sign; they were wrong.

In late January, Lieutenant Anthony Deane-Drummond, one of the six officers of X Troop, was informed as to the true nature of the real target. He was to leave England immediately and proceed to Malta where he would act as the unit's liaison office in establishing an advance base. Deane-Drummond also learned that the plan called for the paratroopers, once their demolition mission was complete, to move west from their target to the Italian coast, some 50 miles away. There they were to be picked up by a submarine. Soon after his briefing, the signals officer left for Malta. He had to find accommodations for the unit, draw explosives and other necessary supplies, and arrange for the unit to be transported to the airfield on the night of the operation. A late change in the plan called for the paratroopers to go in under the cover of darkness.

On 4 February, X Troop departed Ringway by special bus, bound for Mildenhall RAF Base. Before leaving England, X Troop conducted a parade inside a hangar for Admiral Keyes, who offered a few encouraging words to the unit after inspecting it. On the morning of 9 February, X Troop and all eight Whitleys arrived on Malta and were met at the airfield by Deane-Drummond.

On the 10th, X Troop studied an aerial photograph of the target area taken on the day before. The photograph showed that there were actually *two* aqueducts across the Tragino. They were situated about 200 yards apart and one was larger than the other. In the end, the larger one, on the east, was designated as the target.

Final supplies were issued to the men. These included food, a six-day supply of water, and cigarettes. Each man carried three hand grenades. Personal weapons issued to officers included .38 caliber revolvers while each man carried a .32 caliber Colt automatic with four extra clips. Each man strapped a Commando knife to one leg. Explosives, rifles, and sub-machine guns were loaded into weapons containers stowed in the Whitleys' bomb racks. In an effort to anticipate every feasibility, the paratrooper battle uniform was augmented to hide a variety of escape-related items, including: 50,000 lire in notes sewn into shirt collars and trouser waistbands; two silk maps (one of north Italy, the other of south Italy) sewn into sleeve linings; a hacksaw blade sewn into the left breast pocket of each shirt; and a special metallic collar stud was added that contained a small compass.

At 1700, X Troop had a meal of hard-boiled eggs and hot tea. As they ate, Major Pritchard briefed the men, telling them where they would be going and detailing the escape items in their uniforms. During their training, the men of X Troop had been led to believe that they would be blowing up a bridge in Abyssinia. Now they all knew they were headed for Italy. Many of the men were less concerned about executing their mission than they were about making their escape afterwards. It was obvious that they could only travel at night and through territory where the local military and civilian population would be looking for them. And it was mid-winter. They did not, however, express any reservations about their ability to blow up the aqueduct and make a clean getaway.

At the conclusion of the briefing, the men loaded into the Whitleys and took off. The plan was for the three planes carrying the infantry paras to leave first, followed 30 minutes later by the three planes transporting the sappers (combat engineers who were explosives experts). One of the planes carrying the sappers was delayed further when one of the paras got sick and had to be taken off the plane. Many of the men slept on the way to the target.

At 2137, seven minutes later than scheduled, the paratroopers in Deane-Drummond's plane were alerted that the target was near. Flying on a general southeasterly course, the planes passed over the target area and disgorged their cargo. Deane-Drummond, fifth man out of his plane, made what he called "... the best landing I had ever made." He landed about 100 yards from the target. Within a few minutes, he and the men in his stick had retrieved their weapons and secured the immediate areas above and below the aqueduct. He made a quick inspection of the target and realized that the information from the London engineering firm was wrong in one major respect: the aqueduct was not made of concrete; it was made of *reinforced* concrete. As he made this discovery, the lieutenant could hear the far-off sounds of bombs exploding in the direction of Foggia. That would be the diversionary air-raid.

Soon the other planes began dropping their paras and almost immediately there were indications that things were starting to go wrong. Two planes carrying infantry were late because they had rerouted to avoid flak on their line of flight. Some of the weapons and explosives containers did not release, while others that did release were scattered over a wide area. Finally, the last plane, which was carrying Captain Gerry Daly and five sappers, dropped the paras on board in the wrong valley.

By about 2215, other troopers began to appear at the aqueduct. One of the first to arrive was Major Pritchard. Deane-Drummond immediately briefed his commander on the situation, informing him that Captain Daly and his plane-load of sappers were not yet at the target. Pritchard grabbed an engineer lieutenant named George Paterson and advised him to be prepared to oversee the demolition of the aqueduct should Daly not arrive in time. Paterson immediately reviewed the site and told Pritchard that the original plan would have to be modified because of the reinforced concrete. Furthermore, not all of the explosives had been successfully dropped. Pritchard told the lieutenant, "You're the expert now, and I'll stand by your judgment."

As boxes of explosives were delivered to the aqueduct, Paterson and the 12 sappers who had landed near the target began arranging the material around the base of one of the aqueduct's support piers. This group included Philip Julian and R.J. "Jock" Crawford. Covering parties commanded by Deane-Drummond, Captain Christopher Lea, and Lieutenant Arthur Jowett secured areas on both sides of the aqueduct. About a dozen Italian men, gathered up by the paratroopers for purposes of security were pressed into a labor gang to help. These civilians were later awarded medals by the Italian government for "gallant behaviour in the face of the enemy." Deane-Drummond took the remaining two boxes of explosives and, with the help of two of his men, Lance-Corporal Robert Watson and Sapper Alan Ross, arranged them under one end of a small nearby bridge. This bridge, to the west of the aqueduct, was what had shown up on the aerial photograph of the target area. Deane-Drummond's decision to take out this bridge was intended to stop or delay any vehicular troop movement from engaging and pursuing the British paratroopers.

By 0015, all was ready. The Italian men were moved to nearby buildings and the paratroopers moved to an area a short distance away from the aqueduct. Fifteen minutes later, Paterson and Deane-Drummond lit 60-second fuses at their respective targets. The charge at the small bridge went off. The charge on the main target should have gone off at about the same time but it did not. Pritchard and Paterson, both concerned as to what may have gone wrong, began to advance toward the support pier. They had only covered about a dozen yards when an explosion knocked them both off their feet. This was followed by a series of flashes and explosions that rumbled into the dark, distant mountains. Pritchard and Paterson picked themselves up and went forward to inspect the damage.

When they returned to update the rest of the unit, they were quickly surrounded and barraged by questions from every side. Pritchard held up his hand and said, "Listen to that sound."

As the men quieted down they could hear the constant sound of running water. Half of the aqueduct had been knocked down; one of the support piers was gone and another "leaned at a crazy angle."

Pritchard spoke quietly to his men as they gathered around him. "My thanks to you, you've done a splendid job. I'd just love to see old Mussolini's face when he learns of our raid and what we've accomplished. We must now withdraw—and lose no time about it." He reminded them of the plan for a submarine to pick up all those who could make it to the mouth of the Sele River in four days. Then he organized the men into three groups of roughly ten men and two officers each. All heavy equipment and rifles were buried. Lance-Corporal Boulter, who had broken his ankle during the jump, was left behind. At 0100, the three groups set off, moving west.

In another valley, Captain Daly and his men, including "Jock" Davidson, heard the sound of the explosion and decided that there was no longer a need to advance to the aqueduct. Daly briefed his four men on the submarine rendezvous and they set out. Daly's last words, as they began their forced march west were, "We've got rather a long walk ahead of us."

As a matter of fact, none of the parties involved in this plan made it to the rendezvous point on the Sele River. None of the paratroopers made it nor did the submarine. Within a matter of days, all of the paratroopers had been picked up by either Italian Army or *Carabinieri* units. After their capture and some initial interrogations, the Italians determined that Trooper Dupont was a civilian and a native of Italy. The next day he was executed by a firing squad. The rest of X Troop were sent to various POW camps throughout Italy. In time, some of the paras escaped and returned to England. Deane-Drummond was one of those who escaped; he later took part in the Arnhem jump in September 1944.

An incredible coincidence occurred during one of the escapes. In September 1943, after the Italian government had surrendered to the Allies, the

Germans transported many of the Allied POWs north. "Jock" Davidson and three others were shielded by some Italians in an effort to keep them out of German hands. But the paratroopers got away from the Italians and headed south on their own. During their trek through the central mountains they saw a German plane towing a glider pass overhead. Three days later they were informed by some villagers in Tussio about Skorzeny's raid on Campo Imperatore to free Mussolini. The paras had witnessed a part of Skorzeny's assault force dispatched to the resort where Mussolini was being held!

Even if any of the paratroopers had actually made it to the rendezvous site after attacking the Tragino Aqueduct, they would not have been picked up according to the operation plan. One of the Whitleys that took part in the diversionary bombing raid over Foggia on the night of the attack lost an engine on its return flight. The crew bailed out safely but the plane crashed— *at the mouth of the Sele River!* Nervous staff officers at Malta believed that this crash caused too much attention to this area and cancelled the submarine pickup.

Mission Critique

The theme for this mission is that a special capability, that is, a fledgling parachute force, has been raised and trained. The planners then had to find some mission to test this capability and thereby justify the time and expense in it. This mission would determine if the special capability is worth having and if it is worthy of continued support.

Put in these terms, there is always some thought, as Vandenbroucke would say, that this justification, based strictly on a first mission result, may be mere *wishful thinking*. The desire is to see the mission succeed so that the original decision in creating such a force is proven correct. This desire may have entered into the line of thinking that finally resulted in the approval to execute the Tragino Aqueduct mission.

There seems little doubt that this mission was carefully considered by the planners as one that was directed against a necessary target and probably one that was within or contributed to the overall battle plan at the time. However, some juxtaposed reasoning was involved here. The planners took a target, the aqueduct, that was to be destroyed by aerial bombardment and decided, since the target was approved anyway, that the new paratroop capability could be used against it. It is this logic in the decision making process that seems faulty. A suitable target for one capability does not make that target suitable for any capability. When you compare the two capabilities being discussed here (aerial bombardment versus parachute force attack), the differences are startling. There is a saying among men who must be put in harm's way that should be considered an axiom by all planners; it goes "Never send a man where you can send a bullet." Had this principle been applied properly, the planners would have chosen a different target for X Troop.

So, while there appears to have been some justification for this target (however faulty the logic for choosing it), the question still remains as to whether using special operations forces to conduct the operation was necessary. In this case the answer should be an immediate "NO." There are two things working to support this negative conclusion.

First is the fact that the target was approved for aerial bombardment—it had already been through a planning and approval process that brought it to that point. This does not mean that it should be automatically suitable or approved for attack by any method.

Second, we can see that what at first appeared to be a simple tactical plan was rendered almost completely worthless by a complicated and virtually unsupportable exfiltration plan. Only one method for getting the paratroopers out was considered. This plan necessitated the Commandos to move 50 miles through mountainous terrain during winter. The men were further limited to nighttime movement and evasion tactics. This limitation was a major hindrance even if the enemy was not aware of their presence. However, when the mission was executed, the men had literally announced their presence to the Italians. There was no external support until they would reach the coast. Now, this is definitely the kind of challenge that special operations forces can overcome, especially when they enter the target from an unexpected or unguarded approach. However, once the mission was underway, the exfiltration plan was scrubbed by a nervous planning/operations staff. Because of the lack of communications with X Troop, there was no way to tell them about this change.

While some mission had to be found for X Troop, there must have been a target available that gave them a better chance of getting out. Why go to all the trouble of investing these men with their specialized training if they are just going to be thrown away on the first plan that comes along? Why was the plan that was developed not reviewed from a critical perspective? This mission should have remained an aerial bombardment target.

Since it was more than one year before the next parachute operation was executed by the British—what was the almighty rush to conduct *this* one against *this* target? It seems that the unit was a solution looking for a problem. The planners were anxious to test the skills of the soldiers and prove the principle of airborne units. It seems to be a shame to have wasted such highly skilled and trained men on this mission. Yes, it produced a propaganda *coup* of sorts—but this *coup* could have been even more significant with a more suitable target *and* an attacking force that made it back. Special operations forces should not have been used against this target because such soldiers are not easily replaced.

Before examining this operation using the Vandenbroucke and McRaven criteria, the mission results must be analyzed. The aqueduct, which was the target, received some damage but not what the planners or the paratroopers expected. The damage was repaired in about three days, long before the local reservoirs were in any danger of drying up. The aqueduct was not of any strategic or tactical value. Photographic interpreters, after reviewing pictures taken almost two days after the raid, could not find any damage. The planning staff did not know if the paratroopers even got to the target until later in the month, when the Italians trumpeted the capture of the raiding force.

In a review of the criteria for failed operations several apply to this mission.

Inadequate intelligence on the aqueduct's construction led to insufficient explosives being taken with the paratroopers. All that could be rounded up at the time of the attack had to be used to do the damage that was done.

Poor coordination was evident in several places. The paratroopers took no communications equipment with them and were thus unaware that the submarine pickup had been canceled because of the plane crash. There were no plans for an alternate pickup point.

Wishful thinking apparently guided the planning staff in its target selection. Too little time was spent looking at the plan as a whole to see that another target, closer to a pickup point (especially more than one possible point), should have been selected. After all, this mission was supposed to be a proof of principle type operation. If so then *every* effort should have been made to make it completely successful.

Cancellation of the submarine without a mechanism to notify the paratroopers heading to the pickup point was a classic case of *inappropriate intervention of mission execution*.

Conversely, most of the criteria for a successful mission were also present. The issuance of communications equipment with X Troop could have made the plan *simpler* than it was. Only the evasion and pick-up portions of the plan were complicated. The *security*, especially once the force was on the ground at the target, was a high point in the execution of the raid. All of the other criteria were definitely present, which should have made the mission one that the planners could look at with pride. After all, the paratroopers did their part very well. The fault was primarily with the planners and those over-seeing the operation. Additionally, why the paratroopers said nothing about the lack of communication equipment is a puzzle.

Overall the execution was good and the planning was poor. The planning objective was to show that Britain could still project a force and cause troops to be tied up trying to protect potential targets. This mission only partly suc-ceeded in the former and failed in the latter. The poor target selection was almost too big a hurdle to overcome.

Good lessons for future operations came from this raid. Probably most noticeable was the increased number of volunteers who wanted to join the parachute forces. News of the mission was released in response to an Italian news story that downplayed the damage and crowed about capturing the en-tire force. From an operational point of view, planning staffs learned to ask for and get more photo-reconnaissance of target areas and get it earlier in the planning process. Several changes were made in the procedures dealing with night jumps, although this continued to be a problem throughout the war. This first operational parachute mission also pointed out inadequacies with equipment containers. Eventually, both the equipment containers and release mechanisms on the planes were re-designed and improved. All of these changes were based on a good after-action review.

SOURCES

Books:
Deane-Drummond, Anthony; *Return Ticket;* London; Collins; 1952
Foxall, Raymond; *The Guinea Pigs—Britain's First Paratroop Raid;* London; Robert Hale; 1983
Newnham, Maurice; *Prelude to Glory—The Story of the Creation of Britain's Parachute Army;* London; Sampson Low, Marston; 1946
Norton, G.G.; *The Red Devils—The Story of the British Airborne Forces;* Harrisburg, PA; 1971
Otway, Terence B.H.; *Airborne Forces;* London; Imperial War Museum Books (reprint of a volume in The Second World War, 1939–1945, Army series); 1990
————— (unattributed); *By Air to Battle—The Official Account of the British Airborne Divisions;* London; His Majesty's Stationery Office; 1945

Saunders, Hilary St. G.; *The Green Beret—The Story of the Commandos 1940–1945;* London; Michael Joseph; 1949

——————— *The Red Beret—The Story of the Parachute Regiment 1940–1945;* London; Michael Joseph; 1950

——————— (unattributed); *Combined Operations—The Official Story of the Commandos;* New York; MacMillan; 1943

Articles:

Author unknown; "British Airborne Assaults 1940–45"; in *WWII* magazine; July 1976; pages 14–21

Hill, Adrian; "Where Pegasus Might Fly"; in *Journal of the Royal Services Institute for Defence Studies;* June 1979; pages 45–52

Ramirez, Roland J.; "British Airborne Forces"; in *World War II Journal;* Volume 2, Number 3; pages 50–51

Interviews and letters with:

R.J. Crawford in Scotland

R.D. Davidson in New Zealand

Peter G. de Lotz in London

Philip D. Julian in England

CHAPTER TWO

THE RAID TO KILL ROMMEL

The initial success against the Italian forces in North Africa was one of the few glimmers of light in an otherwise bleak situation for Britain in 1940. In February 1941, *Generalleutnant* Erwin Rommel and his *Afrika Korps* began arriving in Tripoli, and the entire situation in North Africa would soon change.

In March 1941, Colonel Robert E. Laycock arrived from England with Number 7, 8, and 11 Commandos. They would be joined by 50 and 52 Commandos, which had been raised in the Middle East, to form a unit that was to be known as Layforce.

By June of that year, the British had been pushed out of Libya, except for the garrison in the fortress of Tobruk, which was firmly under siege. Layforce had been busy conducting small operations throughout the Eastern Mediterranean, including Crete and Syria. The Germans had taken Yugoslavia and Greece, and stood at the border of Egypt when Layforce was disbanded because of a high casualty rate and not receiving any replacements. Laycock was left with a force of 6 officers and 53 men.

British Eighth Army was planning an offensive, named Operation Crusader, for 18 November 1941. British and Empire forces in Egypt would begin Crusader with the objective of relieving Tobruk after a seven-month siege and driving the *Afrika Korps* and its Italian allies out of Cyrenaica. During the planning, Army headquarters had learned about a house at Beda Littoria in Libya, where it was believed that Rommel had his own headquarters. Surmising that a decapitation operation would severely weaken and demoralize the *Afrika Korps*, these planners ordered Laycock to conduct a raid at Beda Littoria; he was to kill or capture "the Desert Fox," who was now approaching the height of his popularity.

The Rommel mission was given the name Operation Flipper. The raiding force was divided into four detachments, each with a specific mission. Lieutenant Colonel Geoffrey Keyes would lead one detachment to Rommel's headquarters just outside Beda Littoria, also taking out communications in the vicinity. Lieutenant Sutherland's detachment was to hit the Italian headquarters in Cyrene, blowing up telephone and telegraph lines in the area. The detachment led by Lieutenant Chevalier would raid an Italian intelligence center near Apollonia. If they were unable to carry out this mission, they were to attack an airfield and adjacent buildings, including a power station, in the same area. The last detachment was under Captain John E. Haselden, an intelligence officer who would prepare the reception committee for the raiders' infiltration. This detachment would sabotage communications sites near Fuidia and Lamluda.

On the afternoon of 10 November, the Commandos loaded aboard two submarines, HMS *Torbay* and HMS *Talisman*, and departed Alexandria for the almost 500-mile trip to a promontory on the Libyan coast known as Chesem-el-Chelb. Just after dusk four days later, the submarines surfaced about two miles off shore at their designated rendezvous spot.

Both the Navy and Army had expected the weather conditions in that part of the Mediterranean at that time of year to be ideal for a seaborne infiltration. But heavy seas and dark clouds greeted the Commandos that night as they clambered onto the submarines' decks. This was nothing like the calm waters they had experienced during rehearsals. Now they were tossed about dangerously as they attempted to lug their gear and equipment up on deck and to inflate the slippery two-man rubber dinghies that would be their transportation to shore. Keyes, on board *Torbay*, the closer to shore of the two subs, made out Haselden's blinking flashlight signal and ordered his men to proceed with the landing.

As the Commandos began loading the dinghies the wind picked up. Captain Robin Campbell, Keyes' second-in-command, wrote later, "An extra large wave washed four of our boats into the sea with several men. We were delayed a long time by this accident." Valuable time was lost trying to get everyone ashore. The Commandos had estimated it would take about an hour for each sub to disembark the raiding force and paddle to shore. It took *five hours* to unload the first sub. Laycock, on *Talisman*, was growing concerned about the delay when he received the signal from Keyes that those on *Torbay* had linked up with Haselden. The Commandos with Laycock had an even tougher time getting ashore. Many of the small boats capsized, forcing the

Commandos to swim back to the submarine or drown. Only Laycock and seven of his men made the landing.

The raiding party initially assembled in a stone ruin where Haselden had a fire going to help warm and dry the bedraggled Commandos. Laycock hoped that others from his party would eventually make it to land but none did. Since he was reluctant to postpone the operation further, he moved his force to a nearby wadi and spent several hours with Keyes, Campbell, and Haselden restructuring the plan. Fewer than half of the Commandos had made it to shore. The new plan called for two assault detachments and a small stay-behind crew to secure the landing site. The mission of the larger detachment, led by Keyes, would not change—attack the house at Beda Littoria, looking for Rommel. This detachment included Keyes, Campbell, and 17 other Commandos. The other detachment, consisting of Lieutenant Roy Cook and six Commandos, would cut telephone and telegraph lines in the vicinity of a crossroads south of Cyrene. Laycock and three Commandos comprised the beachhead element.

The weather on the 15th, a Saturday, was cold and rainy, further chilling and dampening the spirits of the Commandos. They realized, however, that the weather could be an ally, keeping German and Italian units inside instead of outside and watchful. Early that evening, Keyes led his raiding party out of the wadi and headed in a southerly direction towards Beda Littoria. The Commandos were glad of the chance to move, bringing them some warmth. By the morning they were well on their way across a plateau beyond the first line of cliffs they would have to scale between the beach and their target.

Just before dawn Keyes ordered his men to disperse among the scattered scrub in the area. Within several hours the raiders were discovered by curious Arabs. Using an interpreter provided by Haselden, Keyes convinced the Arabs that the Commandos were on a mission against the Italians in the area, whom the Arabs hated. Later that afternoon the Arabs brought Keyes and his Commandos a warm goat meat stew. The food was a welcome respite from the continuing cold rain. As night fell, the Commandos continued on their way. Their movement that night was steady and undetected. During the hours just after midnight they found a cave—warm and dry—where they stayed until daybreak. Keyes was concerned that Arabs in the area would use the cave to warm themselves and moved his men to a nearby wood.

Back at the beach, Laycock and his party visited the beach landing area each night, waiting for signals from the submarines that the Commandos still aboard were ready to attempt another landing. Each night, however, rain

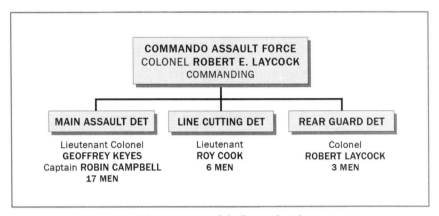

Final force structure of the Rommel raid team.

and heavy surf hammered the area, making any further landings impractical.

As the day wore on the rain became heavier, driving Keyes and his force back to the cave. During the afternoon, Keyes took Sergeant Jack Terry, from his party, and Lieutenant Cook on a reconnaissance of their target. While they were out, the recon party found an Arab boy and persuaded him to go into the village near Rommel's HQ and tell them what he saw. The information this boy brought back confirmed much of what Keyes already knew and enabled him to prepare a sketch for his men of the buildings and guard posts in the area.

Following a quick meal, Keyes briefed his raiders and they prepared for their assault—strapping on equipment, readying weapons and explosives, blackening their faces, and inspecting each other. At dusk they moved out. The rain had not let up at all, making their going very tough in heavy mud. It took the Commandos almost five hours to reach their last obstacle, a cliff that would bring them within a mile of their objective. The cliff was treacherously slippery. Halfway up, someone slipped badly, slamming his rifle onto one of the rock outcroppings. Immediately a dog began barking. Everyone froze.

In the darkness an Arab shouted at the dog. Eventually the dog stopped barking and the Commandos continued climbing. Once on top of the cliff, the party moved closer to the area where the buildings stood. They stopped about a quarter-mile away, where Lieutenant Cook and his detachment moved off in the direction of their targets. The main party went forward most of the remaining distance. Keyes halted the group, and he and Sergeant Terry went for one last recon.

The rest of the raiding party stayed put. In the dark another dog barked. An Arab and Italian soldier came outside to find out what had caused the disturbance. Captain Campbell, chosen for the mission because he was fluent in German, growled at the two that he and his men were a German patrol. He ordered them to go back inside and shut their dog up. The two went meekly back to their hut.

Keyes and Terry returned and led a small party to deal with a guard tent. Only one guard was inside and Keyes took care of him swiftly. When they rejoined the main body, Keyes dispatched his teams throughout the area. One team went to a truck park area, one moved to the front of Rommel's HQ building to cut off any German reinforcing party, another team began looking for power generators, and a team set up in other perimeter positions. Keyes took his raiding team, consisting of Captain Campbell, Sergeant Terry, Corporal Drori, Bombardier Brodie, and Commando Coulthread, to the main building. Just before midnight, at the time when Eighth Army was to kick-off its offensive, everyone was in position.

Keyes moved to the back of the house and found that the door was locked and the windows shuttered. Moving quietly, he led his team to the front of the house. Keyes and Campbell climbed the front steps and discovered that this door was also locked. Campbell pounded on the door, yelling in German for someone to open the door and let them in. The rest of the raiding team crowded onto the porch, waiting tensely for someone to answer Campbell's demand. Soon, a German guard, in overcoat and helmet, opened the door, reeling back in surprise as the raiders pushed inside led by Keyes, whose pistol prodded the German soldier's stomach. The German grabbed the pistol and began wrestling for control of it. Campbell shot the German over Keyes' shoulder.

The team moved into a large hall just as two Germans came down the main stairway. Terry and Coulthread fired bursts at them from their Tommy-guns. Outside the house two Germans with lights came running toward the HQ building. One of the Commandos guarding that approach shot them both.

Keyes began to open doors off the main hallway. The first two rooms were empty. When he opened the third door, the Germans inside began shooting. Keyes fired several shots from his pistol before Campbell shouted that he would throw in a grenade. Keyes closed the door. Campbell pulled the pin, counted two, opened the door, and tossed in the grenade as Terry fired a burst from his Tommy-gun. Several shots came from the room, one hitting and dropping Keyes. Campbell slammed the door, and he and Terry fell to the floor just as the grenade exploded in the room. Silence followed.

Campbell and Terry picked Keyes up and carried him outside but he was dead in less than a minute. Running to the back of the house, Campbell was ready to give the order to begin demolitions. In the heat of the moment, he forgot the password and was shot by one of his own men, the shot shattering his leg. The wounded captain sent for Terry and gave him command of the raiding party. Terry ordered the explosives to be set. Now the Commandos at Beda Littoria discovered what Cook's men were finding at the same time. All their fuses, matches, and even the self-igniting incendiaries had been badly damaged by the rain. Each detachment then pulled out their remaining grenades in an attempt to do at least some damage and began to return to the beach. Campbell ordered Terry to leave him behind. Cook's team was partially successful in its mission, their grenades destroying parts of the electric generating equipment.

Terry succeeded in getting to the beach in two days but Cook and his men were captured. On Thursday night, the 20th, there were conditions better suited to the Commandos' exfiltration, though several factors (such as friendly Arabs moving Laycock's rubber boats to a "better" hiding place, rough seas where the submarines were surfaced, and the general debilitated condition of the raiders) contributed to the failure of any of them to get off the beach. By the following day, German search parties were out in force looking for the Commandos. Laycock ordered his men to split up in small parties and evade back to friendly lines—400 miles away.

On Christmas Day, Laycock and Terry linked up with advancing British forces west of Tobruk. They were the only members of the raiding force to evade successfully. All the rest had been caught or killed. In the aftermath of Laycock's return, Geoffrey Keyes was awarded the Victoria Cross, Britain's highest award for valor, for his gallantry and leadership. Intelligence developed after the raid showed that Beda Littoria was a German and Italian supply point but had never been used by Rommel, as a headquarters or anything else. One report stated that on the night of the raid Rommel had been visiting German positions near Gambut, 200 *miles from Beda Littoria*. Another report placed Rommel in Rome from the 13th to the 15th celebrating his birthday, and that he was stranded in Athens with aircraft trouble on the 17th, not returning to North Africa until the day after the raid, as Crusader was beginning.

In late 1942, Geoffrey Keyes' brother found his grave marker and added the letters "VC" after his name, to indicate Keyes' award. He was the first Commando to be so recognized.

Mission Critique

What had the raid accomplished? Very little, actually, except the inconsequential items of enemy equipment destroyed. It appears to have given a morale-booster for the British at home. It may have also made German commanders regard themselves as unsafe far behind their own lines. Nevertheless there can be no way around a conclusion that this mission was a major catastrophe waiting to happen.

The Rommel raid is an example of a direct action mission but one of dubious necessity. Soldiers on the battlefield, from private in the rear ranks to commanding general, all ran the risk of being captured or killed, regardless of the depth of the battlefield. The justification for this operation was that it would decapitate the *Afrika Korps* and demonstrate that no one was safe. The death of any commanding general will, of necessity, decapitate the command—but only temporarily until the deputy takes over or another commander is appointed. A chain of command is established to preclude the death of the commander from leaving the organization without anyone in command. The fact that no one is safe is a given for any soldier.

The justification for the operation was that this operation would terrorize Rommel's command and therefore demoralize it and perhaps weaken it. While this *may* be true, it was a flimsy justification—soldiers generally fight for each other, and not necessarily for the general in charge. This type of operation does not warrant the time and effort that was put into it.

Even given that such a decapitation operation was deemed necessary, should special operations forces be used to carry it out? The answer is not necessarily. When there are so many varied alternatives available, even in November 1941, such as by an aerial bombing operation (*a la* Ghadaffi), or by a sniper, or by a command-detonated or time-delayed bomb, the use of special operations forces here should have been questioned. The biggest problem with this operation is the same as with the Tragino Aqueduct mission—little attention is paid to the exfiltration of the forces involved.

Consider one last argument against this mission by examining another decapitation attempt. The U.S. Navy in the Pacific planned to kill Admiral Isoroku Yamamoto, the commander of the Pearl Harbor attack. The operation succeeded in its mission (which was to revenge the attack) but what else did it do? Very little; the raiders were even required to make it look like an accident that they shot down this particular plane so that the Japanese would not realize that the U.S. was reading its encrypted message traffic. All that resulted was that the U.S. did exact its revenge on Yamamoto. The Rommel mission should not have been approved and definitely not approved for execution by special operations forces.

The *intelligence* for this operation was extremely poor. The camp that was raided was not what the planners claimed it was and there seemed to be no way to pinpoint when Rommel would be there. In addition, if the planners had known more about the supply/logistics functions at Beda Littoria, they could have planned for broader destruction of this target. This would have been a better contribution to the overall Eighth Army plan of attack and would have coordinated the Commandos' role into the larger plan, instead of the raid being merely an after-thought.

Poor intelligence was not even the worst part. Why no one—from the Commandos who went to the commanders who approved it and all the staffers in between—asked any of the obvious hard questions about this operation is strange.

Wishful thinking played too large a part in this operation and common sense too little. There was too much *one-sided information* that was not critically examined.

Poor coordination is evident in several places—poor rehearsals and none in bad weather conditions; the inadequate packing of equipment, especially the explosives, and poor to no communications between the Headquarters and the raiding parties.

Finally, when bad weather hit the landing site and too few Commandos made it to the beach, the operation should have been called off. Once the smaller force was assembled on the beach and a decision to go ahead with the mission was made, it seems that someone should have checked the explosives and fuses one last time. With all the experience different Commando units had up to this point in the war, this seems like a failure of some pretty basic techniques, one that should not have happened.

McRaven's criteria do not fare any better in this operation. The plan tried to do too many tasks—there were three other missions in addition to killing Rommel, none of them anywhere near the primary objective. There were no realistic rehearsals. Practicing a plan under expected conditions (and good weather was not a given for this operation) can point out basic weaknesses. Changing the plan once the under-strength landed force was assembled proved to be disastrous because it was not part of the operation preparation. And, as with the Tragino operation, there was no alternate exfiltration plan except the one devised on the spot—evade as best you can!

Surprise at the main target was lost when the first shot was fired and the Commandos could not make up the subsequent loss of *speed*. The Commandos did, however, display good *security* and *purpose*.

One of the biggest problems on the planning side was the infiltration procedures. It appears that at least two alternate means of delivery (by parachute or by truck, *a la* the Long Range Desert Group) could have been used but there is no evidence that these were even considered. It seems that this plan was put together by staffers with no special operations background or experience.

As a result of this failed mission special operations forces demanded and later received better target intelligence and more of a hand in planning their own missions.

SOURCES

Books:

Cook, Graeme; *Commandos in Action;* London; Hart-Davis MacGibbon; 1973

Ladd, James; *Commandos and Rangers of World War II;* London; Macdonald and Jane's; 1978

Mason, Herbert M.; *The Commandos;* New York; Duell, Sloan and Pearce; 1966

Messenger, Charles; *The Commandos, 1940–1946;* London; William Kimber; 1985

——————, George Young, and Stephen Rose; *The Middle East Commandos;* London; William Kimber; 1988

Saunders, Hilary St. G.; *The Green Beret—The Story of the Commandos 1940–1945;* London; Michael Joseph; 1949

—————— (unattributed); *Combined Operations—The Official Story of the Commandos;* New York; MacMillan; 1943

Articles:

Pitt, Barrie; "The Keyes Raid"; in *War Monthly;* March 1980; pages 34–39

CHAPTER THREE

THE LOCUST WARRIORS

The Soviet Union was one of the first countries to realize the unique potential of parachute forces. As early as 1927 there were reports of parachute troops being used against bandits in Central Asia. Within the next two to three years Leonid G. Minov began to organize the first military parachute units. He traveled to the United States to study parachute strategy and techniques employed in air rescue missions. He returned to his country with a supply of American-made Irvin parachutes. In April 1930, Soviet industry produced its first run of domestic parachutes, not surprisingly patterned on the Irvin style.

In a parallel development, General Mikhail Tukhachevski, commander of the Leningrad Military District, began theorizing about and earnestly exploring the plausibility of using airborne troops. Tukhachevski was one of a group of farsighted Soviet military officers who developed the concept of deep battle. This military concept seemed ready made for the employment of parachute troops.

The earliest Soviet involvement with parachute operations went through several phases of development. This was especially true with air delivery techniques. As with many novel developments in military planning, airborne troop theory outpaced the practical aspects of plane design and implementation. The first paratroopers exited their transport plane by climbing through a hole in the top of the fuselage. They then had to crawl along the spine before making their way out along a wing. From the wing the paratroopers rolled off and deployed their parachutes using a rip-cord system. Later Soviet plane designers added small compartments that were constructed under each wing. Paratroopers were then transported to the target areas and dropped like bombs over their drop zones. Still later, Minov switched from the rip-cord method of opening parachutes to the static line concept. This method consisted of hooking deployment lines attached to the backpack of the parachute to a fixed cable inside the airplane. The act of jumping out of the plane stretched the static line to its maximum length and the falling paratrooper's body pulled the parachute pack opening tie loose, thus deploying the parachute.

Stalin's military purges of the late 1930s robbed the Red Army of its top leadership. The parachute force was especially hard hit and lost virtually all of its leadership down to about the rank of major. Included in the first round of purges was Tukhachevski himself. Despite the severe impact of the purges, experimentation with unit size or mission types continued. Parallel studies were conducted as to methods of transport and coordination with other units in the Army. By June 1941 there were five airborne corps in the Red Army, each consisting of about 10,000 troopers. These corps had been built from the cadres of the five Airborne Brigades (the 201st, 204th, 211th, 212th, and 214th). These brigades had been the standard unit until changes were initiated sometime in 1940. The corps consisted of three airborne brigades, each composed of four battalions of 678 men each. The organization of airborne forces looked like this:

1st Airborne Corps   (Kiev Military District)
            1st, 204th, and 211th Brigades

2nd Airborne Corps   (Kharkov Military District)
            2nd, 3rd, and 4th Brigades

3rd Airborne Corps   (Odessa Military District)
            5th, 6th, and 212th Brigades

4th Airborne Corps   (Western Special Military District)
            7th, 8th, and 214th Brigades

5th Airborne Corps   (Baltic Special Military District)
            9th, 10th, and 201st Brigades

202nd Brigade   (Far Eastern Military District)

The most immediate problem faced by the Soviets, which was problematic to most of the countries that employed parachute forces, was the lack of transport aircraft. Soviet production of transports had to be cut in order to satisfy a more pressing need for fighters and bombers. Among the few transport crews available most had no experience in formation flying, night navigation, or combat operations. To complicate things even more, the *Lutfwaffe* had maintained complete dominance in the air since the German invasion in June 1941. This air superiority severely restricted the use of Soviet airborne troops in their original capacity.

The Soviets were now confronted with the necessity of employing the deep battle concept. Soviet parachute forces, or "Locust Warriors" as they were called, were now deployed on missions that required them to link up with local partisan units in the areas where they were active. The paratroopers then became responsible for supplying, training, and leading these partisans in combat operations. All these operations were coordinated within the framework of larger army battle strategy or front missions.

Soviet airborne forces were first employed on a major scale during the defense of Moscow. In the early winter of 1941, the German Fourth Army and Fourth *Panzer* Army ground to a virtual halt just 25 miles from Moscow. Facing the Germans were the Russian Tenth and Thirty-third Armies. German forward advances were thwarted and the battle lines became stabilized just east of the area that included Vyazma and Yukhnov. The supply trucks, on which the Germans relied heavily, had to pass through these towns. To arrive at their forward positions, these German convoys had to pass several pockets of partisan activity. These partisan forces began to grow more active. Soon they were conducting raids to interdict the supply routes in the areas west and south of Vyazma and in the area of Yukhnov.

In order to assist a counterattack forming on its left wing, the Red Army's West Front (Army Group) ordered an airborne assault to seize key air, road, and rail transport facilities. The goal was to block any further movement of German supplies, equipment, and reserves from reaching the front. For the next two months, the Soviets began conducting airborne assaults. These were conducted mostly at night and against targets along both supply routes. Most of the airborne units involved belonged to 4th Airborne Corps. Original plans called for the entire corps to be dropped but combat developments, as they so often do, forced a change in these plans. One of these developments was weather. By early January 1942 the temperature had dropped to minus 44 degrees in the area around Vyazma.

On the evening of 2/3 January 1942, the airborne phase began when 348 men of the 1st Battalion, 201st Airborne Brigade, under the command of Captain I.A. Surzhik jumped in the vicinity of the airfield at Myatlevo. This was east of Yukhnov and along the southern supply route. The airborne unit's mission was to clear and secure the airfield for the air-landing of the 250th Rifle Regiment. In addition, the battalion was to capture and hold the bridge over the Shanya River. Surzhik's battalion landed successfully but then the weather quickly worsened. The next two days were spent clearing snow from the airfield while also repulsing several counterattacks by the Germans.

Eventually the Soviet high command decided not to send in the 250th. The parachute battalion was ordered to begin independent activities. For the next two weeks the battalion conducted several guerrilla-style raids, overrunning several German garrisons near Gribovo and Maslovo. Since holding the Shanya River bridge was now implausible, Surzhik and his men blew it before infiltrating back to their lines.

On the night of 3/4 January, the remnants of an improvised airborne detachment under the command of Captain I.G. Starchak was deployed. This unit, originally composed of 415 men plus 50 men from 214th Airborne Brigade, had been used in a combat jump to the northwest of Moscow in December. The current plan called for Starchak's men to jump near the Bolshoye Fatyanova airfield. The transport, however, dropped the paratroopers over a widely scattered area due mainly to heavy German antiaircraft fire. In fact, six of the planes returned to their airfields without having dropped their paratroopers. On the evening of 7/8 January, Starchak and his unit seized the Myatlevo train station and blew up all the rolling stock to be found in the vicinity. By 20 January, Starchak was wounded and had only 87 men left under his command. Remnants of his unit finally were able to join up with elements of advancing army units near Nikolskoya.

In the early morning hours of 18 January, 1/201st and part of 2/201st Airborne Brigade jumped into a scattered area between Znamenka airfield and the village of Zhelanke. This area was about halfway between Vyazma and Yukhnov. Their mission was to seize and secure this airfield for a follow-on air-land operation that was to bring a rifle regiment into the field. The units were then to move south to Yukhnov and cut off the supply route. This action was designed to support the advance of the 1st Guards Cavalry Corps against Myatlevo. The jump operation was unopposed. Surzhik's unit formed up first and attacked a German unit at the airfield. The Germans, however, held. Rather than suffer further casualties in an attempt to capture the airfield, Surzhik and his men created an improvised airstrip near the village of Plesnovo and radioed that they were ready to receive the air-land elements. Immediately, the remaining 200 men of 2/201st air-landed, accompanied by the control group for the overall operation. Between 20 and 22 January, the 250th Rifle Regiment also landed in force.

The Germans, noting the volume of nighttime air activity, became concerned about a railroad bridge on the Ugra River, south of Vyazma. Virtually all of their important supply trains, running south, had to use this bridge and to have it captured or destroyed would seriously interrupt this logistical flow. Therefore, four rifle companies were dispatched to secure the bridge. Their movement was essentially lateral traffic behind the German front. However, when the Germans arrived on 1 February they were immediately attacked by Surzhik's battalion. Although they could not destroy this enemy threat, the Soviets had the Germans surrounded and railroad traffic was effectively stopped.

According to plan, 2/201st and most of the 250th Rifle Regiment units fought their way south toward Yukhnov and the supply route. The rest of the Soviet forces remained at the airfield to block the north-south road between Vyazma and Yukhnov. On 25 January, 1st Guards Cavalry Corps broke through the German lines, crossed the southern supply route, and continued north to link up with the airborne units.

Between 27 January and 4 February 1942, the three brigades of 4th Airborne Corps (7th, 8th, and 214th) were dropped piecemeal in the general vicinity of Vyazma. They landed along the northern supply route with the mission to cut the northern *rollbhan* that ran from Smolensk through Vyazma. Most of the drops were not very concentrated due to the inexperience of the Soviet transport pilots. During the day *Luftwaffe* bombers attacked airfields that were being used to drop and resupply the paratroopers. By night, the airfields were repaired and put back into use. Bad weather finally put a stop to all air operations.

On 3 February, the Soviet Thirty-third Army drove a wedge five miles deep between the two German armies. The Germans quickly regrouped, cutting this salient and sealing it off. A five-division corps was then assigned the mission of reducing this pocket and clearing the parachutists who were threatening Vyazma and the northern supply route. Despite horrid weather, some of the pockets had been eliminated and supplies were rolling into Vyazma on a regular basis by mid-month.

From 17 to 23 February, more Soviet paratroopers (2/8th Airborne Brigade, 4/204th Airborne Brigade, and all of 9th and 214th Airborne Brigades) had jumped into the general areas of Staritsa, Monchalova, Okorokova, and Zhelanye. Of the 7,373 dropped, some 5,000 paratroopers managed to quickly assemble and continued on their mission to attack toward Yukhnov. Once the drops had been completed the units moved quickly. The recently arrived airborne units linked up with the 1st Guards Cavalry Corps and the remnants of the airborne units that had parachuted in earlier. Another attack against the southern supply route was launched. The road was cut and held by the Soviets for two days. A strong German counterattack again reopened the road.

The Red Army paratroopers maintained heavy pressure on the Germans and forced them to withdraw from Yukhnov on 3 March. On 6 March, the Russian airborne and cavalry units drove to within four kilometers of the southern supply route before being stopped. At the same time, a parachute battalion of 450 men jumped near Yelnya, farther to the west. A link-up with local partisans was effected. The combined force attacked and seized a supply base in the railroad center at Yelnya. They also succeeded in surrounding the fairly small German garrison in this area.

On 7 March, another German front line corps, the XLIII, was taken off the line and committed against the Soviet cavalry, airborne, and partisan forces operating in their rear. By 19 March, the Soviets were slowly, but steadily, driven into the forests around Lugi. A reinforced German company was also sent to relieve the besieged units at the Ugra River railroad bridge, but this effort failed. Then, beginning 25 March and lasting for one month, the two German armies (the Fourth and Fourth *Panzer*) coordinated a strong, slugging, give-no-quarter attack against the encircled Soviet units.

On 19 April, 4/23rd Airborne Brigade of the 10th Airborne Corps jumped into the area around Svintsovo. They were to reinforce what was left of the 4th Airborne Corps, which was now down to about 2,000 effectives with perhaps another 2,000 sick or wounded. By 23 May, the corps strength was 1,565 with 470 sick and wounded. A final effort to reinforce the remaining paratroopers was launched between 29 May and 3 June. The remaining battalions of 23rd Airborne Brigade and 211th Airborne Brigade were dropped into the western end of the pocket at Dorogobuzh. But this effort was mostly to no avail.

On 25 April, the Thirty-third Army surrendered. The Germans spent May and June systematically destroying the remaining airborne and cavalry units still operating in the area. It was only during this final drive against the paratroopers in Yelnya and those that had surrounded the Ugra River bridge, that the Germans could boast of finally defeating this enemy.

The German commanders who survived the war tended to minimize the role of the Soviet airborne in this battle. This was not, however, the prevailing opinion at the time of the fighting. The Germans then had admitted that the presence of the Soviet parachute units in their rear area was the chief cause of their withdrawal from Yukhnov in March. One German unit claimed the paratroopers were the very best of the Soviet infantry.

Mission Critique

As with the Allied Market-Garden operation in 1944, military writers are split on the issue of whether using Soviet airborne units in the Vyazma-Yukhnov battles was successful. The mixed opinion regarding this subject is precisely because this military action was more a campaign than an operation. It was part of a mighty struggle to drive the Germans away from Moscow. From the Soviet perspective, this fighting in the Vyazma-Yukhnov area was an overwhelming victory *in the defense of Moscow.*

This campaign was justified by a political decision based almost entirely on desperation. It required that the Soviet high command use all of the capabilities at its disposal. Because it was required, the high command then employed conventional infantry, at least two corps of cavalry, and as much of its parachute forces as could be conceivably jammed into the battlefield.

To highlight this sense of desperation, there have been stories recounting the fact that the Soviets dropped paratroopers into the snow without parachutes. This is in fact known to have happened on at least two occasions. The first was in Finland. The second was during the Vyazma operation. In both cases the planes were flying low and slow, and the drops were made into deep snow drifts. In the Vyazma operation, discussed here, there is even a mention that some of the paratroopers were wrapped in burlap sacks before they were dropped. The mere existence of these stories should point out the utter desperation in which the Soviet high command found itself while defending Moscow. In a desperate situation such as this the necessity of using special operations forces, regardless of the outcome, should not be second guessed.

Employing Vandenbroucke's criteria, there are negative observations to be made in two areas of the campaign. There was a good deal of *wishful thinking* on the part of the Soviet high command that the airborne portion would have great success.

The planners, however, seem to have overlooked or disregarded several things. First and foremost, was the general lack of transport aircraft available to bring in airborne forces in strength. Additionally, the pilots of what transports were available had not flown jump operations before. This prevailing negative also applied to many countries in the course of the war. Departure airfields, to be used by the paratroopers, were constantly being changed due to tactical considerations. Granted, not much could be done about this. However, moving the paratroopers from one place to another, on short notice, just delayed their arrival at their targets. Many of the transports that were available in early 1942 were also used to evacuate the wounded, thus causing scheduling nightmares. In the final analysis, *wishful thinking* or not, the supply routes were bona-fide military targets and the paratroopers were available.

There is at least one indication of *inappropriate intervention*. Once the operation started the paratroopers were virtually committed to suffer for long periods of time without hope of reinforcement or replacement. Again, however, the desperate nature of this struggle certainly justified this.

Employing the McRaven criteria, only a few problems were to be found and they were in the execution phase. These were problems with the twin issues of *security* and *repetition*. These issues only became problems once the operation began. *Security* was very good until the Germans discovered the presence of the paratroopers. There were only so many places for the paratroopers to be dropped, leading to the *repetitious* use of the same drop zone. The problem of using the same drop zones, on succeeding nights, was just inviting German initiatives and the paratroopers were hit hard once on the ground. Furthermore, German anti-aircraft units were now on the alert and positioned themselves to score several major victories. The element of *speed* was lost when the units and/or their drop zones were discovered. Although the fighting was tenacious and prolonged, the Germans usually destroyed the Soviet units in detail—and not just the airborne units.

One negative assessment of this campaign took issue with the fact that while the organization and planning of the parachute assaults were conducted by the staff of the airborne forces, once on the ground the paratroopers fell under the operational control of the army group, which had taken no part in the original planning. This is really petty criticism. Even though the airborne staff planned the operation the Soviet high command could and did change it to meet operational needs. To be truly effective special operations forces must fill a role in the overall theater operations plan. This means that the ground commander, who may indeed not have helped shape the original planning, must still maneuver all the forces available to him to achieve victory. *That is*, after all, why he is in command—to achieve victory.

In the long run, this campaign was successful. There were local victories in the German rear areas and a German plan to resume the offensive in March had to be discarded because of the imminent threat to their rear area supply routes. The final assessment as to its success lies with the fact that the Germans never again threatened Moscow.

SOURCES

Books:

Beaumont, Roger A.; *Military Elites—Special Fighting Units in the Modern World;* New York; Bobbs-Merrill; 1974

Galvin, John R.; *Air Assault—The Development of Airmobile Warfare;* New York; Hawthorn Books; 1969

Glantz, David M.; *The Soviet Airborne Experience;* Fort Leavenworth; U.S. Army Command and General Staff College; 1984

Gregory, Howard; *Parachuting's Unforgettable Jumps;* La Mirada, CA; Howard Gregory Associates; 1974

MacDonald, Charles; *Airborne;* New York; Ballantine Books; 1970

Reinhardt, Hellmuth et al; *Russian Airborne Operations;* Historical Division, HQ, US-AREUR; 1952

Thompson, Leroy; *Unfulfilled Promise—The Soviet Airborne Forces 1928–1945;* Bennington, VT; Merriam Press; 1988

Tugwell, Maurice; *Airborne to Battle—A History of Airborne Warfare 1918–1971;* London; William Kimber; 1971

Zaloga, Steven J.; *Inside the Blue Berets—A Combat History of Soviet and Russian Airborne Forces, 1930–1995;* Novato, CA; Presidio Press; 1995

Articles:

Dontsov, I. and P. Livotov; "Soviet Airborne Tactics"; in *Military Review*, October 1964

Gately, Matthew J.; "Soviet Airborne Operations in World War II"; in *Military Review*, January 1967

Reinhardt, Hellmuth; "Encirclement at Yukhnov: A Soviet Airborne Operation in World War II"; in *Military Review*, May 1963

Turbiville, Graham H.; "Soviet Airborne Troops"; in *Military Review*, April 1943

————; "Soviet Airborne Forces: Increasingly Powerful Factor in the Equation"; in *Army*, April 1976

CHAPTER FOUR

THE RETURN OF THE GOLDEN KITE

By 1940, the embargo against Japan of raw materials by several European countries and the U.S. was beginning to be effective. So effective that Japanese military planners decided that war against the interests of those countries imposing the embargo was inevitable. The planners began to look for targets and some of the early ones on the list were the rich oil fields and refineries of the Dutch East Indies.

The German use of airborne forces during their campaigns in the Low Countries and Norway in 1940 led to a major revolution among military thinkers around the world. At that point, Japanese parachute forces did not exist. As early as September 1940, Major Takedanomiya Tsuneyoshi, a member of the Imperial family and an officer on the General Staff of the Imperial Japanese Army, recommended that the Imperial Japanese Army begin developing parachute forces, to be known as Raiding Regiments. Tsuneyoshi also proposed that an assault of the important Palembang refinery complex, on the island of Java, might be accomplished with the use of these paratroopers. Mr. Sato, of the Imperial Japanese Army Air Headquarters, was one of the pioneers in the training, planning, and organization of the Japanese parachute force

As initially set up, the training lasted for six months and was conducted in great secrecy. This secrecy included sending soldiers, disguised as university students, to an amusement park in Tokyo to practice on the parachute tower there. There was no centralized training center but, rather, four locations where training was conducted. These four sites expanded to as many as 15, including several outside of Japan. Eventually, training was shortened to two months and was centralized. Training was given to both Army and Navy candidates, as each service had an airborne arm. Training for Army personnel was eventually conducted at one location, Nyutarabu in Miyazaki Prefecture. Training for Navy personnel was held at the Tateyama ordnance school in Tokyo Bay.

Army paratroopers adopted as their sleeve insignia a design of the 'Golden Kite.' This was a legendary bird in Japanese history which, by the dazzling light of its plumage, so blinded the enemy army facing the Emperor Jimmu Tenno that the outcome of the battle brought victory to the emperor, who founded the Empire of Japan in 660.

In August 1941, the General Staff of the Imperial Japanese Army began the detailed planning of attacks throughout Southeast Asia in earnest. An airborne operation at Palembang was included in this general plan even though members of the General Staff were concerned that the paratroops would not be ready by the time the war began.

On 28 October 1941, Japanese paratroopers conducted an exhibition for senior commanders at Takanabe, Kyushu. This exhibition was part of a considerably bigger exercise and only included one company sized parachute element. The successful drop persuaded those commanders who witnessed it that the paratroopers were making sufficient progress. As a result, a parachute assault was included in the plans that were finalized by the end of October.

By November 1941 the Japanese Navy had three groups which had received training. These units were designated the 1st, 2nd, and 3rd Yokuska Special Naval Landing Forces. The 1st and 3rd were later known as the Hariuchi or Karashima Force and the Fushumi Force. The 2nd, which had received parachute training, was only deployed in an amphibious capacity and not by parachute.

On 1 December 1941, the Imperial Japanese Army parachute forces were mobilized but still did not know what part they would play in the fighting ahead. One week later Japan was at war. The invasion plan for Java called for simultaneous amphibious landings from both the east and west. However, before the island could be captured, air superiority had to be wrested from the Dutch Air Force. In order to accomplish this, Japanese air strength had to move down into southern Sumatra and consolidate new bases for the Java invasion. One of the airfields selected for capture was at Palembang, the area previously recommended by Major Tsuneyoshi that included two oil refineries near the town. The paratroops were to be attached to the South Army commanded by General Terauchi, who was in overall command of the Southeast Asia conquest, and were assigned the Palembang complex as their objective.

Maps and aerial photographs of the area were sent to the Raiding Brigade headquarters and the staff began reviewing the problem of attacking and capturing both the airfield and the nearby refinery complex. The 1st Raiding Regiment was to execute the parachute assault. The code name for this operation was L.

On 19 December, the 1st Raiding Regiment left Japan for Indochina on the transport ship *Meiko Maru*. The trip was without event until the morning of 3 January 1942. At 1130, the *Meiko Maru* caught fire and sank very quickly. Although no reason was ever determined for this fire, one explanation given credence at the time was that the paratroopers' munitions caught fire spontaneously. All of the members of the regiment were rescued by the fleet of escort ships but were exhausted by their ordeal and virtually all of their equipment had gone down with the ship.

As a consequence of this incident, the General Staff decided to use the 2nd Raiding Regiment, at this time only a reinforced battalion of about 800 men. The regiment's mission was to assault and hold the airfield and oil refineries until they were relieved by ground troops who would make an amphibious landing within 48 hours of the parachute drop. Enormous pressure was placed on Colonel Seiichi Kume, commander of the 1st Raiding Brigade, the parent unit of the two raiding regiments, because the 2nd Raiding Regiment was not yet at its planned strength nor did it have the equipment it would need to be combat ready. Colonel Kume was given the highest supply priority by the General Staff for parachutes and weapons. Within a matter of days Kume reported the 2nd Raiding Regiment ready and, on 15 January, the regiment left Japan, bound for Phnom Penh, Cambodia, where it arrived 18 days later.

The plan was for the Japanese Imperial Forces to land on Sumatra on 15 February 1942. The main landing force was the 38th Division. The 38th was to reach Palembang in two days. The 15th was designated in the plan as L-Day. In order to achieve the maximum in surprise, the first of two airborne drops was scheduled for L-1, the 14th. Colonel Kume and his paratroopers would have to take their objectives and hold them for almost four days, until they would be relieved by the 38th on L+2.

The reason for two parachute assaults was that the planners at Japanese South Army did not believe that the 2nd Raiding Regiment, as understrength as it was, could seize and hold both the refineries and the airfield. Accordingly, they placed priority on seizing the airfield first with the refineries as the second priority. Therefore, most paratroopers would jump onto the airfield with a smaller-sized element assaulting the refineries. In addition, a follow-on jump was planned for L-Day itself, bringing in a company of about 90 paratroopers to reinforce the attack on the airfield.

South Army planners finalized their plan on 1 February, issuing orders to all units involved. The Raiding Brigade staff immediately began to make plans for the airborne operation. They first began looking for areas that could be used for drop zones. Although it appeared that the most effective DZ was the airfield this also looked as though it was the most dangerous one. Machine gun pillboxes and anti-aircraft gun positions would hamper the effort of the landing paratroopers to get to their weapons and any cargo or equipment containers that were dropped with them. The landing paratroopers would only be armed with automatic pistols. All of their rifles, automatic weapons, and other infantry gear had to be dropped in cargo containers. In the end, Colonel Kume picked out two areas located away from the airfield as the principal DZs, one about 1,200 meters to the southeast and one about 200 meters to the west.

The refineries proved to have different problems, with pipes, towers, and electric power lines all over the place, but a similar solution. The selected DZs included one about 700 meters south and the other about 500 meters west of the refineries.

Eighteen transport planes, supported by an escort of 6 bombers, would drop paratroopers in the DZ southeast of the airfield and 6 transports escorted

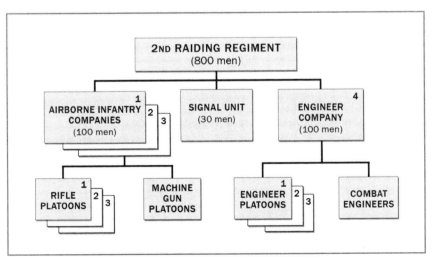

Organization of the IJA 2nd Raiding Regiment.

by 3 bombers would drop at the DZ to the west. At the refineries area, 6 transports and 6 bombers in escort would drop on the DZ to the west and 3 transports with an escort of 3 bombers would cover the southern DZ.

On 11 February, the paratroopers and their planes moved from Phnom Penh to Sungai Petani, Malaya. On the 13th, those paratroopers who would jump on L-1 moved south to the Keluang and Kahany airfields while the others remained at Sungai Petani. The stage was set for Japan's first combat parachute assault.

High altitude bombing, strafing, and pre-jump bombing were conducted for 11 days prior to L-Day. Even though this aerial attack took away the element of surprise for the invading Japanese units, it did succeed in affecting adversely the strength and morale of the British and Dutch forces on the ground.

On L-1, at 0830, planes at both airfields took off. They were to rendezvous at Batu Pahat. Once airborne, the sky train consisted of more than 150 aircraft, including 34 transport planes and 27 heavy bombers. The escort included 80 Type-1 fighters and 9 Type-99 light bombers. A single Type-100 Scout plane led the way. Flight altitude on the way to Palembang was 3,000 meters (about 10,000 feet).

The sky route was clouded by smoke and haze from the fires in Singapore, making flying difficult but also protecting the formation from observation from the ground. At 1120, the formation divided over the mouth of the Moesi River, one section headed for the airfield and the other to the refineries. Six minutes after the formation divided, the planes began descending to drop altitude, 600 feet, over the drop zones. Inside the planes the paratroopers were hooked up, waiting for the two-second buzzer to sound. This would be their command to jump. Suddenly, ground antiaircraft picked several targets out of the overflight, including one of the two equipment planes and two planes with paratroopers. The pilots, many of whom did not have previous experience under fire, took evasive maneuvers once they detected the incoming fire. The jump buzzer finally sounded and the planes were quickly emptied. The evasive maneuvering had the obvious result of scattering the paratroopers over a wide area, thus delaying assembly. Within four minutes paratroopers were descending over both targets. The transport aircraft returned to their departure airfields without sustaining a single loss.

As soon as the paratroopers were clear of their aircraft the heavy bombers dropped their cargo loads and began attacking the ground defenses. RAF Hurricanes attacked the bombers over the airfield and individual dogfights ensued. Light bombers attacked barracks areas and anti-aircraft positions around the airfield. No air resistance was met over the refineries. In all the Japanese lost one heavy bomber to ground fire at the refineries while downing a total of four Hurricanes at both sites (airfield and refineries).

The drop at the airfield went almost as planned. All but one team landed within three kilometers southwest of the airfield. The one team, from 4th Company, led by Lieutenant Okumoto, was delayed because of trouble with the plane door prior to the jump. They landed on a road between the airfield and Palembang city. Once out of their chutes, Lieutenant Okumoto and four others assembled and began moving toward the airfield. They were met almost immediately by four trucks transporting about 40 native militia troops. The paratroopers had only their automatic pistols but they attacked vigorously and quickly captured the demoralized militia soldiers.

Soon more of Lieutenant Okumoto's men began to assemble. At about noon more Dutch troops came from the direction of the city in two armored cars and four trucks. The paratroopers repeated their earlier attack, armed only with automatic pistols and hand grenades. The shock of the paratroopers' attack drove the Dutch troops away, leaving one of the armored cars and three trucks. Two paratroopers were killed in this action and Lieutenant Okumoto was wounded. As would happen years later at Normandy, the fortuitous and off target drop of their group of paratroopers paid dividends because, following these two fights, Lieutenant Okumoto and his men established a road-block between the city and the airfield.

The photos of the drop zone showed low vegetation covered the area. This vegetation was, in fact, trees, which became traps for the falling cargo containers. Retrieving these containers was time-consuming and, in frustration, some of the paratroopers began moving toward the airfield armed only with their automatic pistols, assembling into their combat formations as they moved. The paratroopers near the airfield began to assemble as soon as they were free of their parachutes. By 1330, Major Komura, commander of the 2nd Raiding Regiment, had assembled about 40 of the 180 paratroopers who jumped. Lieutenant Okumoto arrived in the captured armored car and passed on the information about his unit's road block.

Major Komura sent out Lieutenant Mitsuya, commander of 4th Company, and Lieutenant Ooki and 20 men to attack and secure the control tower at the airfield. Along the way, at the road between the airfield and the city, the small group of paratroopers encountered about 300 Allied soldiers who were moving from the airfield. A fierce fight followed and soon the Allied soldiers were fleeing back in the direction of the airfield, pursued by the Japanese paratroopers. Eventually, the control tower was captured at around 1830.

In the meantime, Major Komura continued toward the airfield through the trees, picking up cargo containers and small groups of paratroopers along the way. His progress was slow because of the thickness of the jungle and occasional brief fire fights with Allied soldiers who were trying to get away from the airfield. By 1800, Major Komura had reached the east end of the airfield, where he encountered Lieutenant Komaki and the Signal Platoon. At about 2100, Major Komura was at the control tower, where he met Lieutenant Mitsuya and his force. Major Komura began consolidating the paratroopers into positions around the airfield, spending the night prepared to throw back counterattacks that never came.

The aerial photos of the DZ that was located about 800 meters west of the airfield showed the area to be grassland. When the 60 paratroopers under Lieutenant Hirose, commander of 2nd Company, landed there they found themselves in Kunai grass, some as tall as six feet and with sharp edges. Once again, the conditions on the ground prevented the paratroopers from finding each other or their cargo containers. Nonetheless, separately and in small groups they advanced on the airfield. Lieutenant Gamo collected about 16 paratroopers during their advance. Suddenly they found themselves almost on top of an antiaircraft position; Lieutenant Gamo threw a grenade and rushed the position but was killed before reaching it. His men pulled back.

Further west, Lieutenant Hirose could only find two paratroopers but he moved to the airfield anyway. At about 1400, he was at the front of the west barracks, which, he found, held about 350 Allied troops. Lieutenant Hirose immediately pulled back out of sight. Sometime later one other paratrooper wandered into his area. At about 1700, Lieutenant Hirose again approached the west barracks. This time he found the barracks deserted, and when he and his men entered the building they found food still being cooked. Lieutenant Hirose could only guess that the Allied troops had left in a hurry. He and his men ate a hearty meal before moving on.

The two refineries that were targeted were located along both sides of a branch of the Moesi River. The easternmost refinery was designated by the Japanese as NKPM while the larger, western refinery was called BPM.

The DZ for the BPM refinery was a light marshy area but this did not prevent the 60 paratroopers from 1st Company, under the command of the company commander, Lieutenant Nakao, from locating their cargo/weapons containers. Lieutenant Tokunaga and six paratroopers immediately attacked a pillbox located in the southwest part of the refinery, capturing it by the surprise and speed of their attack. Next these same seven paratroopers moved in a northerly direction until they encountered 60 Allied soldiers, some armed with machine guns, and engaged them in a fire fight. While this fight was at its fiercest, two additional squads of paratroopers, under Lieutenant Ogawa and Lieutenant Yosioka, joined Lieutenant Tokunaga's small force. By splitting his now larger force Lieutenant Tokunaga eventually overcame all opposition and raised a Rising Sun flag over the BPM refinerys central topping installation.

When Lieutenant Tokunaga saw the flag he moved his force to the area at once, closing boiler valves and shutting down the refinery. By this time, Lieutenant Nakao, commander of 1st Company, had joined the force at the refinery. Soon after, an Allied counterattack was launched against the paratroopers, with fire fights raging at close range. The pipe lines were hit several times by bullets, causing oil to leak out. Lieutenant Nakao sent Lieutenant Tokunaga's platoon to push the Allied soldiers back.

Sometime during this fight, the Allied troops fired mortar rounds at the pipeline, destroying a portion and setting fire to the oil. Though the ensuing fight lasted through the night, the paratroopers held their gains, repulsing all counterattacks and preventing further damage to the refinery.

At the DZ for the NKPM refinery, Lieutenant Hasebe's platoon found that the grassy area they were expecting, based on overhead photos, was a deep swamp. Two paratroopers landed almost on top of an Allied pillbox and attacked it immediately, armed only with their automatic pistols and grenades. They killed eight of the defenders and then advanced along the road to the refinery. Shots from a nearby barracks area wounded one of the paratroopers so they both turned back to find the rest of their platoon.

Lieutenant Hasebe and his men had commandeered a native boat they found near the DZ and used it to collect the unit's cargo and weapons containers. As soon as he accounted for his men, Lieutenant Hasebe ordered them onto the road to the refinery. This road ran straight for almost 300 meters, with no place to hide along the route. This made any advance along this road a very dangerous one. Lieutenant Hasebe looked for another way into the refinery but could not find one. He was therefore forced to attack along the road.

The platoon made it to within 100 meters of the refinery before the attack ground to a halt by enemy opposition. Lieutenant Hasebe was killed in the fight and Sergeant Tanba, who took command of the platoon, ordered the men to halt and wait for orders to conduct a night raid. Sergeant Tanba kicked off this raid at 2300 and the paratroopers were able to occupy the refinery almost immediately, the Allied defenders having already retreated. At 0600 the next morning a huge explosion, from a time bomb left behind by the Allied soldiers, set the refinery on fire. The explosion and fire destroyed almost 80% of the refinery.

On L-Day, 15 February, a scout plane was sent out from Keluang airfield. It landed at the Palembang airfield at about 1030. Major Komura gave the pilot a progress report of the actions by the paratroopers, emphasizing that they had not been able to locate very many of their cargo containers. When the pilot returned to Keluang, his report was the first word that General Sugawara had of the success of the previous day's operations, because there was no radio communications between Keluang and the paratroopers in the Palembang area. As soon as he received the report, General Sugawara ordered additional weapons and equipment to be loaded onto transports to be sent to Palembang.

Just before noon, Colonel Kume finally reached the airfield. His plan had included crash landing a transport plane several kilometers southeast of the airfield. This crash landing was conducted because the transport plane carried an anti-tank gun that would not fit into any of the unit's cargo containers. Because of the dispersion of the drop aircraft, Colonel Kume and his party had landed almost 10 kilometers from the airfield. He spent the intervening day crawling through swampy terrain and spent a mostly sleepless night being attacked by swarms of mosquitoes.

About an hour later, the reinforcing element of 90 paratroopers from 3rd Company, commanded by Lieutenant Morisawa, jumped onto Palembang airfield. Colonel Kume sent Lieutenant Adachi's platoon to Palembang to conduct a reconnaissance. By the time they reached the city it was almost 1730. Lieutenant Adachi send word back that the city was mostly empty and that they had destroyed one of the armored boats they found along the Moesi River. When he received this report, Colonel Kume sent 3rd Company to occupy the city. Later that evening, the paratroopers at the refineries sent runners to report on their missions. During the night, soldiers from the 38th Division, which had come in over the beach, linked up with the paratroopers at the airfield. Colonel Kume and his men were relieved in place on 20 February, when the 38th Division took over operations in the area.

The Palembang operation was a great success for the Japanese airborne units. The paratroopers had captured the airfield and one refinery intact on the first day, even though the Operations Plan called for their capture after the reinforcing unit jumped in on the second day. The refineries held almost 250,000 gallons of refined oil. Thirty-nine paratroopers were killed in action, 2 died from parachute malfunctions, and 48 were wounded. General Terauchi, commander of the Japanese South Army, sent a letter praising the action of the paratroopers to the Raiding Brigade Headquarters. The first action of Japanese paratroopers was completed, successfully.

Mission Critique

The Palembang operation was rather tidy and of short duration. For the most part careful planning marked the operation. The paratroopers accomplished their ultimate goal at the airfield, the capture of the oil refineries, and linked up with the forces that landed over the beach.

This mission demonstrates the first solid use of parachute forces of the missions discussed so far. The target assigned to the paratroopers was critical to the plan and appropriate to their capability. While there were some weaknesses in the plan it was better than the two other options that seem to have been available—bomb the airfield and refineries from the air or try to capture them with troops from the amphibious landings. Aerial bombing was not precise and even if it was anywhere close to the capability that exists today, the antiaircraft guns in the area would have contributed to many problems and perhaps even destroyed the refineries, the very targets of the whole operation. As for the amphibious forces, they took two days from their landing to get to the refineries. Who can know how long it might have taken them to fight their way to the refineries and in what condition they would have found the refineries if the parachute forces had not been used? This operation is a suitable use of special operations forces and the mission results support this conclusion.

There were, however, some problems. The pre-operation *intelligence* was either insufficient or incorrect in the estimate of the strength and composition of forces on the ground. This led to an assumption that the airfield would be easier to capture than it was; the relative speed with which the ground forces were able to mount an effective, albeit short-lived, opposition to the Japanese paratroopers contributed in large measure to the problems of capturing the airfield and nearby refineries. Additionally, interpretation of aerial photographs of the drop zones was very deficient in not determining what the ground conditions were that made up the various drop zones. This failure led to the paratroopers not being able to locate most of their cargo containers.

One of the biggest failures, one which could have had much more serious consequences than it did, was a matter of *poor coordination*. Prior to the jump, the pre-raid air attacks on the airfield did not target the anti-aircraft guns at all. Although the paratroopers did not suffer as a result of this major failure, it could have been much worse. Once again luck played a part in the execution of the operation. In this same area, the lack of communications between the paratroopers at Palembang airfield and the rear area command at Keluang airfield was another example of the systemic problem for many of the missions discussed in this book.

Other *coordination* problems evident in the execution of the mission were of a lesser order and, eventually, led to changes in airborne procedures. There were three of these minor problems worth mentioning. First was the size of the initial assault force. If a more accurate assessment had been made of the ground situation it seems logical that a larger force would have jumped in, a force of sufficient size to exploit some of the initial gains. Training had a bearing on this problem. Although Colonel Kume commanded a brigade, he was unable to assemble more than a battalion-sized regiment for this mission. Other missions will show how executing forces were task-organized to make up for an apparent lack of sufficient forces. Apparently this was not considered by the Japanese planners of the Palembang operation. A larger force would have led to a speedier capture of the refineries and probably would have meant that the forces on the ground would not have had as much time to damage the refining equipment.

The second and third items refer specifically to the jump operation in its execution. All of the equipment loads that the paratroopers would need once on the ground were concentrated in just two airplanes instead of being spread out among many more of the planes. The interval between jumpers as they exited the planes was too long, contributing to the unit's dispersion on the ground. Given the German experience in airborne assaults at this point in the war, it is surprising to find these last two items.

There appears to have been some *wishful thinking* in the planning of this operation only in asking the parachute forces to take all of its objectives and hold them until they linked up with the forces from the amphibious landings. Despite some problems the paratroopers did just that, overcoming an apparent weakness.

From the McRaven criteria most of the operation would be termed as well planned and executed except as any previous comments apply. There is no evidence of any rehearsals for this operation. This is not meant as criticism here since much of what would occur in rehearsals is really covered in unit training once an airborne unit is formed. Some *surprise* was undoubtedly lost because of the length of the pre-launch bombing but since the defenders on the ground didn't expect a parachute assault, there was some trade-off in this criterion.

The widespread dispersing of troops and equipment impacted on the *speed* of execution. The *purpose* displayed by the Japanese paratroopers in this operation was excellent. Despite obstacles, they fought against a force better than twice their size and carried out their mission. They operated for two days without resupply, until weapons and equipment arrived from Keluang to replace that which couldn't be located. All in all, this was a very successful operation.

SOURCES

Books:
Galvin, John R.; *Air Assault—The Development of Airmobile Warfare;* New York; Hawthorn Books; 1969

McLean, Donald B. (ed.); *Japanese Parachute Troops*; Wickenburg, AZ; Normount Technical Publications; 1973

Rottman, Gordon L. and Akira Takizawa; *Japanese Paratroop Forces in World War II*; New York; Osprey Publishing; 2005

Tugwell, Maurice; *Airborne to Battle—A History of Airborne Warfare 1918–1971;* London; William Kimber; 1971

Articles, other material:
Donaldson, Graham; "The Japanese paratroopers in the Dutch East Indies, 1941–1942"

The author is greatly indebted for the loan of interview material provided by George F. Cholewczynski, which included interviews between Mr. Cholewczynski and Akira Takizawa; this material provided much of the detail of the operation.

CHAPTER FIVE

STEALING HENRY

B efore any serious strategies for the implementation of mass Allied airborne invasions into France, the Mediterranean, or even across the
Rhine could be seriously considered, the principle of a successful parachute
raid had to be demonstrated. Just as it was first necessary to conduct the di-
vision-size raid at Dieppe in August 1942 before D-Day plans could even
be envisioned, so it was that the same rationale was applied to the fledgling
British airborne force. The raid to destroy the Tragino Aqueduct in Italy
ended with mixed results. Although the target was temporarily destroyed,
the attacking force was captured while trying to make its way to the evacuation site. And so Combined Operations HQ decided to try again. This time
they chose a target in France. The actual place was Bruneval.

Bruneval was picked because "Henry" was there. "Henry" was the codename applied to a piece of German radar equipment. During the early part
of World War II, scientists in England and Germany were simultaneously
racing to develop equipment that could be used to guide friendly fighters
and bombers to their targets, and could also detect incoming enemy aircraft.
One of the significant scientific contributors in this effort was Dr. Reginald
V. Jones, who had been posted to an intelligence position in the Air Ministry.

In November 1939, Jones benefited from an intelligence coup that was
rather startling. British intelligence concluded that "the Germans had two
kinds of Radar equipment, that large rockets were being developed, that there
was an important experimental station at Peenemunde, and that rocket-pro-
pelled gliding bombs were being tried there." By late June 1940, when Dr.
Jones presented the results of his painstaking research, he concluded that the
Germans had a better developed radar system than previously believed pos-

sible. It was not until June of the following year that Jones determined that the German radar consisted of two types of transmitters: a long range system which was designated *Freya;* and a short range system designated *Wurzburg.*

Jones knew quite a bit about the *Freya* system but very little about *Wurzburg.* He especially knew little about the *Wurzburg* antenna. Although at least two people had described this antenna to him, Jones had never seen one. Never, that is, until November 1941, when a friend showed him a high altitude photograph of two radar sites near Le Havre, France. Jones asked for, and got, low-level oblique photos of the same sites. He soon detected some differences in the antennas. One of them was obviously a *Freya.* Since Jones believed the two types of German radar operated in tandem, he concluded that the other was, therefore, a *Wurzburg.* When he and his deputy examined blown up versions of these low-level photos, Jones exclaimed, "Charles, we could get in *there;* there's a beach only a few hundred yards from the objective." *There* was Bruneval. Thus the idea for a raid to capture the *Wurzburg* antenna was hatched.

Acting Vice Admiral Lord Louis Mountbatten had recently taken command of Combined Operations HQ from Admiral Keyes. He was receptive to the Bruneval idea and ordered planning to begin immediately. The planners quickly realized that they had before them all the elements to make this raid a true combined operation. In short order they developed a plan that employed units from the Army, Navy, and Air Force. The naval force, which included motor gunboats of the 14th Flotilla, was to be commanded by Commander F.N. Cook, an Australian. The air element, consisting of 12 Whitley bombers from 51 Squadron, was under Wing Commander P.C. Pickard. The army element was to be a company of paras reinforced by an element of Royal Engineers and a radar expert. The engineers were a sapper unit commanded by Lieutenant Dennis Vernon. The radar expert was Flight Sergeant Charles Cox of the RAF, who knew only that he had volunteered for hazardous operations.

In mid-January 1942, Major John D. Frost, newly appointed to command C Company, 2nd Parachute Battalion, was alerted that his company was to conduct a demonstration jump for a group of distinguished visitors during the last week of February. C Company immediately departed for its designated training area in Tilshead. This site was selected because it most resembled the area where the demonstration jump was to take place. The company shared this training area with the newly activated Glider Pilot Regiment. Frost had not completed all of his qualifying jumps and was told that if he could not do so within a week, then the previous commander, Major Philip Teichman, would take charge. Frost was determined to complete his training in two days. Foggy weather and winds, however, intervened to slow his progress. Eventually, on the fourth day, as Frost recalled, ". . . in perfect weather I completed my course with great relief . . . The intense satisfaction I now felt was in great contrast to all the worries and doubts . . . and it far excelled the mere lifting of the proverbial load from the mind." Major Teichman "found it hard to disguise his disappointment" when Frost re-joined C Company.

Soon after the company's arrival at Tilshead, Major General Frederick A.M. "Boy" Browning, commander of all British airborne forces, came for an inspection. Browning confided to Frost that he would have anything he needed since it was likely that the entire War Cabinet would be there to see the jump and subsequent exercise. The next day a liaison officer from 1st Airborne Division arrived to discuss the exercise. He took Frost to an area about 20 miles away. Frost later described the area as "similar to the terrain on which our demonstration to the War Cabinet was to take place. The steep hills rising from the canal were to represent the cliffs at the edge of the sea and we were to practise a landing by night behind the imaginary enemy defences, the destruction of an enemy headquarters, followed by a move down a gully between the cliffs from which we were to be evacuated by small naval craft."

After reviewing the plan, Frost decided that he didn't like the way his company was organized. He rewrote the plan to fit three well-balanced platoons and tried to persuade division headquarters to change the organization. Since this was ostensibly only an exercise he did not understand the vehement opposition he and his ideas encountered. Within a few days, however, he was briefed on the real mission for C Company and told that if he "still did not like the plan, someone else would soon be found who did." Frost decided that he "had no further objection to raise."

Frost next took his company to Scotland for additional training with the type of naval craft that would be evacuating them back to England. This training was hardly satisfactory as something always seemed to go wrong. Undaunted, C Company returned to Tilshead for a company jump on 15 February. This was the first jump to include the entire raiding force as by now Vernon and his sappers and Flight Sergeant Cox had joined the paras. The training jump went successfully. The last rehearsal with the boat crews ended miserably. However, the time for any additional training had run out.

The estimated window for successfully executing the mission, code-named Operation Biting, was upon them. It was 25 February and there were only four days that the planners thought had the best moon and tide schedules for the operation. If the operation wasn't conducted during this period, it would have to be put off for about a month. Frost was not sure that security would hold for that long. It had to go in February.

A model of the operations area was given to the now-secluded C Company. No real location was given and places were designated by their function, such as "beach fort," "redoubt," "rectangle," and "lone house." The *Wurzburg* apparatus was labeled "Henry."

Company officers and noncommissioned officers studied the plan so they could brief their men. C Company was split into three teams. The teams were named after famous sailors, as a measure of solidarity with the naval crews who would be bringing the paras back from their raid.

Team "Rodney" was led by Lieutenant John Timothy. It included 30 men and was the reserve element, ready to be used where needed.

Team "Nelson" under Lieutenant Euen Charteris, had 40 men who were responsible for taking out the beach defenses. Captain John Ross, Frost's second-in-command, was part of "Nelson."

Finally, Team "Drake" was the main assault element and was led by Lieutenant Peter Young. Team "Drake" consisted of the remaining 50 raiders and was further sub-divided into three assault parties, named "Jellicoe," "Drake," and "Hardy."

Assault party "Hardy," led by Frost, was to surround the chateau near the antenna and nullify any German threats emanating from there. Assault party

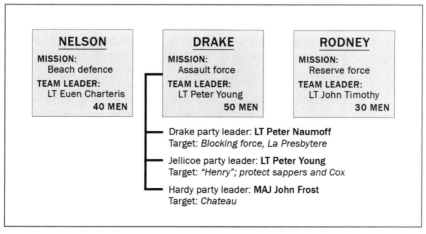

Organization of the raiding force which stole "Henry."

"Drake" was led by Lieutenant Peter Naumoff and was to be a blocking force between the German garrison at La Presbytere and the radar antenna. Assault party "Jellicoe," led by Young, was to surround the antenna and protect Cox and Vernon's sappers while they photographed, dismantled, packed for movement, and set charges to what remained of the installation.

Weather again interfered with Frost's plans. The operational window for conducting the raid was shrinking as postponements were announced with each passing day. On the last day, 27 February, Frost prepared to move his company back to Tilshead when word came that the operation would go as planned later that night. The weather relayed to the raiders promised "no wind . . . and a bright moon with a little cloud and a very light haze . . . visibility in the area was found to be two to four miles, with excellent definition." Frost reviewed the plan one last time and told his men where they were actually going. He explained that the attack would begin when he stood at the front door of the chateau, blew his whistle, and kicked in the front door. One of his men asked Frost what he would do if the door was locked. "Ring the bell, I suppose," was the immediate answer.

As the sound of bagpipes filled the air, the raiders assembled near the 12 Whitley bombers that would carry them to France. There was time for a last mug or two of tea, liberally laced with rum. Before boarding his plane, Frost learned that the target area was now covered with a layer of snow and that his naval support had departed that afternoon. At about 2230 that night the raiders loaded into their planes and settled in for their ride across the Channel. Many of them crawled into sleeping bags for warmth and, in an effort to ease the tension, sang bawdy songs during the trip. As the planes approached the French coast, antiaircraft batteries opened fire. Some of the planes were hit but none was damaged. The accuracy of the antiaircraft fire prompted two of the planes carrying "Nelson" team to take evasive action. While successful these maneuvers caused the pilots to eventually drop their sticks on the wrong drop zone.

Just after midnight the red light came on and the paras prepared to jump. The hole in the belly of the Whitley was uncovered and they moved forward to their prearranged places. The planes approached their drop zones at a height of 500 feet. In the lead plane the light turned green and Frost was the first to drop. The others quickly followed. The ground below was bathed in a bright light and it was easy to identify landmarks. While still in the air, Frost began mentally planning for assembly and movement to the target. Flight Sergeant Cox remembered afterward, "The first thing that struck me was how quiet everything was and how lonely I felt . . ." But, first things first. The plane had no facilities on board and the tea drunk prior to departing was now screaming for release. Once on the ground, Frost and his men stood in a circle and urinated in the snow, both for relief and as a gesture of defiance. They watched as "Rodney" team jumped. They then saw two of the planes carrying "Nelson" team fly over. Frost was not aware that the other two planes had already dropped their paras. The mis-dropped element was then about two miles away and included Lieutenant Charteris, the "Nelson" team leader.

Within ten minutes the raiders had recovered their equipment and assembled at their rendezvous point. As they approached the villa, Frost and his assault party broke into a run, fully expecting to be discovered at any moment. But they were not. Lieutenant Naumoff led his team off in the direction of La Presbytere and Lieutenant Young's team surrounded "Henry." When everyone was in position, Frost approached the front door of the chateau and found, to his astonishment, that it was open! He was so surprised that he almost forgot to blow his whistle. As soon as the signal was given, Young's party began firing and Frost and several men burst into the chateau. They found that it was empty, except for one German soldier standing at the top of a stairway who was quickly shot dead. Major Frost left three men inside to search the chateau. He immediately proceeded to the radar antenna site. He saw that most of the Germans there had been killed in the first few moments of the attack. However, two had been taken prisoner and were now being interrogated by Corporal Newman. Cox was photographing and sketching the antenna set-up. When he finished, he and the sappers began to disassemble all the parts that they could. The sounds of a heavy engagement were heard from the direction of La Presbytere area. Occasional incoming fire from that direction was also received near the antenna.

One of the German prisoners confirmed the order of battle information that Frost had on the area. He also told them that the troops at La Presbytere were equipped with mortars. In the meantime, Cox had discovered that the antenna was warm to the touch and, through the interrogator, learned that their planes had been spotted and tracked by "Henry." The fighting in the area of La Presbytere continued. Soon shooting was heard from the southeast, from the direction of the village of Bruneval. Frost urged his men to hurry. He found that his radios were useless and resorted to using runners to communicate and stay informed. Vehicles were reported near La Presbytere. By now, all parts of the antenna that could be dismantled were loaded on carts. Frost ordered the group to head for the beach.

As they neared the edge of the cliffs, a machine gun opened fire severely wounding Company Sergeant Major Strachan in the stomach. Captain Ross, yelling from the beach, informed Frost that the assembly area on the beach had not yet been secured. At the same time, Frost learned that a German force of unknown size had assembled near the chateau and was advancing on his position.

Frost personally led an assault on the attacking Germans and drove them off. When he returned to the edge of the cliff, he found the sappers moving the carts down to the beach. Ross and Naumoff had joined forces and were about to assault the German beach defenses when they heard gunfire on the German positions coming from the *south*. Fire on the German positions was now converging from both directions. Frost came on the scene to learn that Lieutenant Charteris, whose team had landed on the wrong drop zone, had arrived just in time. During the fighting Corporal Stewart was struck in the head by shrapnel. From the ground he called out to his friend and handed him his wallet, filled with recent gambling winnings. "I've had it," Stewart said. "Here's my wallet." His friend, Lance Corporal Freeman, checked Stewart out and told him, "You've only a scalp wound." "Give us me bloody wallet back, then," Stewart immediately responded.

Charteris explained to Frost that he realized right away that he and his men were dropped in the wrong place. They ascertained their location and took off at a run to find the rest of C Company. Along the way they ran into German gun fire from a patrol near Bruneval. They persisted in their effort to join up with the rest of C Company and their arrival coincided with Ross' attack. Their arrival was timely indeed.

By now it was about 0215 and almost all of the raiders were assembled on the beach. They tried to radio the landing boats to come in and pick them up, but with no success. Frost resorted to firing several flares, which had been agreed upon as a strictly emergency signaling method. However, there was still no response from the Navy. Frost began preparations for a defensive perimeter, thinking that he had been left high and dry. Then, one of Frost's men yelled, "Sir, the boats are coming in! The boats are here! God bless the ruddy Navy, sir!"

Frost had anticipated the boat formation to approach the beach two at a time. Instead all six of the landing craft hit the beach in unison. When the raiders, with their two German prisoners and most of "Henry" were loaded aboard, the boats quickly departed. They soon rendezvoused with gun boats and two destroyers. This was their escort back across the Channel. They were heading for home.

Frost and his men returned to a tumultuous welcome. After almost six weeks of secret planning and training, their exploits were now front page news in the evening paper. The official history described C Company's success this way: "Surprise and speed were the essential requirements of ... [the] raid." But Frost, whose men had just earned the first Battle Honors for the Parachute Regiment, summed it up best. "All we really wanted," he wrote, "was dry clothes, bed and oblivion; but before that there was some serious drinking to be done."

Mission Critique

This operation was one of the true gems of small force special force operations conducted during World War II. The success of the mission to steal "Henry" hinged on the issue of specific target identification. The objective to steal "Henry" also came with an almost built-in justification; and it was a hugely strategic one at that. Therefore, there was universal acknowledgment as to the necessity for this operation. The scientific need to examine a major component of German radar equipment in order to determine how it worked, how it might be duplicated, and how countermeasures might be developed against it were paramount because of how the scientists envisioned it could be used by the military in the future. The execution of the mission relied heavily, though not exclusively, on the employment of special operations forces which, in this case, were carefully and properly chosen.

This is an excellent example of a direct action mission that fits only within the range and capabilities of special operations forces. In all probability a conventional force could not have conducted this operation successfully. In addition, the operations security techniques gave it an added advantage that contributed to its success. A lingering and very significant question is why couldn't the planners find a mission like this one for X Troop, instead of sending them against the Tragino Aqueduct?

There are but a few minor comments to offer when using either the Vandenbroucke or McRaven criteria. The Bruneval raid is an operation that should be examined for all the good aspects it presents. The mission's good aspects include: its success in bringing back photographs of "Henry" assembled; bringing back major hardware components of "Henry"; and bringing along a German soldier familiar with "Henry's" operation. Perhaps the only thing lacking in this operation was something that was not available then; namely a heavy-lift cargo helicopter that could have brought back "Henry" in its entirety.

Also lauded must be the alert, and sometimes improvisational, efforts of the paras of C Company *during* the course of the entire operation. These efforts contributed to the mission's success. Two details amplify this point. First is the on the spot interrogation conducted of each captured German soldier in order to confirm or refute the pre-launch *intelligence*. Second is the *purposeful* action of Lieutenant Charteris and his force. Even though they jumped wide of the target, these men never gave up on their mission. They kept going on to their objective and, in the final analysis, played a critical role in the exfiltration of the entire force. Therefore, these two items, along with the *operations security, repetitious rehearsals, the surprise* element of the raid itself, and the *simplicity* of the plan were all key factors in the mission's success.

A critical factor, which played a very important role in the success of the Bruneval raid, was the operations security techniques employed throughout the mission; from initial planning and scheduling to C Company's safe return back to England. The term "operations security" or OPSEC wasn't used at the time of this mission. However, its principles (what must be protected, what is the threat, how is the operation vulnerable, what is the assessment of the risk, and what countermeasures can be employed) were certainly evident in the planning and execution of this raid. The assessment of the risk by Combined Operations HQ relied on two things: the belief in the countermeasures employed (cover story for the units taking part; no locations briefed to the raiders until just before take-off; night training; brevity codes for radio communications; flares as back-up to radios for signaling; and integrating formations of planes filled with jumpers with the planes destined for a conventional bombing run) and the timing of the raid. As evident from Frost's comment, *security* was critical but could not be maintained over too long a period. There is little doubt that OPSEC contributed to the success of the raid.

This last countermeasure (mixing special operations planes in with a bombing run) can sometimes be a two-edged sword. This technique can backfire because planes flying overhead will definitely cause soldiers on the ground to look up at them. The simple act of looking up will detect any jump operation. Hence, this is not always an effective countermeasure but one that must be assessed any time it is to be used or even considered.

Did anything *not* go according to the plan in the execution of the raid?

At least two things did not. One was radio communications, which didn't work at several points. Communications seem to be a constant problem in special operations, even in today's world of long-life batteries, encrypted transmissions, and satellites to relay signals. Fortunately the back-up plan, using signal flares, did work. The other aspect that did not go according to the plan was the departure order. In response to the signal flares, all boats beached at once. During rehearsals, boats beached two at a time. This proved to be a minor glitch that was partly overcome. Even so, this disorderly withdrawal prevented an accurate head count, resulting in eight of the raiders being left behind. Of the eight, two were dead and six others had not yet reached the beach. This was the only failing in the operation but one that could, and should, have been avoided.

SOURCES

Books:

By Air to Battle—The Official Account of the British First and Sixth Airborne Divisions; London; His Majesty's Stationery Office; 1945

Davis, Howard P.; *British Parachute Forces 1940–45;* New York; Arco Publishing; 1974

Ferguson, Gregor; *The Paras—British Airborne Forces 1940–1989;* London; Osprey Publishing; 1984

Frost, John; *A Drop Too Many;* London; Buchan & Enright; 1982

Galvin, John R.; *Air Assault—The Development of Airmobile Warfare;* New York; Hawthorn Books; 1969

Gregory, Barry; *British Airborne Troops 1940–45;* Garden City, NY; Doubleday; 1974

Harclerode, Peter; *Para! Fifty Years of the Parachute Regiment;* London; Arms and Armour Press; 1992

Millar, George; *The Bruneval Raid—Flashpoint in the Radar War;* London; The Bodley Head; 1974

Newnham, Maurice; *Prelude to Glory—The Story of the Creation of Britain's Parachute Army;* London; Sampson Low, Marston

Norton, G.G.; *The Red Devils—The Story of the British Airborne Forces;* Harrisburg, PA; Stackpole Books; 1971

Otway, T.B.H.; *Airborne Forces;* London; Imperial War Museum (reprint); 1990

Saunders, Hilary St. G.; *The Red Beret—The Story of the Parachute Regiment at War 1940–1945;* London; Michael Joseph; 1950

——————— (unattributed); *Combined Operations—The Official Story of the Commandos;* New York; MacMillan; 1943

Short, James G.; *The Paras—The British Parachute Regiment;* London; Arms and Armour Press; 1985

Thompson, Leroy; *British Paratroops in Action;* Carrollton, TX; Signal/Squadron Publications; 1989

Articles:
Author unknown; "British Airborne Assaults 1940–45"; in *WWII* magazine; July 1976
Hill, Adrian; "Where Pegasus Might Fly"; in *Journal of the Royal United Services Institute for Defence Studies* magazine; June 1979
Vail, Jason; "Raiders Clockwork Plan"; in *World War II* magazine; date unknown

CHAPTER SIX

THE GREAT JEEP RAID

In June 1941, a young British lieutenant found himself laid up in a Cairo hospital following a parachuting accident. The lieutenant had until recently been a member of No. 8 Commando, a unit in Layforce. He was a man of action whose pre-war ambition had been to be the first to climb Mount Everest. Instead, when the war broke out he just couldn't wait to get into it. He volunteered for one special unit after another. The parachuting had been conducted on his own time and now all he had was time on his hands. It was during this period in the war that the *Afrika Korps* had been steadily pushing east toward Egypt. Propelled by an immediate sense of urgency, this man of action put his creative and energetic mind to work, thinking of nothing else but how the war in the Western Desert could be turned around.

He soon concluded that a small force, parachuted behind the lines, could do a lot of damage to lightly guarded German airfields. He had even worked out a plan to extract this force once its mission was completed. He would use the Long Range Desert Group, a truck mounted intelligence-gathering "private army" to rendezvous with his raiders and drive them out from behind enemy lines. The force must be small, responsible for its own training, and work directly for the Commander-in-Chief, HQ Middle East.

The problem now was how to get the C-in-C to approve the idea. After all, lieutenants don't just call on the C-in-C to announce that they have a plan to help win the war in the Middle East. But David Stirling was not just any lieutenant.

The following month, Stirling, now on crutches, bluffed his way into the office of the Deputy Chief of Staff, Lieutenant General Neil Ritchie, confident in his proposals. He announced to the startled general that he had a plan that would help win the war in the Middle East. Ritchie, a fellow Scot, listened with interest and then read Stirling's detailed plan. He agreed to discuss the plan with General Claude Auchinleck, the C-in-C. Three days later Stirling was back at HQ Middle East. It seemed that Auchinleck liked his idea. Stirling was promptly promoted to captain and given the authority to raise a unit consisting of 6 officers and 60 men. The unit was to be called L Detachment, Special Air Service Brigade. Except for this detachment, the brigade did not exist. The unit's first mission was to conduct a parachute raid on German airfields immediately behind the lines during the planned November offensive.

Stirling established his base camp at Kabrit, a town to the east of Cairo on the edge of the Great Bitter Lake. He began his recruiting efforts by contacting officers he had known in the Commando units in Layforce. Subsequent rumors, circulated later by British staffers unfriendly to the SAS, claimed that Stirling had done his recruiting at the bar in Shepherd's Hotel in Cairo. The first recruit was Jock Lewes, an Australian member of the Welsh Guards. Lewes was an Oxford graduate and was once a member of the university's rowing team. Other officers and men were recruited. The last officer Stirling recruited was to become an SAS legend. He was Blair "Paddy" Mayne, a former star member of the Irish Rugby team, who had distinguished himself in international competition before the war.

Training began immediately. Stirling emphasized that he was not interested in his men being tough in bars or while engaged in idle talk with others. He expected their toughness to be directed at the Germans. The training program evolved and was built on several priorities, to include: map reading drills; forced marches; demolitions training; weapons familiarization including Italian and German weapons; and parachuting skills. Stirling assigned Jock Lewes the task of developing a bomb type the SAS could use on its raids. The basic rudiments of this bomb design would require it to be small enough for several to be carried by each man. Yet, while compact, it also had to meet the requirement for explosive and incendiary potential. One trial after another failed until Lewes came up with just the right combination of oil, plastic, and thermite to do the job. Appropriately enough this innovation later became known as the Lewes bomb.

The training intensified as time passed. Although the SAS had the support of HQ Middle East, there were many persistent critics. One outspoken RAF Group-Captain insisted that the unit's mission was unrealistic. Hoping to silence some of these critics and at the same time advance the cause of the unit, Stirling enticed the Group-Captain into a wager. The premise for the bet was that the SAS could raid a friendly airfield, affix labels (not bombs) to planes on the field, and escape undetected. Heliopolis, the main airfield in Cairo, was selected as the target. The security force there had foreknowledge of the bet.

The raiding party consisted of four groups of ten men each. The RAF sent out reconnaissance planes to try to spot the raiders. The mission took three days and covered a distance of 90 miles. The raiders moved by night and rested in camouflaged positions during the day. All four groups of raiders got onto the airfield. They plastered 45 planes with labels (some planes had more than one label!), and departed, undetected. The following morning there were many red faces and heated reprimands at HQ Middle East.

In the November offensive, the SAS parachute raid was a disaster. Several groups of raiders were dropped from planes that were off course and caught in a sandstorm. In total, thirty-eight raiders were lost, killed, captured, or seriously injured. This marked a turning point in SAS operations. Stirling decided that there was too much hazard and uncertainty in this method of delivering his men to their assigned targets. He concentrated on rebuilding his unit and formed a close working relationship with the Long Range Desert Group. For the next six months the two units operated together conducting raids which were characterized by very long approach drives and escapes into the desert.

In January 1942, Stirling was promoted to major. He expanded his unit by arranging with HQ Middle East to have a company of Free French paratroopers, the *Ie Compagnie de Chasseurs Parachutistes*, transferred to the SAS. He also had two unit insignia approved. The SAS cap badge, worn first on caps then later on beige or sand colored berets, was designed by Stirling in the form of a flaming sword of Damocles with a scroll across the blade containing Stirling's motto, "Who Dares Wins." The Cairo tailor who produced these badges made the blade look more like a winged dagger than a flaming sword, and so it remained. The other insignia was the SAS wings. The wings were designed by Jock Lewes based on the symbol of Aten, an Egyptian sun god of the 18th Dynasty. One story of the original SAS wings design was that it was copied from a frieze found on the floor of the lobby of Shepherd's Hotel in Cairo. The origins of the SAS and Shepherd's Hotel seem forever entwined. The wings were awarded to men who had completed seven parachute jumps and were worn on the upper right uniform sleeve. Stirling allowed these wings to be transferred to the left breast for conspicuous operational service in the SAS.

On 2 July 1942 Stirling moved the SAS from Kabrit to a base camp in western Egypt near Bir Chalder. Later that same month, Stirling returned to Cairo to get his unit's replacement jeeps. In the late afternoon, eight days after Stirling's departure, one of the SAS base camp sentries reported moving dots on the horizon. The camp immediately stood to. As the moving dots became more visible, it was obvious that they were jeeps. Stirling had returned and brought with him twenty new vehicles. As they came into view it was obvious that these were not ordinary jeeps. Each was armed with two pair of Vickers K aircraft machine guns. The Vickers' rate of fire was 1,000 rounds per minute or better. One pair of the machine guns was mounted in a steel upright in front on the passenger side. The other pair was mounted on the right side, in the back. In addition to the equipment, Stirling also brought along a plan to use his new equipment.

Eighteen jeeps were consigned to take part in a raid targeting an airfield in the vicinity of Fuka, on the Mediterranean coast. The airfield was at Sidi Haneish. The German designation was Landing Ground 12 and it served as a main staging area for aircraft bound to or from the front.

During the afternoon of the 25th, Stirling explained the tactics to be employed against the Sidi Haneish airfield. New tactics had to be devised out of necessity. It was known that the Germans had been implementing various measures to counter the effectiveness of SAS raids. Some airfields had their sentries sleeping beneath the wings of parked aircraft. When this did not prove successful, the Germans then increased the size of the perimeter guard. Some bases even mounted searchlights on armored cars for additional security.

Stirling wanted to overwhelm the defenses with a frightening and lethal display of firepower. He explained that as soon as the patrol approached the perimeter of an airfield, the jeeps were to deploy in a line abreast and open up with all guns blazing. The intent was to send a steady, deadly stream of tracers into the airfield. He would then fire a green Very light as the signal for his unit to reform.

The new formation resembled an arrowhead. Seven jeeps each were to form into two columns. There was to be a gap of five meters between jeeps and fifteen meters between columns. The remaining four jeeps formed the tip of the arrow. These four vehicles were to ride between the columns. At the front was Stirling, with one jeep on each side and the fourth (the navigator's jeep) in line behind Stirling. The basic premise was for the three jeeps at the tip to fire straight ahead and the jeeps on the flanks to fire out to the open side. This was the formation that would ride onto the airfield proper. Stirling envisioned these jeeps crashing the airfield with all guns firing at once, with the forward jeeps clearing a path and those in column taking out as many planes as they could.

The plan was reviewed several times during the afternoon to insure that each man knew his role. Later that night, the jeep patrol went back into the desert to rehearse the attack in the dark. They practiced forming a line abreast and firing off their weapons. Then, after Stirling fired a green Very light, they practiced moving to the arrowhead formation and firing their weapons again. There was more to the practice than just attempting perfection. Sixty-five guns would be firing all at once. One false move, particularly by a driver, could prove fatal. The drivers had to be especially cautious because they had the twin tasks of maintaining their formation over irregular terrain and not getting in the way of their gunners. One of the drivers, Carol Mather, was in the last jeep of the left column. He wrote later that "my front gun fired across my face and my rear gun behind my head, so it was important to sit very still and not to lean forwards or backwards."

The rehearsal, which had begun at midnight, lasted until almost three in the morning. Finally Stirling was satisfied. He fired a red Very light to signal the end of rehearsal. His signal was answered by two more red lights glistening in the sky, fired by the leaders of each column, Paddy Mayne and Sandy Scratchley. All shooting stopped immediately. The formation returned to line abreast and the patrol returned to base. George Jellicoe, Scratchley, and several other SAS raiders laughed heartily at the idea of having held a full dress rehearsal behind enemy lines.

At dawn on the 26th, the base camp came alive. All work was directed toward getting the patrol ready for the coming night attack. Ammunition was drawn; fuel tanks and fuel resupply cans were topped off; and food, water, and camouflage material were all packed onto the tiny quarter-ton jeeps. Each vehicle was given a thorough mechanical going-over. Just after 2100, as a full moon began to rise, the raiding party left the base at Bir Chalder bound for Sidi Haneish, 65 kilometers to the northeast. A loose formation was adopted for movement with each jeep traveling just to the right or left of the one in front and attempting to maintain a speed of 30 miles an hour. Stirling had planned to arrive at the airfield around one in the morning. This schedule would give the patrol a good three hours of darkness, following the raid, to evade out of the area.

Steve Hastings, a driver from near the rear of the right column, said afterwards, "Mostly we rolled along at a good 20 mph over flat shingle or sand. Every now and again we would come to small escarpments and then bunch together until we found a way up or down. The dust rose thicker and engines revved as they changed gear." After about an hour's drive over the relatively smooth desert surface, the patrol crossed the Siwa track. The column then halted. Mike Sadler, the navigator, set up his theodolite and took a bearing. Sadler had the most important job in their approach to the target. It was imperative that he bring them right onto the airfield. The slightest miscalculation, right or left, would ruin the element of surprise and lose time.

The terrain became rougher as the patrol moved out again. Jeeps began to get flats and each took at least five minutes to fix. Over an hour was lost. Then, about midnight, the patrol was confronted by a prominent ridge across their line of movement. Stirling sent out scouts to the right and left searching for a way to bypass this obstacle. The rest of the raiders took a break in place, smoking and stretching their legs. Fifteen minutes later the jeeps returned. One of them had found a possible route about a quarter mile further on. With much grinding of gears and slithering over the slippery track, the jeeps eventually bypassed the ridge. Soon after, Stirling gave the signal to stop. Sadler took another theodolite bearing and laid his map over the hood of Stirling's jeep to examine their progress. Raiders from other jeeps gathered around. Sadler finally announced that the patrol had come thirty miles and that the target was now only ten miles due north.

Stirling ordered a final check of guns and ammunition. He then announced that there would be one more stop, just short of the target, to deploy into the extended line formation. During the next 45 minutes, the terrain became more rolling and the moon ducked in and out of clouds, causing nocturnal shadows to move across the passing landscape. The patrol then happened onto the site of a recent battle. Burnt out trucks and tanks, and sprawling dead bodies comprised the debris of battle. Thirty minutes further on Stirling again halted. Silence and the desert wilderness surrounded the raiding party. Sadler dismounted his jeep and approached Stirling. "By my reckoning," he said, "we're less than a mile short of the field. It's right in front of us."

Stirling's faith in his navigator was complete. He accepted Sadler's verdict and ordered the patrol into line abreast formation and to advance. The going was now slow as they encountered rough ground. The clouds had by now dissipated and all the jeeps showed up clearly under a full moon. The drivers struggled to maintain control of their vehicles. The gunners sat tensely, fingers on triggers and weapons level to the front. Suddenly, the dark night was transformed to light. A half-mile ahead was the airfield; now flood-lit from one end to the other. Had they been spotted? Had the Germans been expecting them?

Hearts pounded. Pulses raced. A collective breath was held. Within a matter of seconds the sound of an airplane engine could be heard muffling the noise of the jeep engines. They had not been seen. In fact, a bomber was coming in for a landing. At that moment, with not a flicker of hesitation, Stirling headed straight for the runway. He was about 100 yards short when the bomber's wheels chirped down onto the runway. The gunners on the lead jeep opened fire and the 34 other gunners followed suit. The airfield became a "fantastic slanting cascade" of red and white tracers. And as suddenly as they had come on, the airfield lights went off. A green Very light arched skyward and the jeeps moved into their arrowhead formation and quickly picked up speed. Sadler had the patrol medic in his jeep. He slowed his jeep down and dropped out of the formation. They remained on the edge of the airfield throughout the fight that followed.

There seemed to be a wide assortment of planes at this airfield. *Stukas*, *Messerschmidts*, *Heinkels*, and *Junkers* transports lined the runway. The planes did not immediately catch fire, as the raiders had expected. Despite the immediate proximity and impact of the gun fire, it took almost 30 seconds for fires to start. However, the sound of muffled explosions could soon be heard to the rear of the attacking formation. Some of the planes actually crumbled under the onslaught of bullets ripping through them. While burning airplanes signaled the evident success of the raid, they also lit up the night, making the attacking jeeps better targets.

The Germans began to recover from their shock and scampered for their weapons. A mortar and a *Breda* 8mm machine gun opened up on the SAS jeeps. The front gunner in Sandy Scratchley's jeep slumped forward, "his back curiously straight and the head and shoulders resting on the guns." The first mortar round had found a victim.

Hastings, in the rear of the formation, said later that he felt something hot pass beneath his seat. "There was a clang, and my face and that of my front gunner were covered in oil. There was a moment of blindness and incomprehension; we wiped the oil out of our eyes and the jeep swerved violently, hit a bump, recovered itself and continued miraculously!" Stirling's jeep was soon hit and put out of action. The column immediately came to a halt. Stirling and his two gunners, Cooper and Seekings, jumped out and moved to other jeeps. Stirling shouted for gunners to concentrate their fire to take out the *Breda* machine gun. As it turned out, the *Breda* and the mortar were both being fired from the same position. Tracers from the *Breda* made it a good target and it was silenced very quickly.

Stirling then ordered the drivers to shut off their engines. He received a quick personnel count and cautioned the gunners to slow down their rate of fire to conserve their rapidly diminishing ammunition. He also directed the patrol to complete the circle of the airfield, taking out any plane they saw. After that they were to begin their escape. As the patrol moved around the airfield and headed for the desert, one obviously unscathed plane remained silhouetted against the sky. Suddenly a man ran toward the plane. Reaching up, he placed something into the cockpit and then ran back to his jeep. Paddy Mayne wasn't carrying a rugby ball but an incendiary bomb. As he got back into his jeep, the plane exploded.

The jeeps soon cleared out from the airfield and dispersed into the dark. As the attack was winding down and jeep fatalities were recorded, one of the last jeeps in the column had its engine seize up just past the runway. The raiders from this jeep jumped out and were quickly picked up by vehicles behind them.

The first jeep raid was over. Three jeeps had been put out of action on the airfield and six others had taken hits. One raider (Scratchley's front gunner) was killed during the raid and one other would be killed in the evasion phase. It took two days for all of the raiders to return to their base at Bir Chalder. What had the raid accomplished? Stirling estimated that the SAS had destroyed 25 planes and damaged at least a dozen more. Most of those destroyed had been the highly-prized *Junkers* transports. The success of the raid was credited as much to the tactics as to the element of surprise.

Less than six months later, David Stirling was taken prisoner. He made several short-lived escapes. On one of these escapes, he came upon an airfield he had not known about and immediately began sketching it for a later raid. The raid, however, never took place because he was recaptured. Stirling eventually wound up in Oflag IV-B (Colditz Castle), a prison reserved for the very hard core Allied prisoners. He remained there until the end of the war.

As for the SAS, perhaps the unit was rated best by Field Marshal Erwin Rommel, who described it as "the desert group which caused us more damage than any other British unit of equal strength."

Mission Critique

The determination as to the necessity David Stirling's first jeep raid relies on the rationale used to create his organization, the Special Air Service, in the first place. The same determinations of necessity may be applied to the unit's continuation in the field, and of missions and equipment assigned to it. Middle East Command granted it a rather wide-ranging warrant when it authorized the creation of the SAS. The SAS was authorized to conduct operations on targets that it found or that were assigned to it. The necessity or justification for missions was approved in advance, either individually or in blanket form. The SAS target in this instance was a German airfield and the primary mission was to destroy planes. Even though the location of the airfield was far from the front lines, the target mission could have been executed by either conventional or special operations forces.

The obvious disadvantages of using conventional forces (either aerial or naval bombardment) were getting a force close enough to the target and for the force to go undetected. Additionally, for optimum success it needed to be executed at a time when there were a lot of planes on the ground. These disadvantages became advantages when the SAS was given the mission. However, the timing of so many planes being on the ground at the time of the raid was almost certainly serendipitous.

The SAS raid on Sidi Haneish is a good example of a compact operation that was well-planned and well-executed. You would have to dig pretty hard to find anything negative to say about this raid when referring to any of Vandenbroucke's or McRaven's criteria.

None of the sources mentioned any pre-operation *intelligence* of the target. It is quite possible that Stirling knew as much about this airfield as there was to know. At the very least he knew all that was necessary to conduct the raid, namely: where it was, how long it would take to get there and back, and the anticipated plan of action at the target.

It is quite apparent that Stirling had spent a lot of time working out the details of what he wanted his men to do once they arrived at the target. He also spent a lot of time reviewing his plan with his men. In addition, they rehearsed it in meticulous detail in conditions of both daylight and darkness. The mission was not launched until Stirling was satisfied that his men were ready. These *repetitious rehearsals* paid off during this raid and many others. The fact that Stirling conducted his rehearsals behind enemy lines has always amazed me as a stroke of both genius and bravado. The apex, however, of both Stirling's bravado and confidence was stopping *in the middle of the raid* to get a situation report.

Stirling's innovation and tactics developed out of necessity. These innovations were necessary to overcome German responses geared to fend off his unit's attacks based on tactics used on previous raids and were hallmarks of subsequent SAS operations. His insistence that each man be completely familiar with his role in the operation will also be evident when discussing another one of the British desert units, Popski's Private Army. In Stirling's case this need for detailed knowledge on each man's part in the mission was not only an operational necessity but was also an issue of safety as well.

This operation is exactly the type that enabled Stirling to be given almost complete *carte blanche* when picking his targets and even to execute raids without prior approval from HQ Middle East. There is a story, probably apocryphal, that because of the number of planes destroyed in this raid Stirling asked that his men be declared "aces." Nothing official has been found to confirm this story, however.

SOURCES

Books:

Calvert, Michael; *Fighting Mad;* New York; Bantam Books; 1964

Chapman, F. Spencer; *The Jungle is Neutral;* New York; W.W. Norton; 1949

Cowles, Virginia; *The Phantom Major—The Story of David Stirling and the S.A.S. Regiment;* London; Collins; 1958

Geraghty, Tony; *This is the SAS—A Pictorial History of the Special Air Service Regiment;* London; Arms and Armour Press; 1982

Gordon, John W.; *The Other Desert War—British Special Forces in North Africa, 1940–1943;* New York; Greenwood Press; 1987

James, Malcolm; *Born of the Desert;* London; Collins; 1945

Ladd, James D.; *SAS Operations*; London; Robert Hale; 1986

Saunders, Pete; *Special Air Service;* London; Outline Publications; 1983

Shortt, James G.; *The Special Air Service and Royal Marines Special Boat Squadron;* London; Osprey Publishing; 1981

Swinson, Arthur; *The Raiders: Desert Strike Force;* New York; Ballantine Books; 1968

Warner, Philip; *The Special Air Service;* London; William Kimber; 1971

Articles:

Fugelman; "Beyond the Last Blue Mountain"; *Combat Illustrated* magazine; April 1981

CHAPTER SEVEN

TARGETS X, Y, AND L

The German airborne invasion of Crete in May 1941 had diametrically opposite effects among the Allied and German strategists. The Germans, responding to tirades by Hitler, decided never again to commit large scale parachute forces. The American and British military leaders believed that the airborne assault on Crete was vindication of steps both countries had taken to create airborne forces.

The creation of the American airborne force had its beginning in World War I. In October 1918 Brigadier General William Mitchell received approval to proceed with planning on a proposal he had made to drop the 1st Infantry Division by parachute into the German rear near Metz. The responsibility for detailed planning was given to one of Mitchell's young staff officers, Lewis H. Brereton. The plan was to use bombers as platforms from which the infantry would jump. The Armistice to end the war intervened and planning for the Metz operation stopped.

Almost 20 years would pass before the U.S. Army again seriously considered delivering troops to the battlefield by parachute. A 1928 demonstration at Brooks Field, Texas in which a three man fire team jumped from four planes and assembled a machine gun on the ground was the only sign of interest shown in using parachute forces; little attention and no further action resulted from this brief experiment.

In 1934 and 1935, Major William C. Lee, a U.S. Army officer serving as a military attaché in Paris and London, observed German military training. This training included soldiers jumping by parachute to capture objectives and equipment, and men being delivered to the battlefield by glider. Lee's interest was immediate. Later, as an instructor at the Infantry School and as a student at the Command and General Staff College, Lee wrote articles and talked with his fellow students about his ideas for vertical envelopment. He refined his ideas based on discussions with staff and fellow students.

In a later assignment to the Office of Chief of Infantry, Lee, now a lieutenant colonel, continued to push his ideas for airborne infantry. This was to the dismay and displeasure of his boss, who wanted Lee to concentrate on coordinating armor projects and to be the resident expert on foreign military armor forces and organizations. However, when President Roosevelt saw a newsreel about German parachute forces and inquired about the American capability with such forces, Lee was given his dream project, on 25 June 1941. Others were also working on this project, including the Infantry Board, which had made several proposals to the Chief of Infantry on size of units, equipment, and how they should be employed.

On 26 June 1940, the Parachute Test Platoon was created at Fort Benning, Georgia with a strength of 2 officers, 1 warrant officer, 6 sergeants, and 42 enlisted men. This unit inaugurated many of the training doctrines employed by the U.S. airborne program during the remainder of the war.

Since there was no formal training course, the original test platoon got its training where it could. This included several trips to Washington Township, New Jersey for training on the 125-foot jump towers there that were owned by the Safe Parachute Company; towers based on this design, but 250 feet tall, were eventually built at Fort Benning. The Test Platoon also sent representatives to Chanute Field, Illinois to learn rigging, sewing, and maintenance of parachutes. The Test Platoon later passed this training on to other units as they were activated. The first jumps were conducted at Fort Benning on 16 August. Soon thereafter the Provisional Parachute Group was activated at Fort Benning to supervise the activation and training on the battalions and, later, regiments of parachute and glider units that would follow.

Over time training settled on a six-week course, which was conducted in several stages. 'A' Stage lasted three weeks and was almost exclusively devoted to physical training, especially running; the physical training did not stop when this stage was completed but carried over into all of the stages. 'B' Stage lasted one week and consisted of aircraft exit techniques from mockups of plane frames and from the 34-foot towers, controlling the parachute in the air, parachute landing falls, and parachute packing techniques. 'C' Stage lasted one week and included more parachute packing, the suspended harness, and the 250-foot towers. 'D' Stage was jump week. Five jumps qualified a trooper for jump wings, the badge of the paratroopers that had been designed by one of the early airborne officers, Lieutenant William P. Yarborough.

The parachute battalions, which would form the cadre of the regiments, were designated in the 500 series; thus, the first battalion activated was originally designated as the First Parachute Battalion, then redesignated as 501st within two weeks; the second was 502nd, and so on. 501st Battalion was later redesignated as 1st Battalion, 501st Parachute Infantry Regiment and formed the core of the 501st Regiment.

The entire redesignation and activation process was generally a smooth operation but there were several gyrations that were mind-boggling. For sake of continuity and lack of confusion, the unit involved in the operation in this discussion will be referred to by its final designation: the 509th Parachute Infantry Battalion. In June 1942, the 509th was sent to England and attached to a British airborne division for training. The battalion commander was Lieutenant Colonel Edson D. Raff.

The decision to commit parachute elements to the North African campaign was not made until early October 1942. The only American unit close enough to be considered for use in Africa was the 509th. When presented with the proposed mission for his unit, Lieutenant Colonel Raff told his theater commander he had no doubts about his unit's ability to accomplish the mission. His only provision was that he be permitted to command the paratroopers once they were on the ground.

Raff made this condition because the plan called for the 509th to fly 1,500 miles, at night, in planes belonging to the 60th Troop Carrier Group. The 60th had been hastily assembled and its training had not reached the level that its cargo, the paratroopers, had. Since there were no plans to refuel after leaving England, Raff wanted it clear from the beginning that the paratroopers would be under his command on hitting the ground, not the Air Force commander's in case he happened to land at the objective.

The plan for employment of the 509th was written by Raff and the airborne staff officer for Operation Torch, Major William Yarborough (who, in addition to designing the U.S. paratroopers' jump wings, had also been instrumental in designing the special jump uniform American paratroopers wore during the period). Raff and Yarborough were friends and both wanted the airborne concept to work so they spent much time refining and reworking the plan. The plan called for the 509th to accomplish three objectives: destroy enemy fighters at an airfield designated "X"; seize and hold an airfield designated "Y"; and cut communications west of a town designated "L", located east of airfield "Y". All the maps, photographs, and terrain models used in the training were marked with these letter designations. The vital necessity was to gain air superiority. There was a strong possibility that the French would remain loyal to their puppet government at Vichy and oppose the Allied invasion in North Africa, and attention was focused on the two airfields.

Just after dark on 7 November 1942, the longest uninterrupted flight by paratroopers during World War II began. This had followed weeks of special training and rehearsals. Raff and his men were ready to show what they could do. The sky train consisted of 39 C-47s, each loaded to the brim with fuel for the long flight. The pilots, although fairly competent at beam-riding on airline routes, had little practical experience at dead reckoning or astro-navigation. They were, however, determined and adaptable. The planes maintained good order until they approached Spain. After the fighter escort turned back, the transports hit clouds that were moving lower just as the sky was getting dark. As they climbed through the clouds the planes became separated. The pilots continued to fly south while their loads of paratroopers, wrapped in blankets, slept in the cramped aircraft cabins.

By morning, 33 of the 39 planes were still within sight of one another but there was a bigger problem—the pilots weren't certain where they were. The men of the 509th were also uncertain as to whether they would land to French cheers or drop by parachute between two fields and march against French guns. The answer was to have been radioed to Raff as his unit flew across the Strait of Gibraltar but, if sent, the signal was not heard. In the meantime valuable fuel was being burned while the pilots continued to figure out their location after reaching the African coast. Finally the air commander ordered one of his planes to land and find out where they were; it turned out that they were within about 100 miles of their targets.

At 0845, 8 November 1942, the paratroopers in the main group of planes got their first inkling of what kind of reception was awaiting them when they flew over La Senia airfield (Objective X) as Allied planes were bombing it. Confusion followed. Several of the troop carrier planes were short on fuel and landed in the desert. Twelve flew to an area between La Senia and Tafaraoui (Objective Y) where Raff ordered the paratroopers to jump. First the supply containers, then the troopers left the planes and floated to the ground underneath parachutes. Once assembled, the 509th quickly linked up with an armor force of the 1st Armored Division, which had arrived from the beaches near Oran, and together they occupied the airfields. A quick check of casualties among the paratroopers showed that, although about 20% of the unit was missing, there were no killed or wounded.

Raff considered the result of this operation to be an undramatic end to the first U.S. combat jump. In fact his paratroopers played little role in the objectives assigned to them. Although it was an inauspicious opening combat assault for American paratroopers, they were destined to do better.

Mission Critique

The North African use of American airborne troops was, in some respects, similar to the Tragino Aqueduct mission. The targets in this case given to the paratroopers were appropriate and the justification for the targets was also good. However, because of the distance they had to travel from departure airfields in England, and the fact that when they arrived at the targets there was already an armor force on the ground, should cause a question as to whether this was a good use of special operations forces. Indeed, many things could have delayed the armor force, which would then have made the employment of airborne troops seem to be the correct decision. The answer, in this case, to the necessity of using special operations forces is fuzzy. The event shows they probably did not help much in capturing some of their assigned targets.

Since the U.S. planners were anxious to include paratroopers in this operation, assuming the risk of such a long flight to the target was definitely *wishful thinking*. A better use of these specific forces may have been to hold them in reserve and stage them out of Gibraltar, much closer to where they were to be used and more flexible in terms of what targets could be assigned to them.

This criticism of the plan is based on the flying distance from departure airfields to the targets, lack of navigation aids along the way, lack of updates on the ground situation while in flight, and the expectation that the ground battle plan would not impact on the airborne targets. This last must always be prominent in plans for parachute operations; if the airborne assault is into friendly lines it is probably an expensive waste of time and effort, unless it is planned that way from the start or is used to reinforce the ground situation.

On the other hand, some things went correctly in this operation. The *intelligence* on the targets was correct in that these sites were key military objectives. Several other forces (including air and armor) were either assigned the targets as well or simply went after them as targets of opportunity.

The use of untrained air crews to conduct the U.S. Army's first airborne operation was not a decision that the parachute planners or troopers could change. It is one of three major instances of *poor coordination* in this operation;

the others being the poor communications among the aircraft once they took off and the fact that the long pre-jump flight put most of the planes at the edge of their fuel capacities. As mentioned in the Tragino operation, why not pick a better mission to prove the principle? The obvious answer is that they had to accept what was available. However, that's too pat an answer because in both cases it was the airborne advocates that were pushing for a chance to prove the usefulness of an airborne capability.

The plan was far from *simple*. It involved dropping paratroopers onto three separate targets after having flown all night to get there and receiving no tactical update. Even these days that would not have been a *simple* plan.

While there is no doubt that the 509th *rehearsed* operations while in England, those *rehearsals* did not involve enough complications to train the men to make adjustments to the plan once over the target or on the ground, or to take into account the long flight to the drop zones.

The presence of friendly armor forces at one of the targets removed any element of *surprise* for the jump operation. In addition, Raff really had no idea of the tactical situation on the ground when the jump sequence was conducted. This could have proved entirely disastrous to his command; fortunately it did not.

Many of the problems with this operation can be attributed to the communications (especially the lack thereof) that I mentioned earlier. If the airborne planners had examined this operation with more of a critical eye, they would have made a better plan, one that would have highlighted the new U.S. airborne capability better. In the event the problems mentioned did get taken into account on subsequent jump operations, which more than proved the principle of the airborne force capabilities.

SOURCES

Autry, Jerry; *General William C. Lee—Father of the Airborne;* Raleigh, NC; Airborne Press; 1995

Galvin, John R.; *Air Assault—The Development of Airmobile Warfare;* New York; Hawthorn Books; 1969

Huston, James A.; *Out of the Blue—US Army Airborne Operations in World War II;* West Lafayette, IN; Purdue University Studies; 1972

Lassen, Don and Richard K. Schrader; *Pride of America—An Illustrated History of the U.S. Army Airborne Forces;* Missoula MT; Pictorial Histories Publishing; 1991

MacDonald, Charles; *Airborne;* New York; Ballantine Books; 1970

Raff, Edson D.; *We Jumped to Fight;* New York; Eagle Books; 1944

Tugwell, Maurice; *Airborne to Battle—A History of Airborne Warfare 1918–1971*; London; William Kimber; 1971

CHAPTER EIGHT

POPSKI'S PRIVATE ARMY: SPREADING ALARM AND DESPONDENCY

Included in this book are several overviews or histories of special units. Those discussions will start here with Popski's Private Army. The histories tend to stray from the key thrust of discussing in detail just one operation or mission. Most of the units chosen for these overviews are not particularly well known by the reading public. They are sometimes little known even in military history circles. Including some or all of the operations of the units belonging in this category amply demonstrates the wide diversity of missions that special units are capable of performing.

A critique of such units, and their operations, would probably not be as useful. However, a short discussion, after each history, of the critical factors that characterized each unit and its ability to execute its mission is probably more useful.

CNN described parts of Operation Desert Storm as the new look of war: FAVs and HMMWVs conducting desert patrols behind the lines in Iraqi territory to gather intelligence, conduct sabotage, and rescue downed airmen. To students of special operations forces, this was nothing new. For example, Mike Hoare's jeep-mounted mercenaries of 5 Commando, who fought in the Congo in the early 1960s, used similar tactics, although on different mission, whether they knew it or not. Mounted cavalry over the past several hundred years had actually established many of these tactics and missions. And, more recently in the mechanized transportation age, there have been various units that refined cavalry tactics and established jeep tactics—Ralph Bagnold's Long Range Desert Group, David Stirling's Special Air Service, and Vladimir Peniakoff's No. 1 Demolition Squadron.

Peniakoff was born in Belgium but his Russian parents insisted that he learn English as his first language. During World War I his Cambridge education was shortened by service as an artilleryman in the French Army. In 1918, he was invalided out and finished his schooling, studying engineering. After several moves, he settled in Egypt in 1924 and remained there until the outbreak of World War II. In October 1940, he was commissioned in the British Army and posted to the Libyan Arab Force, formally designated as 102 Military Mission. For the next two years he did pretty much as he pleased, spending as much time as he could in the North African desert fighting with the Libyan Arab Force and the Long Range Desert Group, and as little time as possible in garrison. It was during this period that he became known as 'Popski' because it was easier to say and understand on the radio than his own last name. After being wounded in a Long Range Desert Group raid in October 1942, he was sent to a hospital in Cairo. Upon release, he was assigned to Middle East HQ.

When he reported in, Peniakoff sought out a sympathetic ear, and found one in Colonel Shan Hackett, head of Raiding Forces department. The two had known each other for about a year. Hackett had summed up Peniakoff's previous military 'escapades' on their first meeting, "Now, Popski, for your private reasons you fade out into the desert. You go and fight a private war with your private army for your private convenience, taking orders from no one, and when you choose to come back you expect H.M. Government to pay you for your fun!" Despite this, Hackett now needed to supplement various special units fighting in the German rear. He agreed with Peniakoff's plan to raise a small unit and authorized him to begin recruiting. The initial authorized strength was 5 officers, 18 other ranks, 4 jeeps, and 2 three-ton trucks; the unit's provisional designation was No. 1 Demolition Squadron.

The first two men Popski recruited had both worked with him in the Libyan Arab Force. They were Captain Bob "Park" Yunnie and Lieutenant Jan Caneri. Regimental Sergeant Major G. Waterson came from the King's Dragoon Guards, a regular army unit. While these three looked for other possible unit members and worked on the vehicles, Popski reported back to Hackett. Middle East HQ was anxious for Popski to decide on an official unit name but he could not make up his mind. In a moment of exasperation, Hackett said, "You had better find a name quick or we shall call you 'Popski's Private Army'." "I'll take it. I would like to be known as that," was Popski's reply and so it became.

Popski, as all of his men would call him, contacted a silversmith and had him make cap badges in the form of an astrolabe, an astronomical instrument used for navigation by measuring the location of stars. This was worn on a black tanker's beret. An epaulet flash, dark blue with red letters "PPA" (this was later changed to white letters on black cloth), completed the unit insignia.

Even though he had only put together 17 men, Popski was anxious to get going. He arranged for Stirling's SAS to train his men in the use of explosives. His jeeps were armed with one pair of Vickers K aircraft guns and were modified to carry 12 four-gallon gas cans. These latter gave the jeeps a range of between 600 and 700 miles. Without any further training, Popski took his unit into the desert. He believed that the best training would come from actual experience. This shakedown patrol also developed several practices that became standard throughout the history of Popski's Private Army.

At each stop, several things happened at once. Several men jumped out and set up stoves made from tin cans filled with sand and a small amount of gasoline. Their job was to brew up tea for the patrol. As security was established on the perimeter of the rest stop, the navigator designated their location. Equipment was checked to make sure that none of the gas cans had developed leaks, that emergency rations were easily located, and that the vehicle's map case had not been torn off. Popski insisted on frequent vehicle and weapon maintenance and that each man could locate on his jeep whatever equipment a situation might require. Only then would he allow a meal to be prepared. Popski summarized his philosophy this way: "In action, untroubled with mechanical difficulties, my ideally-trained soldier would be free to apply his mind to the fundamental problems of his trade, and be ready with an answer to the ever-recurring questions: 'Where am I?' 'Where is the enemy?' 'Where are my friends?'"

On his first several patrols, Popski took time to train each man on all of the unit's weapons, allowing many thousands of rounds of ammunition to be fired into the desert. Mock jeep battles were staged to develop battle craft in both the drivers and the gunners. It became a unit rule that if jeeps had to be abandoned where an enemy could get to them, they would be set on fire. Patrol procedures for dismounted fighting, with soldier afoot and jeep supporting, were practiced. If a patrol became dispersed, the rendezvous for the next day would be 15 miles back the way they had come.

During one of PPA's early patrols, several men became pinned down in a fight with Germans. Waterson, the sergeant major, and Henderson, a navigator, shot their way in to the pinned down patrollers to lead them out. On the way in, Henderson was shot in the stomach. Waterson gathered the other men and planned their escape. Since Henderson could not move, his wound received special treatment and he prepared to remain behind. At the last moment, one of the PPA men, Binney, lost his nerve and refused to leave. Waterson led the patrol out of the German trap, leaving Henderson and Binney behind. The two were captured. Following this action, Henderson died on the way to a German hospital and Binney was mistakenly sent on to a German hospital in Tripoli. Several months later, after Tripoli was liberated by the British, Binney returned to Popski and asked to rejoin the unit. Popski refused to take him back.

PPA's first big mission was assigned in early January 1943. The British Eighth Army, fresh from its victories at El Alamein and Cyrenaica, planned to push past Tripoli and into Tunisia. Tripoli would be outflanked by an armor force, making capture by the main forces moving along the coast much easier. Montgomery wanted to push his armor force on to pull off a "left hook" around the south and west end of the Mareth Line, a heavily fortified defensive area southwest of the port city of Gabes. But Eighth Army had no idea whether the terrain in front and around the west end of the Mareth Line would support movement by an armor force. The planned attack was ten weeks in the future.

PPA and a New Zealand patrol of the Long Range Desert Group set out to reconnoiter the Mareth Line area. Popski was told that once his intelligence role was ended, "I should have a free hand to operate in any area *behind* the Mareth Line and do what harm I could . . ." In an interesting departure from his usual procedure, Popski arranged for this roving commission to be put in writing. This served him well following the action by permitting him to requisition equipment from British and American units in Algeria.

The unit moved gradually to an area south of the Mareth Line and set up a base camp at Qaret Ali. Captain Yunnie remained with a small force to secure the base and Popski, forming his party in two groups, set out for Matmata, a small town on one of the last spurs in the area.

The reconnaissance lasted four days and was successful in finding a route "of terribly bad going, but just practicable . . ." Getting the information to Eighth Army became a problem because, while Popski's force was conducting its reconnaissance, most of the vehicles in Yunnie's force had been destroyed by German air attacks. Lieutenant Tinker, in command of the New Zealand patrol, drove 140 miles westward across the desert to deliver the intelligence.

In the meantime, Popski and his unit set out in the same direction with two jeeps, little fuel, and many men walking. The jeeps ran dry on the third day and were left behind with a party of bedouins. On the sixth day, they were met by Tinker, who had come back to drive them in to the town of Tozeur.

Six weeks after this reconnaissance, the New Zealand Corps, which included the New Zealand 2nd Division, the British 1st Armor Division, the 8th Armor Brigade, and a force of French units advanced along the route Popski laid out. They forced Rommel's right flank and compelled him to withdraw, sowing seeds for the final victory in North Africa.

Soon after, Popski arranged to be attached to the U.S. II Corps, which ordered him to take a patrol to the vicinity of the Kasserine Pass. II Corps was concerned that if the Germans forced their way past the floundering U.S. 1st Armored Division, there was nothing preventing them from sweeping to Tebessa and beyond, pushing II Corps further west. Popski had developed an intelligence source in the French Army (a captain on the French General Staff) who told him that the Germans were heading south and thus presented no danger to II Corps. The purpose of his patrol was to confirm that information.

This patrol lasted two days. It succeeded in planting mines along the rough road, a job led by Lance Corporal A.W. Locke, a short, feisty, one-eyed (he wore a black patch over his empty right socket) former member of the Long Range Desert Group. After the patrol had pulled away some distance from the mines, they set up a watch over the road. They knew that if the Germans intended to go south, they would soon be hearing explosions. The Germans were not long in coming. Locke said later that he heard so many bangs from the mines that by his reckoning "each of our mines must have gone off twice over." II Corps did not have to withdraw from Tebessa.

Popski's Private Army spent the remainder of the spring conducting harassing raids on airfields and lines of communication in the German rear. When it became obvious to Popski that the war in North Africa was won, he began to work with Allied Forces HQ to see what he could learn of future operations plans. His objective was to "make our choice amongst the countries where the next fighting would take place and train and equip ourselves accordingly."

PPA, for a small unit, had accomplished an incredible amount of damage during its operations in North Africa. It was given credit for destroying 34 airplanes, six armor vehicles, over 110 trucks, and 450,000 gallons of fuel. On the down side, it had suffered one battle death, two men captured, and two men wounded. The battle death, Henderson, died after being captured with Binney.

When subsequent plans for PPA to fight in Sicily fell through, Popski arranged for his unit to receive parachute training from the British 1st Airborne Division. Following this, he decided that if his jeeps were to be of any value, they would have to go in with the men. He therefore scheduled extensive training for his small unit in glider operations, mounting one jeep and crew per glider. This training went on for several weeks and included many night glider landings in unfamiliar terrain. Detailed planning was conducted to have one patrol from PPA (five jeeps) added to the 1st Airborne's invasion of southern Italy by parachute and glider. Late changes caused the airborne invasion to be cancelled and the division, with one patrol of PPA still attached, made an amphibious landing at Taranto, in the heel of the Italian boot.

Popski had planned for operations in Italy for several months, so he was prepared to configure and equip his jeeps according to the changes he wanted. The Vickers K aircraft guns were replaced by two Browning belt-fed machine guns mounted fore and aft on swivels in the jeep. One of these guns was a .30 caliber and the other a .50 caliber. These weapons fired, in succession, tracer, armor piercing, and incendiary ammunition. The load list for each jeep, besides the rack mounted gas cans, included ammunition, spare parts, pioneer tools for the truck for digging and for felling trees, two boxes of compo rations, a towing cable, and two spare wheels. Altogether the list contained over 200 items. Each man carried a .45 caliber pistol and a Thompson machine gun or an American M-1 carbine. Each patrol carried two radios, a mortar, a hand winch, a Bren gun, land mines, and explosives.

As they were loaded aboard the ship to go to Italy, the unit was split. One of the officers, Lieutenant McGillawray, and his gunner, Gaskell, were loaded aboard another ship.

Soon after arriving in Taranto, Popski's jeeps were winched onto the quayside and PPA set out on its first reconnaissance in Italy. The patrol made a wide sweep of the immediate area, contacting and accepting the surrender of several Italian officers, despite the fact that, since Italy had signed an armistice the previous month (August 1943), these officers were not really at war with the British. Popski learned of the German dispositions and reported back to 1st Airborne Division. He acquired much of this information by using telephones to call places in the areas he believed Germans were located and asking the Italian soldiers or politicians who answered where the

German units were and in what strength. When he checked in, some 29 hours after arriving on shore, he learned that the ship carrying Lieutenant McGillawray and Gunner Gaskell had struck a mine and sank, with heavy loss of life, including his two men. The men of PPA took these deaths very hard.

Early the following morning, Popski's patrol again set out, this time to find a way to get behind the German lines. His mission was to avoid contact and concentrate on gathering intelligence. During the ride Popski told his driver, Jock Cameron, "Four hundred miles up this coast lies Venice, an island town of canals and narrow streets, where no wheeled vehicle has ever been seen. One day we shall land our jeeps on the main square, which is called Piazza San Marco, and drive them round and round, a senseless gesture no doubt, an empty flourish—but it has never been done before and at that time we shall be able to afford showing off because the war will be nearly over."

CHAPTER NINE

POPSKI'S PRIVATE ARMY: HIDE AND SEEK

The ten jeeps crossed the Gravina-Foggia road and headed west. This road was the principal German line of communication. The patrol was generally hidden by the dark night. Once across, they maneuvered into the remote hilly area and found a lane between high stone walls. For two hours the patrol wandered in this maze, not certain where it would come out. Finally, the jeeps emerged onto a barren plateau. At the edge of the plateau they established a perimeter security and set up camp with plans to spend the day. The jeep commanders then spent several hours surveying the countryside that they would be entering at nightfall.

Popski called the men together. As they studied the maps spread out in front of them, he explained the plan. The men craved action but to the disappointment of some, they learned that they were not behind German lines to attack any objective or shoot it out with the Germans. Instead, their mission was to collect information. After dark, the patrol wound its way into the valley, found the road, and eased the jeeps onto it. As they drove they looked for the turnoff they would be taking. Just then, some of them in the rear of the formation realized they had missed the turn. Popski stopped his lead jeep and began to turn around. Captain Yunnie, second-in-command of Popski's Private Army, described what happened next. "The German convoy was on top of us before I quite realized what was happening. Twenty trucks rambled round a bend and bore down upon us in the moonlight. My mouth went dry and I felt my stomach turn over. 'What the hell do we do now?' I heard my mind ask."

What they did was a credit to their training and unit discipline. Taking their cue from the lead jeep, the formation drove straight ahead. Popski's unit carried on as if they owned the road and had every right to be there. Popski even waved at the German drivers in the first trucks! Sergeant Beautyman, the patrol's radio operator, didn't forget the intelligence training Popski had given him. He said later, "I counted twenty-eight, and it was a pretty tense bit of counting. They were blacked out, of course, and they never said a word. Neither did we. We could have shot them up, but that would have ended any further snooping in the area." After the convoy went past, the patrol found its turn and headed for Gravina. They spent the following day talking to the local Italians, learning about German troop dispositions. The farmer on whose land the patrol was based served Popski and his men a large pasta dinner.

Over the next several days the patrol continued scouting the same general area. They recruited several local farmers to be their eyes and ears. The locals often brought them good information, all of which was radioed to 1st Airborne Division. Popski started feeling adventurous and just before leaving he split his patrol into two. He sent a road watch team, under Yunnie, one way while he set up a ruse to enter the town. Putting to use some of the intelligence his patrol had gathered, he again demonstrated his prowess over the local telephone network. He telephoned the German quartermaster, a major named Schulz, and pretended to be an Italian sergeant with eight cases of cognac to trade. Schulz agreed to arrange for a captured American car to pass through road control points leading into town. Popski and his driver, Corporal Jock Cameron, immediately stripped down one of the jeeps. Then, later that night, they passed the road-block without incident and parked on the town piazza in front of Major Schulz's office. They carried ration boxes, filled with rocks, into the building and up the stairs. Before the sleepy Major Schulz could react, Cameron bludgeoned him unconscious. Popski immediately began searching the office. He found, to his amazement, the ration breakdown sheets for the German 1st *Fallschirmjaeger* Division and attached units.

To keep up pretenses, Cameron carried in several more ration boxes while Popski continued searching. Once finished, the two men began to set the stage for their exit. To allay the curiosity of the guards, who might otherwise be interested in Schulz' unconscious state, Popski left a partially filled bottle of whisky on Schulz's desk to help explain things. On their way out they even presented the guard a pack of "V" cigarettes. Beautyman was extremely busy that night sending out several messages that contained a fairly complete German order of battle for that area. 1st Airborne HQ was unbelieving at first, but a firm message from Popski ended the discussion. Popski summarized the patrol simply: "With this flourish I considered that my first mission was completed . . ."

There were many patrols over the next several months and not all of them were successful. The unit began to expand as Captain Caneri, the executive officer of PPA, kept scrounging more jeeps and other related equipment. Additional men were recruited and, at its height, PPA had a total strength of just under 120 men. That unit strength did not last long, however. Casualties accounted for some of the losses. There were also some patrol members who just didn't live up to Popski's expectations. The unit eventually leveled off at four patrols of five jeeps each as the field element. Caneri was in charge of the rear support element.

By June 1944, PPA was operating in the Appennine mountains, on Italy's Adriatic side. Near the town of Camerino, about 150 miles northeast of Rome, was the headquarters of a German *Gebirgsjaeger* (mountain) division. Popski decided it was time to put reconnaissance duty on hold for a while. It was time to do some fighting. To set the stage, he began two deception operations. The first consisted of Yunnie's patrol and Popski's patrol sending radio messages to each other but using call signs for British armored units. The messages conveyed the impression that the armored unit, a brigade, was closing in on the German division HQ. More importantly, the signals stated that the armored unit was prepared to engage in battle.

The second deception was a little more elaborate. Popski arranged to interrogate a POW sergeant from the mountain division. Behind the desk in his office was an operational map showing Eighth Army positions well in advance of their actual locations but closing in on the German mountain unit. During the interrogation, other members of PPA entered Popski's office and updated the map. Later that night, the German sergeant was allowed to escape with the hope that he would tell his unit all he had seen.

The following morning at 1000, Popski dispersed his ten jeeps and then opened up on the town with all guns firing. The jeeps changed positions frequently but kept up a steady barrage. Popski was trying to convince the German commander that he was facing the imminent threat of being surrounded. He was actually hoping to encourage the German commander to pull out. Both patrols even conducted a hit and run attack along a road leading into the town. Periodically the Germans fired back with artillery but this was generally ineffective against an enemy on the move. That night Italian partisans reported that German convoys were abandoning the town. Popski had pulled another fast one.

In between operations, the men of PPA trained. Refresher parachute training, jeep tactics, shooting drills, even radio techniques were all on the schedule. One operation called for Yunnie's patrol to be infiltrated, and later exfiltrated, using amphibious vehicles. These landings were a novelty for the unit and called for intensive training. The scheduled mission, however, did not come off as planned. The landing craft assigned to the mission went aground 100 miles behind the German lines. Popski had to destroy 12 fully equipped jeeps before getting out in a hair-raising escape. Committed to the possibility that amphibious tactics could provide for success, based mainly on the element of surprise, he later scrounged his own fleet of landing vehicles. Periodically, he roamed the German rear area at will. But finding the Germans was not always that easy. Popski sometimes found that the only way to locate the Germans was to expose his patrols and to intentionally take fire. These moments were always frightening because of their unpredictability.

PPA continued to function in its unorthodox style, both in terms of its operations and recruitment of unit members. They soon began to work more closely with partisan units in their area of operations. On one mission two escaped Russian prisoners of war attached themselves to the unit. Another time a German deserter, known only as Karl, went along on several missions. Occasionally, PPA even found time to engage in a mission in support of a British unit. On one such operation, near the end of the war, PPA cooperated with the 27th Lancers, the recce regiment for Headquarters, Allied Armies in Italy.

On this mission, an island tower guarded the entrance to the Fiumi Uniti River near the town of Ravenna. A German force had stubbornly defended this outpost and was successful in blocking an approach road into town. It was also forcing PPA amphibious operations to make a wide detour. A new patrol leader, Captain John Campbell, volunteered to take the mission. That night he led a five-man patrol in a reconnaissance of the tower. They trudged through water, sometimes in depths up to their necks. A fisherman volunteered to row them close to the tower for an inspection. This fisherman told the patrol that the Germans locked themselves in the tower in the daytime and posted a sentry inside the door at night. Campbell decided that the door was too thick to be forced and that the only way in was to somehow get past the night sentry. The patrol departed and returned the next night. They hid in a nearby cowshed all the while staying in radio contact with Popski.

At dawn, the guard came out. He stretched and let his dog loose for a run. The dog headed right for the cowshed. The dog sniffed the patrol but, curiously, did not give them away. The guard and his dog soon went back inside. Campbell was betting, however, that they could still get in if they were patient. He was convinced that there were no latrine facilities inside the tower. Sure enough, about an hour later, the guard came back out and began to relieve himself. Campbell and his men were ready. They sprinted to the tower and knocked out the unsuspecting guard with a well-placed blow from a blackjack. They were in!

The patrol quickly and quietly subdued the rest of the German force in the tower. They radioed back to Popski, who brought a patrol up to the cowshed. During the rest of the day, three different German elements went to the tower to find out what was going on. The first two were captured without a shot being fired. The last group, about one-half a platoon, was leery of a possible ambush and fired on the tower. When Popski's patrol fired on the Germans from the cowshed, the group surrendered. The next day Popski learned that the rest of the German units in the area departed during the night.

Several days later, while still supporting the 27th Lancers, Popski and his patrol defended a bridge against a multi-company attack. Popski and his new driver-gunner, Sergeant Sam Taylor, led the furious fire fight and eventually broke the attack. In the battle, Popski's left wrist was shattered and his hand almost blown off. He nevertheless kept on shooting. When he arrived at an aid station later, Popski found that he had also been shot in the right palm.

Popski's left hand was amputated above the wrist and his right hand was put in a cast. He was sent to England to recuperate and a newly promoted Major Caneri took command of Popski's Private Army. Weeks later, when Popski returned with a hook at the end of his left arm, he found little left of the unit. The war was almost over and his "private army" was being disbanded. But his arsenal was still full.

Just two weeks before the end of the war, Popski led a patrol into the town of Chiogga. There he bluffed the garrison commander into surrendering his force of almost 700, including supporting artillery. Soon after this, he loaded five jeeps onto three landing craft and sailed to Venice. He disembarked his patrol at the quay on the Canal San Marco. Popski described what happened next this way: "I started my jeep and, trembling with excitement for the one and only time during the war, drove into the Piazetta, passed between the columns, turned left into Piazza San Marco, and, followed by the others, drove seven times round the square. This was my hour of triumph." He executed the defiant gesture he had predicted almost two years earlier.

The day before the war ended, Popski crossed into Austria and linked up with a Russian force near the town of Voitsberg.

Popski made his mark in military history. He had selected, trained, and led a dedicated band of jeep-mounted soldiers who specialized in intelligence gathering where it counted the most—behind enemy lines. They were trained and prepared to execute their missions by air, by land, and by sea. They could always attack and blend back into the local landscape. But they always knew that, first and foremost, they were there to find the enemy.

When Popski died in 1952, Major Caneri eulogized him this way: "Popski was a funny little man—and a great one. He was a martinet and yet a very human being. Sometimes he would fuss like an old grandmother; then he would suddenly grin and offer to stand you a drink. Although he was an old man, in a war sense, when he began to fight, he never let fatigue or pain slow him down. He constantly drove, led, and encouraged us all . . . He certainly, in PPA's own small way, created a new dimension in military tactics. He made the war—in those years I was with him—a memorable experience."

Major Yunnie, also recently promoted, was transferred home in April 1945, before the war finally ended. He had mixed feelings about leaving but finally accepted the inevitable. He led his patrol into a wooded area and said his farewell quietly, with tears. Years later he recalled his parting. "Tears? Among fighting men? But tears are women's things . . . In war, there is a love of comrade for comrade which far surpasses the love of a man for a woman and it is a love which women do not understand. Having no connection with sex, it is an emotion entirely of the heart, a deep, enduring bond forged from risks taken together, hardships and dangers equally shared, death looked in the face time and time again. There wasn't a man in that patrol but would willingly have given his life for all or any of the other patrolmen, aye, been proud to give it, and would never have counted the cost. Tears? Why not?"

Mission Critique

PPA was given fairly wide ranging authority when it was created by Middle East Command. The targets assigned to PPA were appropriate to special operations forces. In most cases these mission objectives were identified with the sole purpose of intelligence gathering. These mission targets were not targets to be destroyed or otherwise attacked, although Popski had authorization to engage when necessary. Generally decisions to engage were to be only as a last resort.

Virtually the same rationale applies to missions. Missions conducted by the Amphibious Scouts; the Alamo Scouts; the Jedburgh teams; and the OSS Ops Groups will be discussed later in this book. Not all of these units went exclusively on intelligence gathering missions. However, those missions that were not, were reviewed to determine if conventional forces could conduct them. You should note also that the Alamo Scouts had a different category of special missions added to their requirements once the Philippines were invaded. Again, these were good missions for a special operations force.

There is just one significant quality that characterized the operations of PPA. That quality is imagination. It is this characteristic that permeates the unit's process in selection, training, planning, and operational execution. Popski looked for men who could think for themselves. He also looked for men who would accept and apply his concepts for training and operations. He was not content to remain static in his operational concept. Although his unit initially used jeeps to travel to those parts of North Africa where it operated, Popski arranged for his men to also be trained in parachute and glider operations. On several occasions his unit also employed amphibious modes of transport to get to operational areas. The emergency action drills which he had devised and hammered into his men whenever there was a spare minute contributed mightily in several successful encounters with German and Italian units. There is also no doubt that Popski agreed with George Jacques Danton, who, in 1792, said, "Il nous fant de l'audace, encore de l'audace, toujours de l'audace" (. . . we need audacity, still more audacity, and audacity forever).

Popski had an active mind and was always thinking of ways to improve his operations. And he was always looking out for his men's safety. The simplest critique of PPA's missions is to note that McRaven's criteria were essential hallmarks of virtually every operation. Popski constantly reminded his men that they were most successful when the enemy did not know they had been there and then they were able to return safely with essential intelligence.

In applying Vandenbroucke's criteria, I believe that when PPA was first formed, Popski and Hackett may have been subject to some *wishful thinking*. However, this disappeared once PPA began to operate. It became obvious that Popski was serious about gathering intelligence and bringing his men back alive. Except for this, there appears to be little in the way of criticism for Popski and his men.

SOURCES

Books:

Beaumont, Roger A.; *Military Elites;* Indianapolis; Bobbs-Merrill; 1974

Brown, Ashley and Jonathan Reed (editors); *The Unique Units;* Harrisburg, PA; National Historical Society; 1986 (The Elite—The World's Crack Fighting Men, volume 10)

——————; *Desert and Air Services;* Harrisburg, PA; National Historical Society; 1986 (The Elite—The World's Crack Fighting Men, volume 14)

Gordon, John W.; *The Other Desert War—British Special Forces in North Africa, 1940–1943*; New York; Greenwood Press; 1987 (Contributions in Military Studies, number 56)

Hoare, Mike; *Mercenary*; New York; Bantam Books; 1967

Kay, R.L.; *Long Range Desert Group in the Mediterranean*; Wellington, NZ; War History Branch, Department of Internal Affairs; 1950 (New Zealand in the Second World War Official History)

Peniakoff, Vladimir; *Private Army*; London; Jonathan Cape; 1950

Rosignoli, Guido; *Army Badges and Insignia of World War 2*; New York; MacMillan; 1972

Sanderson, James Dean; *Behind Enemy Lines*; New York; Pyramid Books; 1959

Whittaker, Len; *Some Talk of Private Armies*; Harpenden, UK; Albanium Publishing; 1984

Willett, John; *Popski—A Life of Vladimir Peniakoff*; London; MacGibbon & Kee; 1954

Yunnie, Park; *Warriors on Wheels*; London; Hutchinson; 1959

Articles:

Evans, Hoyte; "Popski's Private Army Cap Badge"; *Trading Post* magazine; date unknown

CHAPTER TEN

THE AMPHIBIOUS SCOUTS

The strands that are woven into the historical tapestry of Naval Special Warfare comprise the antecedents of today's SEAL teams. One of the least familiar of these strands is a unit created in the summer of 1943 by Rear Admiral Daniel E. Barbey. The unit was to be the forward eyes and ears of the 7th Amphibious Force. It was officially designated the U.S. Seventh Fleet Special Service Unit #1. To its members it was better known by its classified name—Amphibious Scouts Unit #1.

Barbey chose a Naval officer with a most interesting background to form the Amphibious Scouts, Lieutenant Commander William F. Coultas. Coultas had spent several years immediately prior to World War II traveling throughout the Solomon Island chain in the Southwest Pacific. While he appeared to be a working member of a National Geographic expedition, he was in actuality gathering intelligence for the Navy. This background is eerily similar to that of Ralph Bagnold, the founder of the Long Range Desert Group. Bagnold had spent the pre-war years navigating and charting the desert regions of North Africa. Later, his truck-borne intelligence-gathering unit used his charts to sneak behind the lines of the *Afrika Korps*.

Barbey chose Coultas because of his acquired knowledge and experience, as well as for his familiarity with the operations of the Australian Coastwatchers. Charged with his mission, Coultas soon departed for Australia to begin recruiting. His selections represented curious cross-sections, as the men were recruited from the Navy, Army (32nd Infantry Division), the Marine Corps (1st Marine Division), and from Australian units that had recently returned from fighting in North Africa. Some of the criteria he used for selection included education, intelligence, and previous combat or sea duty. To Coultas, it was also imperative that each man must be a volunteer. Among the U.S. Navy personnel volunteering for duty in this top-secret unit were Ensigns Alva E. Gipe, Rudolph A. Horak, Donald G. Root, and Henry E. Staudt and at least two petty officers, Calvin W. Byrd and John Grady.

Training began once Coultas had assembled a sizeable enough group. For several months the Amphibious Scouts trained in Australia. Their training officer was an Australian Army captain named John Murphy, who had been a civil government administrator prior to entering the Army. In September, the training center was moved to a vacated PT boat base near the village of Kola Kola on Fergusson Island. This island was located off the eastern end of New Guinea.

While local natives assisted in building and refurbishing the training center structures, the volunteers focused on their training activities. Required disciplines included heavy emphasis on swimming and physical training; jungle fighting and survival techniques; hand-to-hand combat; shoreline sketching; measuring beach approaches; and patrolling techniques. At Fergusson Island, transport by PT boat was added to the training regimen. These boats transported patrols to various places around the island and retrieved them when the mission was completed. The students had to use inflatable rubber boats to land ashore and, once ashore, they were required to deflate and effectively conceal the rubber boats. They were then to conduct their assigned reconnaissance. Once their assignment was completed, they were to return to their hidden boats, reinflate them with compressed air, and paddle out to the waiting PT boats. Teams not on patrol were assigned to hide in the vicinity of reconnaissance targets and attempt to ambush the scouting parties. At the conclusion of training, six teams of seven men each were selected to perform operations. Each team contained a mix of nationalities, services, and ranks.

By mid-September, 7th Amphibious Force had completed three invasions, including Woodlark and Kiriwina islands in late June and at Lae in the Huon Gulf area of eastern New Guinea in September. Admiral Barbey was less than satisfied with the way beachhead intelligence had been gathered to this point. He actually categorized it as primitive and haphazard. The planned landings at Finschhafen, on the north coast of Huon Gulf, were next on the timetable. Barbey now decided it was time to use the Amphibious Scouts. The team selected to conduct this reconnaissance was led by a legendary Australian Coastwatcher, Captain G.C. "Blue" Harris. His team included two Australian lieutenants, an Australian sergeant, two Papuan soldiers (named Yule and Masa), and Ensign Hank Staudt, the lone American. The

Harris team was chosen for this mission because Harris had worked in the Finschhafen area before the war and was somewhat familiar with it.

The team was dispatched to its drop-off location in two PT boats. One of these PT boats carried the patrol to its drop-off point while the other continued up the coast, past the actual landing site. The second boat acted in a diversionary capacity in case its movement was being observed by the Japanese.

The Scouts required two inflatable rubber boats to accommodate the whole team and its supplies. The boat to which Staudt was assigned, however, got swamped in the rough surf and turned over, scattering both men and supplies. Once he was close enough to begin walking, Staudt ran into several coral formations that cut up his legs. When the drama on the water was finally mastered, the mission began to reverberate with activities born out of intensive training. Once they hit the beach, the Amphibious Scouts quickly collapsed and buried their boats. Then they moved into the jungle area past the beach, looking for a suitable hiding place. For the next three days the team hid by day and conducted its reconnaissance mission by night. They made hydrographic surveys of the beach area (from the low to the high water marks), checked the water for obstacles, and surveyed the beach for exit areas.

With the landing party safely hidden during daylight hours, intentional bombing raids were conducted in vicinities nearby. These bombing missions were intended, as Staudt later described it, to "keep the Japanese occupied." While these may have been general nuisance missions, they also served to keep the Japanese from becoming aware of the Scouts and their missions. One bombing run dropped its load so close that several Japanese soldiers hid in the very same area the Scouts were using. At one point, Harris and a Japanese soldier found themselves face to face. Before Harris could decide whether to shoot him, the Japanese turned and ran away. Since no subsequent search was ever conducted for the Scouts, they concluded that, in the heat of the moment, they had been mistaken for Japanese.

The team had not taken a radio with them. However, plans for its extraction were preset and all went well during the extraction phase. Ensign Staudt received the Navy and Marine Corps Medal for his work on this mission. Exactly one week after the team completed its mission, Finschhafen was invaded and quickly taken.

It wasn't long before the Amphibious Scouts were tasked with a new mission. This time the target was near Gasmata, on the island of New Britain. Landings were scheduled for December. The team chosen for this mission was led by an Australian Coastwatcher, Andrew Kirkwall-Smith, who was familiar with New Britain. Others on the team included: two Australian radio technicians; two native soldiers (Sabu and Pablo); John Bradbeer of the 1st Marine Division; Army Lieutenant Daily P. Gambill; and Ensign Rudy Horak.

This mission proved to be an adventure from the outset. While the team was still in its rubber boats, two Japanese barges came within sight of the supporting PT boats. Horak said later, "We managed to get between them and the land. They didn't see us [in the dark]." Just prior to landing, however, the native soldiers panicked and flipped the boats over in the surf. As a result, the team lost all of its provisions and for the next 11 days they had to employ their training and live off the land. The patrol eventually worked its way across the tip of the island to Borgan Bay and concluded that the area on the north side of the island was better suited for an amphibious landing. During the course of this reconnaissance, the team was actively pursued by Japanese patrols who had discovered their presence on the island. The Scouts played a deadly game of hide-and-seek throughout their mission on New Britain but managed to elude capture and provide valuable intelligence. Horak happily concluded that, in the end, ". . . the Marines *did* take our account into consideration because they did not land on the southern shore. It was too rocky, too densely vegetated."

Ensign Horak received the Bronze Star for his part in the operation, a significant part of which included pinpointing the locations of two very menacing coast artillery pieces. These installations were later taken out by aerial bombing. The guns actually overlooked the strategic strait that was later used by the invading Marines. In the course of this mission, Horak contracted malaria and "lost 35 pounds from not eating and fear of the Japs." He was evacuated to Australia and, after recuperating, was involuntarily transferred out of the Amphibious Scouts.

At almost the same time as the team was being evacuated out of Gasmata, a second team was going in. And while its point of entry was near the same place as the first team, the focus of this mission was very different. The nine-man team was led by Lieutenant Lindsay C. Noakes, an Australian Army intelligence officer. Also on the team were: Lieutenant Milton H. Beckworth, U.S. Army; Ensign Donald Root; Sergeant "Mike" Mantas, U.S. Marine Corps; and five native soldiers. The team's mission was to land near Luschan Harbor, move across the island, and determine whether the area in the vicinity of Linderhafen Plantation was suitable to sustain an air field. The team estimated that it would take 18 days to complete this mission.

Just after midnight on 7 October, a single PT boat delivered the team to its entry point. The team silently lowered its rubber boats into the water and, with several men in each boat, began loading mission equipment and supplies. When this was complete, the team pushed away and paddled to the beach. Because of the mission's protracted duration, the rubber boats were sent back to the waiting PT boat. The team was on its own. The Scouts quickly found an area to rest and, in the morning, set out for their destination, 20 miles away.

The team moved across terrain that was unforgiving. It was thick with brush and vine, making movement very slow. It became quite apparent that they had underestimated the impact of nature while crossing this area of the island. On the seventh day, things got worse as Noakes and Root became ill. At this point they were not even halfway to their objective. The Scouts reluctantly acknowledged that they had run out of time and would not make it to the plantation and then return in time for their pickup. So, on the eighth day the team rested and, on the following morning, set out on its return trip. By maintaining close contact with the locals, the Scouts avoided the Japanese troops in the area, who seemed unaware of the presence of a reconnaissance team in their midst.

On the 18th and final day of its mission, the team arrived at its pick-up point. That night, the Scouts could hear the low rumbling sounds of PT boat engines echoing across the water but, to their consternation, they could not make radio contact. Even though no one on the team could see the boats they could certainly hear them. The alternate pick-up time was pre-designated for the following night. Yet events on the second night were a repetition of the night before, and they could not make radio contact. Again, the Scouts could hear, but not see, the PT boats. Some of them began to deal with the unsavory prospect that they might have been left behind. On the third night, in what they later found out was a last ditch effort to make contact, the PT boats returned. After two hours of effort there was still no radio contact. The morale of the team slipped to an all time low. Just as they were about to give up hope, Beckworth thought he saw one of the boats. Without hesitation, he signaled with his flashlight. The PT boats moved in quickly and pulled the weary team off the island. For his part in this mission, Ensign Root was awarded the Bronze Star.

During late November and early December, the training center moved to the village of Dowa Dowa, near Milne Bay on New Guinea (Hank Staudt remembers that they were welcomed to their new location by Tokyo Rose). This move was very practical as it actually put the Scouts closer to the planning staff at 7th Amphibious Force HQ and facilitated their involvement in more pre-landing reconnaissance missions. The unit commander and founder, Commander Coultas, had moved on and was replaced by Major M.G. Brown, U.S. Marine Corps.

Even while various teams were out conducting missions, the work at the training center did not stop. At least three different reconnaissance units from the 1st Marine Division were sent through the training, at both the Fergusson Island location and at Dowa Dowa. The practice later spread as other divisions began to use these training facilities for their recon units. Admiral Barbey was more than willing to train the Marines because he believed that "troop commanders usually felt they could get more and better information on matters of particular interest to them, such as trails, defenses, and back country terrain, by reliance on ground reconnaissance."

On their next mission, the Scouts returned to New Britain Island for the third time. This mission's activities put the Scouts in the vicinity of Cape Gloucester. The team for this mission included: two Marine officers (John Bradbeer, who had been on the first mission to New Britain, and Lieutenant R.B. Firm); a Marine sergeant; two native soldiers; a radio technician; and Ensign Alva Gipe.

This mission was conducted in direct support of the 1st Marine Division. As in previous missions, two PT boats assisted in the landing phase. This time, however, one of the PT boats actually took the team in, getting as close to the shore as it could. From there, most of the team loaded onto one rubber boat and continued to the beach with some alarm. Ensign Gipe noted the loud rumble of the departing PT boat's engine, saying "You could hear it all over." The team broke into several functional elements. Gipe began surveying the left side of the beach while the two Marine sergeants did the same on the right side. One of the native soldiers stayed near the landing site with the rubber boat. Firm patrolled inland and Bradbeer remained on the PT boat. The Scouts soon realized that the Japanese were aware of their presence on the island and decided it was time to leave. In a later discussion of the mission, Gipe described the beach as very rocky and concluded, "As far as the Navy was concerned, they wouldn't have gone in with their LSTs. They *couldn't* have gone in. And then the exit out of the beach was steep and they wouldn't have been able to use it." On their leg returning to 1st Marine Division headquarters to file their report, the PT boats were sighted and chased by a Japanese destroyer. They escaped by staying in close to shore at a small, nearby island. For his part in this mission, Ensign Gipe was awarded the Silver Star.

This was the last mission for the Amphibious Scouts in their current make-up, one that would make use of strategies that involved large teams. In December, following a leave in Australia, most of the Scouts were assigned other duties. The team size was reduced to usually two Scouts, one Navy officer and one Navy petty officer. Gipe and Donald Root, each newly promoted to Lieutenant (Junior Grade), were assigned as team leaders. Petty Officer John Grady teamed with Gipe while Petty Officer Calvin Byrd teamed with Root.

In between missions the Scouts were assigned to the staff of U.S.S. *Blue Ridge*, Admiral Barbey's flagship. The teams were usually assigned duties with the Beach Party during landings for which they did not conduct the prior reconnaissance. Following the invasion of the Admiralties by elements of the 1st Cavalry Division in late February 1944, Root and Byrd were sent in to gather tidal data at Bat Island in the Purdy Group, located near the Admiralties. The two-man team left Finschhafen on board U.S.S. *Oyster Bay*, a PT tender that took them most of the way to the Purdies. They then transferred to a PT boat for their infiltration run to the northern part of Bat Island. To gather tidal information, the two Scouts used knotted ropes tied to stakes that required measurements to be taken every hour. They were told that this information was to be used in the planning for the forthcoming invasion at Aitape and Hollandia, scheduled for late April 1944. The measurement lasted only 16 days, although the mission had been planned for 30 days. The mission was curtailed because others on the island (teams of Army plane spotters and Australian Coastwatchers had been assigned there as well) had caught a tropical fever. A decision was made, therefore, to evacuate everyone.

In late March, the Scouts heard some distressing news. A reconnaissance team headed by "Blue" Harris, the leader of the first Amphibious Scouts mission that had included Hank Staudt, had been discovered by the Japanese near the Hollandia area. Harris and several of his men were killed in an ambush during their second day ashore. Three members of the team, however, escaped to tell the story.

It was in the midst of this action that Hank Staudt was to lead a team to gather data in the Aitape area. His team was carried to its objective area by submarine but, prior to launch, Colonel Brown, the Amphibious Scouts commander, told Staudt that the mission had been aborted. "I could never figure out why we aborted this," Staudt said later, "until I found out about "Blue" Harris being picked up in Hollandia. And, no doubt . . . they didn't want the same thing to happen . . ." It turned out that this was to be Staudt's last mission. Soon after, he returned to sea duty (LST 462). He said later, "After that I slept on clean sheets."

A later mission for Root and Byrd to recon Biak Island was canceled when their PT boat hit a partially submerged log and lost a propeller. Both Gipe and Staudt later participated, although in more conventional capacities, in the landings at Biak. They both later said that if the recon by Root and Byrd *had* taken place, the landings would not have taken place at this spot. As it turned out, the beaches designated for the landing operations were terribly unsuited for an amphibious operation.

In June 1944, the Gipe/Grady and Root/Byrd teams were merged by Sixth Army with larger teams led by Alamo Scouts. These teams were also supplemented by Air Corps officers and representatives of the Sixth Army Intelligence staff. Their mission was to conduct reconnaissance operations in the vicinity of Sansapor, at the western end of the Vogelkopf Peninsula of New Guinea. Root and Byrd were attached to Thompson Team of the Alamo Scouts. They infiltrated their mission area by submarine. Later Gipe and Grady accompanied Dove Team and went in by PT boat.

During the long submarine ride to western New Guinea, Byrd said the crew treated the scouting party like celebrities. The landing, on the night of 27 June, missed the target areas by about 500 yards. The teams were forced to carry their boats through the rough surf in order to reach their actual destination, a physically draining task that took almost an hour to complete. Finally, they reached their start point at the mouth of the river.

From there, the teams paddled inland. Just before dawn they reached a spot where they could effectively deflate and hide their boats but halted when they noticed a Japanese barge coming up the river; the barge nearly came to where the teams were hidden. The Scouts remained in hiding until the Japanese departed, which they did at about 1500 that afternoon. Root and Byrd left for the beaches while the Alamo Scouts pushed inland.

On the beach, the Amphibious Scouts "recorded information concerning the condition of the beach, the terrain leading inland away from the beach, the water . . . depth, coral, surf, etc." They noticed a small island nearby and recorded their observations from a distance. The following day they moved further east and continued their survey. Byrd's version of how the mission ended was summarized thus: "After dark the [submarine] was contacted and with the help of their sonar and our radio we had a safe return. We were treated to a good shower, ridded of chiggers, and fed a big steak." For his part in this mission, Calvin Byrd was awarded the Bronze Star.

Gipe and Grady were assigned to go back in to Sansapor, only slightly east of their first mission. The skipper of the PT boat carrying the team from the PT base at Woendi Island was an old college classmate and friend of Gipe. On the night of 14 July, the combined Alamo Scouts-Amphibious Scouts team landed and buried its boat and radio. The Scouts spent the next four days conducting a reconnaissance of the area. There were Japanese nearby but none of the scouting party was ever spotted as the native islanders kept the team well informed of the Japanese patrols and routine.

At the appointed time, they returned to their cache eager to make contact with their pick-up boat, but quickly discovered that the radio antenna was broken. They weighed the potential risk and decided to use their Aldis signaling lamp. They successfully contacted the waiting PT boat and the scouting party was retrieved without further incident. Gipe later talked about the team's concern that it would be spotted while using the signal lamp: "That light looked like Grand Central Station." The subsequent invasion of Sansapor was launched at the end of July. This mission proved to be the last for both Sixth Army's and 7th Amphibious Force's units in New Guinea.

The final mission conducted by the original teams of Amphibious Scouts Unit #1 was in support of the invasion of Leyte, a mission that would mark the return of U.S. forces back to the Philippines. The objective of this mission was very different than those in the past. It required two teams to set up navigation lights that could be seen from the open sea, on Dinagat Island and Homonhon Island. The lights were needed to mark the channel for the invasion fleet. Just as importantly, it was also a signal that the channel was clear of mines and safe to enter. The teams were to go in on 17 October. They would have just two days to complete their mission, as the invasion fleet would be steaming through the channel beginning at midnight, 20 October.

Root, Byrd, and Petty Officer Paul Daugherty were assigned to Dinagat Island and Gipe, Grady, and Lieutenant (Junior Grade) David H. DeWendt were assigned to the mission on Homonhon Island. The marking lights that were to be carried in by the teams were described by Calvin Byrd in this way: "The light poles consisted of three [inch] pipe joints that could be coupled together. The lights could be screwed to the top of the pole. Lights could be adjusted up or down, and from side to side. Power would come from truck batteries."

The poles, lights, couplings, and batteries were disassembled to make transport easier. From their landing points, each team was required to carry its equipment on stretchers to the designated installation sites.

In comparison to previous missions, a veritable fleet transported the Scouts to their mission area. The complexity and significance of this mission required it. This small fleet consisted of 3 APDs (World War I destroyers converted to assault troop transports), 3 destroyers, 12 minesweepers, and a sea-going tug. Included in the force were several hundred members of the 6th Ranger Battalion. It was the task of the Rangers to secure as much of each island as possible and to provide security for the Amphibious Scouts. The convoy had to plough through a rough storm on its way to the mission site. This storm, however, did not unduly impede their progress and scheduled arrival off Dinagat Island. They arrived just before noon on 17 October. It was still raining.

Root's team and about 100 Rangers went ashore. They met no opposition and immediately set out for their destination. Their objective was Desolation Point, which was located at the very northern tip of the island. They were on the move for the rest of that day and made good progress, and spent the night in an empty, shell-blasted building.

At dawn, the Scouts and Rangers continued on their trek and reached Desolation Point while it was still morning. The team immediately began to assemble the signal light. Close by, the Rangers discovered a building where they found charts with silhouettes of American planes, and assumed the site had been used by a Japanese plane spotter. This did not surprise Calvin Byrd who described the view of the ocean from this point as "exceptionally good." Since the teams could not determine when this post had been evacuated, the Rangers remained on alert. With the point secured and the signal light set up, the team spent the rest of its mission in relative ease while waiting impatiently for the invasion force to arrive. There was nothing to do but observe the minesweepers continuing their work of clearing the channel between islands.

On Homonhon, Gipe's team went ashore with its Ranger support led by Captain Arthur D. Simons. They were met at the beach by a small band of Filipino guerrillas who were expecting them. The team moved quickly to the position chosen for its light ("at the water's edge" remembers Gipe) and immediately went to work while the Rangers secured the area. The mission proceeded without incident. On the evening of 18 October, both teams adjusted their lights. The synchronization process was executed by radio with a destroyer positioned in the channel for this purpose. After the necessary adjustments were complete, both lights were turned off.

That night on Dinagat, Byrd heard two shots around 2200. The next morning the Rangers showed him the body of a dead Japanese soldier who had been killed while maneuvering near their perimeter. The mystery of what happened to the plane spotter was solved.

Nothing now remained but for the invasion fleet to proceed up the channel. The invasion of Leyte on 20 October was a huge success. However, the U.S. Naval forces were engaged with the Japanese in a big naval battle in Leyte Gulf. It was several days later, when the outcome of the naval battle was assured, that the Amphibious Scouts and Rangers could be retrieved from their positions.

This ended the missions for those members of the Amphibious Scouts recruited to form the unit. During 1945, several missions were conducted by Amphibious Scouts teams made up of officers and petty officers recruited in the States and trained at Fort Pierce, Florida. These included missions on Luzon, several nearby islands, and even in Borneo. Two of these missions, led by Scouts (both ensigns) Sidney S. Chapin and William C. Sheppard, assisted XXIV Corps in its September 1945 amphibious landing in Jinsen, Korea, where it took up occupation duty.

Both in its training and in the little known details of the execution of its various missions, the history of Amphibious Scouts Unit #1 planted the seeds for the future growth of other Naval Special Warfare units, even to the SEAL teams of today.

Mission Critique

In a sense, the missions of the Amphibious Scouts are similar to those of Popski's Private Army; namely to gather intelligence. In contrast to Popski's Private Army, the targets of the Amphibious Scouts were different and so were the means of insertion. The two aspects of target and insertion means were, however, compatible. The Scouts were specifically raised and trained to obtain intelligence that would support a decision of whether to launch an amphibious landing in a given area.

The last mission detailed, the lights for the Leyte Gulf passage, was an outgrowth of a capability available to a commander.

It seems that several of MacArthur's subordinate commanders considered it necessary to create an intelligence gathering organization to support planning. It is seen here with the U.S. Navy and it will be seen later in the case of Sixth Army. The justification for the creation of the Amphibious Scouts was based on sound reasoning

Referencing the Vandenbroucke criteria, many of these missions demonstrate *coordination* problems that are common to several of those discussed in this book. This is especially true with problems in communications. The need for secrecy while on these operations probably prevented means, other than radios, from being used. Even when used as a back-up, the radios still had many problems.

Two examples of *wishful thinking* apply to the second mission on Gasmata mission (the one that targeted the area around the Linderhafen Plantation) and the two-man mission to Bat Island. The first was planned for 18 days and the second was originally scheduled for 30 days. These were exceptionally long durations to be operating behind enemy lines. How either of these could have been planned better is speculative but the way they were executed shows that they didn't work.

The most gratifying aspect about the missions conducted by the Scouts was the cancellation of landings at sites the Scouts determined were unacceptable for such invasions or altering plans when their reconnaissance showed problems in that area. Nothing else can demonstrate more clearly that these missions were necessary and that they were part, indeed an integral part, of the overall command operations plan. In addition, nothing gives a special operator more satisfaction than to experience command acceptance of a recommendation based on operational results.

A side feature of the operations involving the Amphibious Scouts is the operational and training contact they had with other special purpose, special mission organizations, such as: the Coastwatchers; the Marine Recon units; the Alamo Scouts; and the 6th Ranger Battalion. Such contact was very unusual for special units during World War II. It was probably mirrored only by the SAS and its operational contact with such special units as: the Long Range Desert Group; several Commando units; the Special Boat Service; and various Jedburgh teams.

As with Popski's Private Army, the McRaven criteria were generally evident in all of the Scouts' missions. The exception was perhaps the lack of *repetition*. Once training was completed the Amphibious Scouts did not generally conduct rehearsals for upcoming missions. This lack of *repetition*, however, does not appear to have caused any serious problems on operations. Overall, the missions of the Amphibious Scouts proved successful. These missions were especially successful when the teams brought back intelligence defining why a particular area was not suitable for its planned purpose.

SOURCES

Books:

Barbey, Daniel E.; *MacArthur's Amphibious Navy—Seventh Amphibious Force Operations 1943–1945;* Annapolis, MD; United States Naval Institute; 1969

Canon, M. Hamlin; *Leyte: The Return to the Philippines;* Washington DC; Office of the Chief of Military History (in the United States Army in World War II series); 1954

Dwyer, John B.; *Scouts and Raiders—The Navy's First Special Warfare Commandos;* Westport, CT; Praeger; 1993

Feldt, Eric A.; *The Coastwatchers;* Melbourne; Oxford University Press; 1946

Hochstrasser, Lewis B.; *They Were First—The True Story of the Alamo Scouts;* unpublished manuscript in author's collection

Interviews and letters with:

Calvin W. Byrd (interview on June 2, 1995; letters on July 9 and 26, August 23, and September 15, 1995)

Alva E. Gipe (interview on June 2, 1995; letter on August 9, 1995)

Rudolph A. Horak (interview on June 2, 1995; letters on July 12 and October 9, 1995)

Doris Root (letter on Aug 3, 1995)

Henry E. Staudt (interview on June 2, 1995; letter undated, received about July 18, 1995 and letter dated November 13, 1995)

CHAPTER ELEVEN

'Oil Spot' in New Guinea

General Kurt Student, founder and commander of the German airborne corps, also devised several strategies for his troops. He preferred employing small formations of paratroopers whose goal was to gain and secure footholds in several widely dispersed locations. Student anticipated that this form of attack would initially confuse the enemy as to the size and scope of the operation. This strategy made it hard for the defender to respond with a concentrated force as attackers would be active over a wide perimeter. Student also hoped that these small concentrations would eventually open the way for the troopers in the footholds to link up with each other as well as with conventional forces moving up behind them. Student referred to these airborne footholds as "oil spots."

One of the most ably coordinated air corps/airborne operations in World War II, marking the first use of American paratroopers in the Pacific Theater, was the baptism by fire of the 503rd Parachute Infantry Regiment.

The 503rd, commanded by Colonel George M. Jones, was assigned to the Pacific Theater during the fall of 1942. However, it was not until April 1943 that it was scheduled for use in combat. The invasion of Hollandia was planned to include a parachute assault to complement the amphibious landings but a lack of sufficient transport aircraft necessitated cancellation of the planned drop. It was in mid-September 1943 that plans, including a parachute assault, were made to take advantage of a specific situation—the isolation of Japanese forces in Lae, on Papua New Guinea. To do so, simultaneous strategies had to be executed on schedule.

First, a feint toward Salamaua, involving U.S. and Australian units, would attempt to draw the Japanese toward the feint and away from Lae. Second, the 9th Australian Division would conduct an amphibious assault ten miles east of Lae, at Hopoi. Led by an advance element of Australian combat engineer units, the 9th Division would then move westward to capture Lea. On the following day, the 503rd was to parachute into Nadzab. Its objective was to provide security for Australian engineer units as they put a disused airstrip into service. Furthermore, the 503rd was to block movement of the Japanese into the Markham Valley area, ten miles west of Lae.

The Markham Valley extends in a southwesterly direction from Lae to the Ramu River. The geographic width of the valley varies. At some intervals the width may be as much as 25 miles wide. The valley is bounded by jungle and mountainous terrain at both rims. Once the airstrip was deemed serviceable, the 7th Australian Division would air-land on it and attack Lae from the west.

Since the 503rd had no organic artillery, a troop from the 2nd Battalion, 4th Australian Field Artillery Regiment was attached for temporary service. The Australians were given elementary pre-jump training and made one practice jump supervised by Lieutenant Robert W. Armstrong, 1/503rd. The Australians had modified the 75mm pack howitzers by cutting down the barrel and mounting it on a light carriage, thus making it more suitable for jungle warfare. A pair of these guns was then dismantled and loaded for delivery by parachute. This had never been tried before. Air delivery experts from the Fifth Air Force had, under great time pressure, tested the concept and their effort was a complete success.

The original plans called for the operation to begin on 1 August. It was delayed until 27 August, then to 4 September because of insufficient transport aircraft. Finally, enough aircraft were assembled to put the plan into motion. The amphibious landing took place as scheduled and the Japanese at Lae reacted to the feint in the hoped-for manner.

On 5 September 1943, an early morning fog socked in the departure airfield. The fog lifted by 0800. At 0825, 79 C-47s crammed with paratroopers of the 503rd took off from the airfield at Port Moresby. Each paratrooper carried a combat jump load of 80 pounds. This load included three days' rations in addition to main and reserve parachutes. The supporting Australian artillery would jump from 5 C-47s two hours after the scheduled assault by the American paratroopers. An additional 12 C-47s carried equipment for use on the ground, such as ammunition, radios, tents, medical supplies, and stretchers. The flight to the drop zone included a rendezvous with an escort of 100 fighter aircraft. At the drop zone, B-25 bombers would drop fragmentation bombs and A-20 attack bombers were to lay a heavy smoke screen.

The air train crossed the saddle of the Owen-Stanley Mountains at an altitude of 9,000 feet making it very cold for the paratroopers inside the planes. The cold was enhanced by the fact that the planes were flying without doors. The doors had been purposely removed and the frames were covered with several layers of cloth tape. This innovation was designed to prevent snagging or tearing as the paratroopers and their equipment exited the aircraft.

Soon after crossing the saddle the planes descended to a more comfortable level at 3,500 feet. When the planes were several miles out from the drop zones they descended even lower, to tree-top level. The inside of the planes now became hot and humid. This sudden climate change caused many of the paratroopers, who were loaded down with their parachutes and combat loads, to become physically sick.

At 0948 the paratroopers buckled their helmets, stood up, and conducted final pre-jump equipment and static line checks. Almost all of the paratroopers became concerned with the weight of their loads. Many opted to remove their reserves and shoved them under their seats. The planes then popped up to jump altitude, ascending to between 400 and 500 feet. Just before 1010, the drop zones came within sight and red lights illuminated the interiors of the planes. The lead jumpers in each plane immediately took up their position. They stood in the door while other paratroopers behind them began pushing forward, anxious to get out of their crowded, hot, smelly "flying coffins."

Lieutenant Colonel John J. Tolson III, 3/503rd commander, stood in the door of the lead plane. He had previously accompanied bomber crews on several runs in this region in order to conduct his own personal reconnaissance. When the green light came on, Tolson jumped and his unit followed. The three battalions of the 503rd dropped in a cloverleaf pattern. The planes were emptied in about four and one-half minutes. Some planes dropped their sticks from as low as 175 feet.

Based on airborne observation, the kunai grass on the drop zone was thought to have been only knee high. However, in many places, it was actually as high as 12 feet. The tall grass combined with the hot, humid air nearly exhausted the paratroopers as they struggled to find their assembly areas.

The paratroopers went to work immediately. 1/503rd seized the airstrip area; 2/503rd blocked the western entrance to the area; and 3/503rd blocked the eastern approach. Patrols were sent out to reconnoiter trails and to establish a perimeter. Gliders had been standing by at Port Moresby but were not needed. Two hours later, right on schedule, 17 C-47s, carrying the Australian artillerymen and the 503rd's equipment, flashed over the drop zone and emptied their loads. Later that day the paratroopers made contact with lead elements of the Australian combat engineer units, whose task was to repair the airfield in preparation for air-landing operations the following day. The Australian engineers worked through the night, protected by the American paratroopers.

Early on the morning of 6 September the first C-47s landed at Nadzab airfield. The first flights carried the advance party of the 871st Airborne Engineer Battalion and, later in the day, the 7th Australian Division began landing operations. By 14 September, the airfield had 2 parallel runways each measuring 6,000 feet in length. It was very apparent that the Japanese had been caught completely by surprise.

The 503rd's jump was witnessed by several dignitaries. General Douglas MacArthur observed the operation from one bomber while Lieutenant General George C. Kenney, commander of the Fifth Air Force, watched from another. As the combat assault unfolded MacArthur was reported to have been jumping up and down like a kid. MacArthur later told an aide that the parachute assault of the 503rd was the greatest example of combat efficiency he had ever witnessed.

The success of the 503rd came at a time when the planners of the U.S. Army were considering disbanding the airborne divisions. The precision with which the operation was conducted as well as the close cooperation at the working and the planning levels between the Army ground and air elements proved important factors in the decision not to disband them. Obviously, joint planning and training were the key elements in solving many problems if there was to be a future for large-scale airborne operations. And there was.

Mission Critique

The Nadzab jump was the first combat assault by U.S. airborne forces in the Pacific theater. Within three weeks of the Nadzab mission several parachute operations were conducted in other theaters, including assaults by elements of the 509th PIB and two regiments of the 82d Airborne Division in Italy, near Salerno and Avellino; German paratroopers near Monte Rotondo in Italy and onto Cos Island to conduct operations; and, a small force of British paras from No. 12 Commando who jumped into St. Valéry-en-Caux in France to conduct a raid. From slow beginnings parachute forces were being used more and more whenever possible. In the Pacific the U.S. Army had two airborne units, the 503rd PIR and the 11th Airborne Division, both assigned to Sixth Army.

The Nadzab operation must have seemed like a planner's dream come true. At hand was a real problem, namely to seize an airfield that, by its location, would reinforce an amphibious landing and put infantry troops in a solid position to prevent the rollback of troops coming in over the beach. Also at hand was a solution—an airborne unit on stand-by waiting for a mission.

The planners and higher staff believed that the operation was necessary, a decision that is difficult to second-guess. Since this was not a case where a conventional unit could have executed the mission, it fell to a special operations force.

The plan for the Nadzab mission demonstrated a daring yet economical use of appropriate units to conduct a difficult but tactically necessary operation. Of the Vandenbroucke criteria only two proved to be problems at Nadzab. The error in estimating the height of the kunai grass in the jump area was definitely a case of *inadequate intelligence*. While the paratroopers still operated effectively, this mistake slowed down the operational *speed* of the paratroopers.

The subject of sufficient aircraft availability has been mentioned before as an indication of *poor coordination;* tt is a problem that plagued airborne operations throughout the war. It seems that sufficient aircraft were only mandated by higher command when airborne operations were absolutely essential to the mission. Even then this was not always the case, as can be seen in the Arnhem jump in September 1944. Then virtually as many aircraft as could be made available were and yet this still proved to be not enough.

The only McRaven criteria that applies here is the element of *surprise*. The Nadzab mission was a virtual success because the Japanese did not expect it and were, therefore, not prepared for it. Now, obviously, this is always true for any operation where *surprise* plays such a key part. That does not mean, however, that it should be glossed over, either in after-action reports or in the planning for future operations. Rather, it should be, as McRaven advocates, an essential element in the operations plan. In the case of the Nadzab mission, *surprise* and *simplicity* were both obvious elements in the plan and execution. Both elements proved key to the success of the mission.

This mission, coming when it did and coupled with other airborne operations at about the same time, was instrumental in the U.S. Army's decision not to disband its airborne forces.

SOURCES

Books:

Galvin, John R.; *Air Assault—The Development of Airmobile Warfare;* New York; Hawthorn Books; 1969

Guthrie, Bennett M; *Three Winds of Death—The Saga of the 503rd Parachute Regimental Combat Team in the South Pacific;* Chicago; Adams Press; 1985

Huston, James A.; *Out of the Blue—US Army Airborne Operations in World War II;* West Lafayette, IN; Purdue University Studies; 1972

MacDonald, Charles; *Airborne;* New York; Ballantine Books; 1970

Tugwell, Maurice; *Airborne to Battle—A History of Airborne Warfare 1918–1971;* London; William Kimber; 1971

Others:

1967 Yearbook of the 173rd Airborne Brigade; publisher unknown; the introduction includes a brief history of the 503rd

CHAPTER TWELVE

OPERATION JAYWICK

Ivan Lyon was a man possessed—he wanted vengeance. Lyon had been assigned to the British garrison in Singapore when it was overrun by the
Japanese in February 1942. He escaped on a sail-boat, evading all the way to
Ceylon. That trip alone is a story of survival and endurance. When he learned
that he was to be sent to Australia, he notified his wife and son (who had
fled Singapore and were living in Perth) that he would be joining them. But
the telegram arrived too late. Gabrielle and young Clive had departed for
India several days before, hoping to surprise Lyon in New Delhi. But they
never arrived—the ship on which they traveled was sunk and all aboard were
reported lost.

Lyon, in the meantime, was assigned to Special Operations Executive
(SOE) and reported to the Services Reconnaissance Detachment (SRD) in
Melbourne. Soon after arriving, Lyon was told of the sinking. His only comment was, "War is a grim business, isn't it?" Although appearing calm on the
outside, Lyon seethed with a fury. He decided he would make the Japanese
pay—and his target would be Singapore.

When he had first been sent to Singapore as a young subaltern, he had
been assigned to the prestigious Gordon Highland Regiment. But Lyon grew
weary of the life of a garrison soldier and yearned for excitement. He taught
himself to sail, bought a sailboat, and spent much of his free time sailing the
Java Sea around the Malayan peninsula.

In Australia Lyon was seconded to No. 101 Special Training School,
where he trained students in the techniques of behind the lines sabotage and
wireless communications. He met and worked with several people who became special operations legends in the Far East later in the war, particularly
Michael "Mad Mike" Calvert and Frederick Spencer Chapman. The experi-

ences he gained at this school fueled Lyon's planning to avenge the fall of Singapore and, more specifically, the death of his family.

If he was convinced of his mission, others were not. Lyon had difficulty persuading his superiors at SOE that a raid could be successfully mounted in Singapore harbor, especially from as far away as Australia. His commander at SRD, Lieutenant Colonel G.S. Mott, was at least interested in the concept Lyon was briefing. Since talking had not worked, Mott decided that it would be necessary to demonstrate to SOE and General Headquarters that the plan could work. Knowing that he was taking a great risk, Mott ordered a secret commando attack on ships moored in Sydney Harbor. Lyon and his men successfully attached several limpet mines to ships before the raiding party was discovered. Lyon had made his point.

One final connection led to the approval of Lyon's plan. His sister, Ann, arranged for Lyon to meet Lord Gowrie, the Governor-General of Australia. By now a major, Lyon so impressed Lord Gowrie that he was authorized to recruit and train a raiding force. Lyon christened the raid Operation Jaywick.

In September 1942, two actions began at almost the same time. Lyon established a tent-city training camp at Refuge Bay, north of Sydney, and began to pick his team. He finally settled on 20 men, most from the Australian Navy. Training began immediately with an emphasis on physical toughness and endurance. Much of the training area immediately around Refuge Bay was barnacle-covered rock and cliffs. All training here was conducted bare-footed. Night land navigation courses were conducted without compasses, and the men were taught to rely on the stars and the land around them to find their way. Lyon made sure that he included unarmed combat and swimming in all aspects of training. The swimmers trained in the shark-infested waters of the bay.

Soon after training began the team discovered they had an unofficial mascot in the form of a tattoo. It seems that Lyon, when he was in Singapore, had a tiger's head tattooed on his chest. One writer described the tattoo this way: "a tremendous tiger's head ... in black and yellow, with staring red eyes, stretched almost from his navel to his collarbones ... it was widely admired." Photographs show that the tattoo, centered on Lyon's upper chest, was probably about six inches by six inches. Size notwithstanding, it was an inspiring sight.

Lyon's attack plan was for the team to sail 4,000 miles from Australia to Malaya, then launch six of their number into Singapore harbor in folboats, collapsible rubber two-man kayak-like canoes propelled by paddle. Once launched the folboat teams would have to hide during the day. All travel to and from the target area and the attack itself would be at night. Each folboat team would need to be self-sufficient, carrying everything needed on board, including water, food, weapons, and ammunition. Now the teams understood the emphasis on their training in dead reckoning and celestial navigation.

The folboat teams trained so that eventually they would be able to paddle for *ten-hour* stretches. They rehearsed several different immediate action drills including capsizing, landing, and beach take-off. They even used several types of paddles before settling on one which did not need to be lifted out of the water, thus preventing a phosphorescent blade flash or water swirl. The last stage of training concentrated on the employment of limpet mines.

A limpet mine is "about the size of a dinner plate, in which hangs suspended a container of high explosive shaped like a quart milk bottle. Round the edge are four powerful magnets on hinged springs. They were used in groups of three, joined by seventy-five feet of cordtex fuse." Lyon conducted several training exercises targeting ship crews who knew the attackers were coming—and the attacks always succeeded. During this part of the training Lyon learned that his wife and son had survived the sinking of their ship and were in a prison camp in Japan. While this news gladdened him, Lyon was nonetheless still determined to repay the Japanese for Singapore and for his family's suffering.

Finally, the training was completed. Lyon further trimmed his team to 14. This team would man the sailing vessel, *Krait*, which would take the folboats to their target area. Lyon had planned the attack for 15 February 1943—the anniversary of the surrender of Singapore but several things delayed the team's departure, including an engine failure on *Krait*. By the time a new engine had been installed it was late August 1943; *Krait* set sail for Singapore.

During the first few days of sail, while they were all still getting their sea legs, Lyon briefed the team on their target. It was the first time they knew they were heading for Singapore harbor. During this period the men on the team began staining their skin a dark brown. *Krait* had sailed in waters near Singapore before and Lyon insisted that exposed skin be dyed in the event they were spotted by Japanese aircraft—he hoped the pilots would mistake them for Malayans. On the fourth day under sail, *Krait* passed through the strait between Lombok and Bali islands, entering the Java Sea. This passage was filled with tension caused by guards who kept constant watch on the straits and by the southerly rip tide that hit *Krait* as she tried to pass through on a northerly course. What should have been a two-hour passage took more than nine hours.

Lyon continued to rehearse the folboat operators in their mission. These six and the two reserves spent many hours reviewing the plan and carefully examining maps of the target area, until they all knew the area by heart. *Krait*, meanwhile, had turned northwest and was sailing near the southern coast of Borneo. Along the way they encountered several other sailing and fishing vessels but with no untoward incident. During the afternoon of 18 September, they passed the island of Panjang, which Lyon decided would serve as the folboat base camp. *Krait* lingered within five miles of the island until dark, then returned. By midnight, a scouting party reported the island clear and the six operators prepared to shove off. The two most disappointed members of *Krait*'s crew were Seaman F.W. Marsh and Seaman M. Berryman, the reserve folboat operators.

Amid good wishes and quiet jocularity, the six raiders (Major Lyon, Lieutenant D.N. Davidson, Lieutenant R.C. Page, Seaman W.C. Falls, Seaman A.W. Jones, and Seaman A.W.G. Huston) pushed away and headed for Panjang Island. Following the attack they were to rendezvous with *Krait* on the evening of 1 October at Pompong Island.

For the next several days the raiding teams rested, redistributed the supplies among the boats, and reviewed their assault plan. They noted Japanese boat patrol routes and times to aid in their movements. Beginning on 20 September, they crept closer to Singapore harbor, moving at night and hiding during the day. They slept very little. They spent the night of 23 September and part of the next day resting and watching, on Subar Island. Several large ships were in the harbor by now. At 2000 on the 24th, they left their final hiding place and launched the raid.

As they approached the harbor, the land lights dimmed out and a searchlight came on. Its beam swept inexorably toward them, finally illuminating all three folboats. All movement in the boats stopped. The searchlight stayed on them for about half a minute, then moved on. Soon after completing the sweep, the light was turned off. As the night dragged on the raiders made little progress—the tide made it difficult for them to make any headway at all. They decided to try again in two nights from a closer launch point.

The disappointment of the first attempt took a stressful toll on the team. They were now behind schedule and the next launch would have to be their last—or they would be stranded without a way back to Australia. *Krait* was not expected to wait and at least one team would have to hurry to the rendezvous to hold *Krait* in the area until the whereabouts of all three teams were known. (At least one team would be late—Davidson and Falls—because they were charged with post-raid damage assessment.) Their visual reconnaissance of the harbor showed little difference in the ships present.

Once again, the teams left their hiding place for the harbor and found their new route in was much easier going. On the east side of the harbor Davidson and Falls were almost run down by a tug but were never spotted. As they pushed closer, they found one end of the harbor boom open and very little evidence of any security force in the main harbor area. This was too good to believe! But since there were no worthwhile targets, they left the harbor and returned to the ships anchored in the Roads area.

Here they found a glut of targets. They drew up alongside one ship, with Davidson steadying the folboat while Falls adjusted the fuse which was expected to go off at five the next morning. Then they slipped the mine under the water and set the magnets. They drifted to the end of the connecting cordtex fuse, set another mine, and repeated their drilled movements once more. Finally, when the third limpet was set, they moved to their next target. They mined three ships and then decided it was time to leave.

Further west Page and Jones found the wharf that was their designated target area. Since it was lit, they kept well out while they searched for ships. Finding a worthwhile ship, they quickly attached their three mines and then moved away. They also had no trouble with a second target. As they approached the third ship, the tide carried them on too quickly and they bumped the hull, loudly. However, there was evidently no guard as no alarm was raised. This ship was then mined, and Page and Jones headed back.

Lyon and Huston found targets among the ships in the northern harbor/Roads area. Unfortunately a spit of land hid the harbor lights, making it difficult for the raiders to pick out ships in the black night. It also did not help matters that all the ships in their area were blacked out—all, that is, but two tankers. Lyon guided the boat to these ships. As he was lowering the second mine under water, Lyon glanced toward Huston and then abruptly at what had caught Huston's attention. Ten feet above them a man was watching them from a port hole! Lyon continued his work, figuring that if they were discovered he might still get the ship. When he finished he pushed the folboat away and they both began paddling rapidly. Lyon whispered to Huston, "He'll soon be dead," referring to the man at the port hole. He was certain they had been spotted. They left without mining any other ships.

By 0500 the next morning the Page and Lyon folboats had reached their island hideout on Subar. As the two teams were covering their boats they heard an explosion from the harbor area. They identified it immediately as coming from the area of Davidson's targets. Soon they heard more explosions. Since they did not see any flashes from these explosions they knew they were all underwater explosions.

The teams on the island waited until daylight and then moved to positions where they could assay their damage. At least one ship was already partially submerged and the only ship that Lyon and Huston had mined was belching smoke. They could see nothing else.

Throughout the day there was furious activity in the harbor area. Planes and patrol boats searched in various patterns, looking for anything that didn't belong. Despite the search efforts, the raiding teams remained undetected. In the early morning hours of 1 October, the Lyon and Page teams made their rendezvous with *Krait*. Two nights later the third team arrived. *Krait* did not wait long once the raiders were aboard and, by 19 October, the vessel arrived back in Australia with all hands.

After-action assessments showed that all seven ships that were mined had been sunk or destroyed. The raid had been a complete success. However, higher headquarters then stepped in to make what can only be described as a typical rear echelon decision—the raid would be kept secret and no one would be given public credit for the damage. One possibility is that more operations were planned and they did not want to reveal the methods and techniques used in this raid. Lyon and his raiders had belled the cat, in his own den, and there was to be no follow-up propaganda victory. The fact that such an announcement would tie up perhaps thousands of Japanese troops guarding many occupied harbors seemed not to concern the generals. The opportunity to tell the world that the Japanese were not invulnerable and that, further, the raid had resulted in no battle losses, was not taken. The people of Singapore paid for the error of not publicizing the raid. The Japanese assumed that the raid was conducted with local assistance and killed many local citizens whom they believed had helped the raiders.

This operation, by itself and as it stands, was successful. The following year Lyon led another raid on Singapore harbor, Operation Rimau. This time the teams went in using small submarines. Unfortunately, all of the raiders were caught and later killed by the Japanese, apparently betrayed by locals who had spotted them. If this second raid had worked, it could have led to a broader plan for such operations. With Lyons' disappearance, any impetus for continuing this type of operation was lost. This, too, should not have happened but is further testament to some of the haphazard special operations that higher commands permitted to happen instead of taking a long-range view and improving their coordination.

Mission Critique

The attack on shipping in Singapore harbor is another of the missions in this book that has caused mixed feelings. Jaywick was the result of one man's obsession. Of course so was the creation of the SAS and PPA. Jaywick, however, did not fit into any overall theater plan nor was it capitalized on by the higher command. It did have an appropriate target, probably one that would have been difficult to reach by other, conventional, means. It was probably only by incredible luck that the operation was successful, considering all of the things that could have gone wrong. This was a good mission—after it was over. Lyons, by his persistence, convinced the special operations community in Australia that this was a necessary mission and even offered the force to execute it, a force he had raised and trained *just for this mission*. The biggest mistake was leaving the Japanese to doubt as to how it was conducted. This could have been anticipated and a solution provided in the operations plan.

Interestingly enough, this is another example of a mission brought to the planners with a force to execute it instead of the more traditional planning method of finding a mission for an existing force. We have already seen this with the SAS and PPA. Although not discussed in this book, this same principle happened in the case of the Cockleshell raid, where a Royal Marine officer, Lieutenant Colonel H.G. Hasler, proposed and later led a canoe attack on Bordeaux Harbor in France. That raid, while not as successful as Jaywick, occurred in December 1942. Comparisons of these two raids are inevitable even though their executions were different.

A problem in the aftermath of this raid is the way the command element put the local populace in harm's way by not explaining what was done. An aspect of this criticism is credit. Yes, the raiders did receive appropriate decorations for their part in the operation and, yes, everything can't always be the way the special operators want it. The point here has to do with morale—the benefits to the morale of many disparate elements, from the raiders themselves to other special units, to the local populace in Singapore, as well as to the overall morale of the Allied forces and their homelands. The command element seemed to be too concerned with secrecy when it overlooked all the

OPERATION JAYWICK • 139

other benefits that a more open discussion of this operation could have provided.

There are only two criteria that are essential for comment concerning this operation, one from Vandenbroucke and one from McRaven. Of the former, there was a good deal of *wishful thinking*, especially on Lyon's part, that provided the basic justification for this mission. There is no doubt that Lyons was a driven man. However, he was not completely reckless. He did put together a good plan, and picked and trained the unit to execute it, thus perhaps providing some balance to his single-mindedness.

Lyon's mind-set did contribute to the unit's *purpose*. One example of Lyon's mind-set can be seen in their first approach; after having rowed for hours yet still unable to reach their target, the men turned around and came back two nights later to hit the target—and continued the attack even after at least one of the boat teams was spotted.

SOURCES

Books:

Connell, Brian; *Return of the Tiger;* Garden City; Doubleday; 1960

Ind, Allison; *Allied Intelligence Bureau—Our Secret Weapon in the War Against Japan;* New York; Curtis Books; 1958

Silver, Lynette R. and Tom Hall; *The Heroes of Rimau—Unraveling the Mystery of One of World War II's Most Daring Raids;* London; Leo Cooper; 1990

Articles:

Wellington, Mike; "The Australian Mounted Z-Force's Kayak Raid on Singapore was Totally Unexpected"; *World War II* magazine (volume 4, number 2)

CHAPTER THIRTEEN

ALAMO SCOUTS: ALAMO
SCOUTS TRAINING CENTER

MacArthur said no—at least twice. Stay out of my theater—I don't want
you here. He didn't want anyone operating in his area of command
who was not under his control, especially an organization that reported to a
headquarters in Washington. By doing so, he barred the Office of Strategic
Services from operating in the Southwest Pacific Area. That did not mean,
however, that there was no need for an organization which conducted clandestine intelligence collection operations behind the lines, supported guerrilla
campaigns, and sent trained saboteurs into enemy-controlled areas to wreak
havoc. In fact, MacArthur was one of the first to see the need for an organization to control all of this activity. As a result, his command, General Headquarters, created its own intelligence and special operations organization, the
Allied Intelligence Bureau.

Lieutenant General Walter Krueger, Sixth Army commander, was no
stranger to directing intelligence collection operations needed to make decisions and he probably did not need MacArthur's precedent to encourage him.
Krueger had taken a personal hand in directing intelligence collection during
the Louisiana maneuvers ("war games") in the late summer of 1941. Krueger
had also seen the results of poor intelligence targeting and collection in the
Kiska invasion fiasco, where it transpired that the Japanese had already pulled
out before the invading forces landed. He was determined that this would
not happen to Sixth Army.

Krueger described what he did next: "Getting information of the enemy
and our objective area had prompted me to issue orders on 28 November
[1943] establishing a training center near Headquarters Alamo Force for
training selected volunteers in reconnaissance and raider work." Specifically,
the order said:

1. The Alamo Scouts Training Center (ASTC) is hereby established under the supervision of Headquarters Alamo Force at the earliest practicable date prior to 1 January 1944, and at a location in the vicinity of the present Headquarters." [Alamo Force, the code name for Sixth Army, was then located on Goodenough Island, New Guinea.]

2. The training center will train selected volunteers in reconnaissance and raider work. The course will cover a six-week period. Specifically selected graduates will be grouped into teams at the disposal of the Commanding General, Alamo Force, and will be designated "Alamo Scouts"; the remainder will be returned to their respective commands for similar use by their commanders.

3. Commanders of combat units will be called upon from time to time to furnish personnel for the above training. Personnel so selected must possess the highest qualifications as to courage, stamina, intelligence and adaptability.

Krueger issued his order after discussions with his G-2, Colonel Horton V. White. They decided that the course would be six weeks long and that it "was not designed to be a basic course ... it was taken for granted that students were versed in many of the basic subjects." Instead, it was to be a "refresher course in map reading, scouting and patrolling, and in weapons ... more time was devoted to message writing, radio communications, aerial photography, intelligence, and the techniques of field reconnaissance."

White chose Lieutenant Colonel Frederick W. Bradshaw of his staff to be the Director of the Alamo Scouts Training Center. Krueger had noticed Bradshaw, a lawyer from Mississippi, during the Louisiana maneuvers where he was the G-2 for the 31st Infantry Division. Krueger believed Bradshaw to be just the man for the job. Bradshaw was given a free hand to establish the ASTC but was told that training must begin before the end of the year.

Bradshaw faced four immediate tasks and set out to accomplish them simultaneously. He must find a training site, gather a staff of administrators to run the place and instructors to teach, design a course of instruction, and select trainees from among the units of Sixth Army.

Because of his position at Sixth Army, Bradshaw was aware that the U.S. Navy's Amphibious Scouts were about to leave their camp at Kola Kola on Fergusson Island, off the southeast end of New Guinea. He quickly recruited two Army officers from this Navy unit, Lieutenant Mayo S. Stuntz and Lieutenant Milton Beckworth, for his staff. Each had extensive training in the business of sneaking and peeping and Beckworth was a veteran of an Amphibious Scouts mission on New Britain the previous October. Stuntz, appointed as supply officer, went to the headquarters engineer of Sixth Army and arranged to have the facilities at the camp rebuilt. This became a familiar pattern for subsequent relocations of the training center.

In the meantime Bradshaw began the process of final selection of trainees. Each division in Sixth Army would eventually establish its own process for choosing candidates to be sent to the Alamo Scouts Training Center but the director always made the final selection. Bradshaw knew that he would not be able to keep all of those who graduated from the training to run missions for Sixth Army but he was determined that those who returned to their units would not be considered second best and, accordingly, he had to start with the best.

Bradshaw had strict criteria for his students. Lieutenant Tom J. Rounsaville, a graduate from Class Four, summarized these criteria this way: "They must be men of courage, stamina, ability, and intelligence. They must be volunteers for dangerous missions into enemy territory. They must be in excellent physical condition, have good eyesight, be good swimmers, know map reading and compass work, be good marksmen."

After many hours of screening, the first class was selected, composed of 6 officers and 38 enlisted men from the 158th Regimental Combat Team (Separate) and the 32nd "Red Arrow" Infantry Division.

Instructors and camp staff personnel were also selected on the basis of their previous records. All, including the medical officer, were combat veterans. The initial group of other officers included: Captain Homer A. Williams, Bradshaw's deputy who would replace Bradshaw as director when he returned to the G-2 staff in June 1944; Captain (Doctor) Richard G. Canfield; Major John F. Polk; Lieutenant Daily P. Gambill; Lieutenant Henry L. Chalko; and Lieutenant Fred A. Sukup. The last three had also served with Beckworth in the Amphibious Scouts. Sergeant David Mackie and Sergeant Leonard Epstein were among the non-commissioned officers who oversaw the running of the camp; they were the mess sergeant and supply sergeant, respectively. Lieutenant Lewis B. Hochstrasser, who graduated in Class Two, wore glasses; because of this, he was not put on an operational team. He was appointed as adjutant and remained at the training center as an instructor in map reading and message writing. He was later appointed executive officer of the Alamo Scouts and was also the unit's unofficial historian.

The training schedule relied primarily on the training of the Amphibious

Scouts as well as readings about reconnaissance work. Another factor was the training and combat experiences of others on the staff, such as Lieutenant Stuntz. Stuntz had taken a group of 50 men and officers of the 1st Cavalry Division to a 30-day commando school in Australia, whose instructors were Australian commandos, many of them former Coastwatchers.

Training for Class One began on 27 December 1943 and was conducted in two phases. Phase one lasted four weeks and consisted of classroom refresher courses. Each day of training included two hours of physical training and swimming. Other subjects included cover and concealment; unarmed combat (Judo); use of rubber boats; map reading; scouting and patrolling; stalking; movement under observation and enemy fire; familiarization with Japanese weapons; range firing; night scouting; boat reconnaissance; observation; combat intelligence; sketching shore line and beach installations; jungle food sources; intelligence reports; night land navigation; ropes and snares; aerial photography; explosives; knife fighting; and booby traps.

Phase two lasted two weeks and included practical application of the previous training woven into strenuous field problems, each lasting three to four days. Throughout the training cycle, team membership rotated. This gave all the students the chance to work with and evaluate the others. The patrols in phase two required the teams to plan, brief, and execute the missions assigned. Support included Navy PT boats for approaches and small rubber boats for landings. Exfiltration varied and was either by boat or overland. Another team assisted the primary team with the infiltration and exfiltration phases of the patrol; this team was called the "contact team."

Occasionally one team was called upon to act as the enemy. In later classes, members of operational teams played that part during this phase of training. The patrols were all marked by combat realism. One team leader, Lieutenant Robert S. Sumner, described the final patrol as ". . . through U.S. units in the . . . vicinity. Our mission was to collect order of battle info which we accomplished. Our infiltration was at night from a rubber boat which we hid. Made our walking recon at night hiding during the day. On the third night . . . exfil almost under the noses of a U.S. Signal Operating Battalion. Recovery by one of the landing craft from Alamo Scouts Training Center—and it was a text book exercise for us, it was that good . . ."

In addition to the instruction staff already selected, Bradshaw drew upon the backgrounds of students and many of them were selected to teach blocks of instruction. A board of observers from Headquarters, Army Ground Forces visited the Alamo Scouts Training Center to monitor and report on the training of the first class. One of the AGF recommendations, which the instruction staff had also observed, was, "Some time allotted to basic subjects in which the students were found to be better prepared than was expected, will be transferred to additional practical exercises." Beginning with Class Two, the field applications phase was extended to two and one-half weeks.

Over time, as the war progressed and Sixth Army headquarters moved forward, the Alamo Scouts Training Center followed. In all, there were five different locations. Two more were eventually located in New Guinea: Mangee Point near Finschhafen, and Hollandia. When Sixth Army invaded Leyte in October 1944, a training center was established at Abuyog where one training class was conducted. Several temporary locations for the Alamo Scouts Training Center were established on Luzon in La Union and Pampanga provinces while a permanent camp was being built. This location, the last one, was at Mabayo on the Bataan peninsula. Altogether, nine training classes were conducted at the different camps.

These nine classes included 250 enlisted men and 75 officers as graduates. Not all of these graduates, however, served on active Alamo Scouts teams. Twenty-one officers and 117 enlisted men composed the various teams who operated under the direction of the Sixth Army G-2. Some of the other graduates remained as instructors or staff members at the Alamo Scouts Training Center. Two of these were Lieutenant Henry L. Baker and Lieutenant Sidney S. Tison Jr. Together with members of the 5217th Reconnaissance Battalion, Baker and Tison infiltrated by submarine to work with Philippine guerrillas on Luzon. Following this mission, they attended training in Class Seven and, because of their previous combat missions, were selected to continue as instructors. Others were returned to their parent units to lead and conduct reconnaissance operations there, such as Corporal Terry Santos from Class Four who served as a member of the 11th Airborne Division's reconnaissance platoon until the end of the war. One officer in class seven, Lieutenant Jay Russell, was told just before the end of training in June 1945 that he could stay with the Alamo Scouts as a team leader or return to his unit and be immediately rotated back to the States. After three years in the Pacific, Russell selected the rotation option with the provision that if the invasion of Japan became a reality Russell could return to lead a team.

The Alamo Scouts teams consisted of one officer and five or six enlisted men and usually operated as single teams. Occasionally two teams operated together or were sent on missions in a close proximity to each other. The teams were named after the officer who led them.

Left: Generalleutnant Erwin Rommel, commander of the German Afrika Korps. His success in North Africa made him a target of Eighth Army planners, who sent in a Commando force to kill or capture him. *Courtesy of the National Archives*

Below: Amphibious Scouts team leader Alva Gipe, left, performing beach master duties on Morotai. The officer on the right is Bob Eiring, the commander of an Underwater Demolition Team. *Photo courtesy of Alva Gipe*

SAS beret flash, based on original cap badge.

Beret badge of Popski's Private Army.

SAS wings.

Insignia of the Imperial Japanese Army paratroopers. The emblem represents the Golden Kite.

Insignia of Japanese Navy paratroopers of the Yokosuka Special Naval Landing Force.

A group of Amphibious Scouts during training in late 1943. Rudy Horak is second from the left in the first row. Hank Staudt is second from the right in the top row. *Photo courtesy of Hank Staudt*

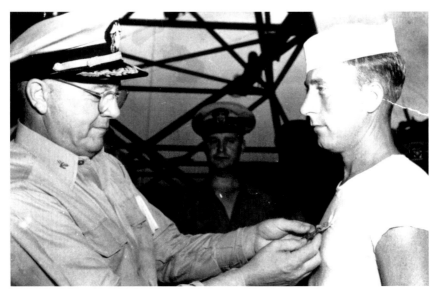

Calvin Byrd, right, receives the Bronze Star for his part in a joint mission with the Amphibious Scouts and Thompson Team, of the Alamo Scouts in the reconnaissance of Sansapoor. *Photo courtesy of Calvin Byrd*

Major General Fred H. Osborn, left, Director of Morale Services Division, War Department, talks with Private First Class Edward Raupa and other students in Class One at the Alamo Scouts Training Center following a swimming demonstration. *US Army Signal Corps photo, courtesy of USAINSCOM*

This photo was taken at Finschhafen, New Guinea, on 22 June 1944, the day that Class Three graduated from the Alamo Scouts Training Center there. Those pictured include staff and graduates. *Front row, left to right:* LT John M. Dove, LT Milton B. Beckwith, LT Donald P. Hart, LT Gean H. Reynolds, LT William B. Lutz, and LT Arpad Farkas. *Back row, left to right:* LT Lewis B. Hochstrasser, CPT Richard G. Canfield, MAJ Homer A. Williams, CPT Gibson Niles, LT Gus Watson (Australian Army), and LT Robert S. Sumner. *Photo courtesy of Lewis B. Hochstrasser*

Two Amphibious Scouts, Rudy Horak and E.J. Foley, on a training mission on New Guinea in 1943. *Photo courtesy of Rudy Horak*

Above: Colonel Horton V. White, right, G-2 of Sixth Army, presents awards to four Alamo Scouts following a mission by Dove Team from 8–11 June 1944 to conduct a reconnaissance of the Toarum River area, between Wadke and Hollandia in New Guinea. Those receiving the awards are, from left: Tech/5 Irvin Ray (Dove Team), S/SGT Vern Miller (Hobbs Team), S/SGT John Fisher (Dove Team), and LT John Dove (Leader, Dove Team).
Photo courtesy of Lewis B. Hochstrasser

Top right: Three members of Sumner Team, following the awards ceremony on New Year's Day 1945 at Leyte. All members of Sumner Team received the Bronze Star for the Pegun Island mission. Left to right: PFC Harry D. Weiland, S/SGT Lawrence E. Coleman, and CPL William F. Blaise.
Photo courtesy of Robert S. Sumner

Bottom right: Sumner Team graduation from the Alamo Scouts Training Center, 22 June 1944. The team consists of, left to right, front row: PFC Paul B. Jones, PFC Edward Renhols, and CPL William F. Blaise; back row: LT Robert S. (Red) Sumner, S/SGT Lawrence E. Coleman, PFC Harry D. Weiland, and CPL Robert Schermerhorn. *Photo courtesy of Robert S. Sumner*

LT Robert S. (Red) Sumner, leader of Sumner Team, Alamo Scouts, in June 1945 just before Sumner moved up to the Sixth Army G-2 staff. Note the Alamo Scouts patch on the right (combat patch) shoulder. Sumner wore this unauthorized combat patch on his uniform until he retired as a Colonel. *Photo courtesy of Robert S. Sumner*

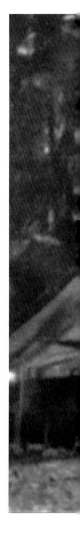

Replica of unauthorized shoulder patch of the Alamo Scouts. This patch was based on the winning design by CPL Harry A. Golden, a medic at the Alamo Scouts Training Center. The contest was held in 1944 and was to find a design for a shoulder patch. The design was submitted to the A.N. Meyer Company, which made 440 patches. The patch was never authorized by the U.S. Army but was worn by Scouts anyway.

Some of the members of the Rounsaville and Nellist teams on the day after the raid on the POW camp at Cabanatuan. Those pictured are, left to right: front row: PFC Galen C. Kittleson, PFC Rufo Vaquilar, LT William E. Nellist, LT Tom J. Rounsaville, and PFC Franklin Fox; back row: PFC Gilbert Cox, T/SGT Wilbert Wismer, SGT Harold Hard, CPL Andrew Smith, and PFC Francis Laquier. Missing from the photo are S/SGT Tom Siason, PFC Sabis Asis, and T/SGT Alfred Alfonzo. *Photo courtesy of the Alamo Scouts Historical Foundation*

An unidentified Jedburgh soldier with his jump suit and rucksack.
Courtesy of the National Archives

Replica of the Special Forces (or S.F.) wing, worn on the right sleeve of dress uniforms by members of the Jedburgh teams. Although this was never officially authorized by the U.S. Army, the insignia was worn anyway. Note that there is no period after the "S".

This shoulder tab was worn on the top of the left shoulder sleeve of the uniforms of members of the 2671st Special Reconnaissance Battalion, Separate (Provisional). This battalion included all of the OSS Operations Groups in the Mediterranean theater. As with many of the insignia of the OSS, this one was never authorized by the U.S. Army. Later in the war, when B and C Companies of the 2671st rotated to the China-Burma-India theater, the soldiers continued to wear this tab.

A stone marker in front of the U.S. Army Special Operations Command headquarters, Fort Bragg, North Carolina, commemorating the part the Jedburgh teams played in the history of U.S. Special Forces.

Left: The shoulder sleeve insignia of the 11th Airborne Division. Note that the "Airborne" tab and the patch are one piece, unlike patches for airborne divisions after WWII.

Right: Replica of pocket patch of the Reconnaissance Platoon of the 11th Airborne Division. Although not authorized by the U.S. Army, platoon members wore this patch anyway.

Otto Skorzeny, taken after World War II while he was in custody awaiting trial as a war criminal. He was acquitted but the Allies refused to release him. He later escaped and was never retaken into custody. *Photo courtesy of the National Archives*

Above: The first enlisted men of the 555th Parachute Infantry Company receive their coveted jump wings at Fort Benning, Georgia on 18 February 1944. The men are, left to right, front row: 1SGT Walter Morris, SGT Jack D. Tillis, SGT Leo D. Reed, SGT Daniel C. Weil, SGT Hubert Bridges, Tech/4 Alvin L. Moon, SGT Ned D. Bess, and SGT Roger C. Walden; back row: CPL McKinley Godfrey Jr., SGT Eliah Wisby (hidden), SGT Samuel W. Robinson (hidden), SGT Calvin R. Beal, S/SGT Robert F. Green, S/SGT Lonnie M. Duke, SGT Clarency H. Beavers, and SGT James E. Kornegay. *Photo courtesy of Bradley E. Biggs*

Below: The first officers of the 555th are awarded their jump wings two weeks later, on 4 March 1944. They are, left to right: 1LT Jasper E. Ross, 2LT Clifford Allen, 2LT Bradley E. Biggs, 2LT Edwin H. Willis, 2LT Warren C. Cornelius, and 2LT Edward Baker.
Photo courtesy of Bradley E. Biggs

Men of A Company, 555th Parachute Infantry Battalion preparing to jump into
a fire area in the Chilan National Forest in Washington state on 22 August 1945.
Photo courtesy of Bradley E. Biggs

Clyde Thomas of the 555th, rigged wearing rugged terrain jump gear designed by the men of the 555th, boards a Troop Carrier Command aircraft prior to jumping into a fire area. *Photo courtesy of Bradley E. Biggs*

A modern-day Special Forces soldier, SGT Patrick Clark of the 7th Special Forces Group (Airborne), Fort Bragg, North Carolina, outfitted in rugged terrain gear patterned after equipment pioneered by the men of the 555th. *Photo courtesy of John F. Kennedy Special Warfare Museum*

One of the most interesting aspects of the teams, though, was how they were chosen. As anyone who has ever spent a day in the Army will tell you, the Army is *not* a democracy. Now the Alamo Scouts were mostly not a democracy either, though selection to a team and team composition were decided by voting on secret ballots. At the end of training, each enlisted man was asked to name three other men with whom he would go on a four man patrol and why; the officers were asked to pick five men. By this time, everyone in the class had worked with everyone else and was familiar enough with to know who they were compatible with. Lieutenant Sumner, a graduate of Class Three, later wrote: "The men I worked with at Fort Pierce were the ones I wanted. I had them in mind when writing up a recommended list and obviously so did they. The final composition was what I had suggested." The training center faculty had the final say on who made an operational team, but their lists were usually very similar to those of the students. From the first day of training to the last, the concept of the team was drilled into the students.

Once they were operational, this concept became a reality for the Alamo Scouts. Every member of the team made a contribution to every mission. Just because the lieutenant was in charge did not mean that he had the only ideas or the final say-so. Every man was expected to speak up when something needed to be said and this did not end when the team was debriefed. Major Gibson Niles, the third and last director of the Alamo Scouts Training Center, wrote after the war, "As the number of successful completed missions increased, the experience gained thereby was put to use in improving the training program. Recommendations and suggestions . . . were carefully considered and included in the training curriculum." Redesign of the training was a necessity as the type of missions given to the operational teams changed over time.

The Alamo Scouts operated behind Japanese lines during the two years of their existence. In many cases, behind the lines consisted of a series of islands, all held by the Japanese, which would be invaded by Sixth Army units in a series of amphibious attacks during 1944 and early 1945. Sixth Army G-2 needed to know not only about unit dispositions on these islands but also beach conditions, such as gradient angle, sand composition, water depth, etc.

Most of the Alamo Scouts' missions were to conduct reconnaissance and gather intelligence. Mission insertion (and later extraction) was by rubber boats launched from Catalina (PBY) aircraft, submarine, or PT boat. Later, following the invasion of Luzon in the Philippines, Alamo Scouts teams worked closely with Philippine guerrilla units, foreshadowing modern day Special Forces operations. At least six of their missions were to capture Japanese prisoners, two were to liberate prisoners of war from the Japanese, and several were to recover downed aircrew or sensitive equipment and codebooks.

When not on missions behind the lines, the Alamo Scouts pulled personal security duty for General Krueger as he visited units at or near the front. To accommodate the additional mission of dealing with local guerrilla units, Sixth Army G-2 established a separate office, the Special Intelligence Section, to coordinate the missions of the Alamo Scouts teams and their work with the guerrillas. Many of the members of the Special Intelligence Section were former team members or instructors, such as recently promoted Captain Stuntz, the former supply officer.

Despite all of these changes, an examination of the training schedules for Class One (conducted from 27 December 1943 to 4 February 1944) and Class Seven (from 23 April to 1 June 1945) shows them to be very similar. This meant that they had it right, from the very beginning. The hours and hours spent swimming and practicing heavy surf landings, in the words of Major Niles, "made possible the success of many missions." As for where the initial training schedule came from, they just made it up like much of what the Alamo Scouts did, such as electing team composition. Since many of the original staffers were from other units or had been to various training schools, they drew on their backgrounds and threw out what didn't make sense. A comparison between the Alamo Scouts Training Center training schedule and the one for the MACV Recondo School from the Viet Nam War shows an incredible similarity.

The first mission for an Alamo Scouts team was assigned in a hurry. As originally conceived, the invasion of the Admiralty Islands was to take place early in April 1944. Class One graduated 5 February. Four teams came from this class: McGowen Team (led by Lieutenant John R.C. McGowen), Barnes Team (led by Lieutenant William F. Barnes), Sombar Team (led by Lieutenant Michael J. Sombar), and Thompson Team (led by Lieutenant George S. Thompson). Soon after graduation, the Admiralties invasion was moved up to late February and Sixth Army G-2 was told to conduct the reconnaissance of Los Negros Island, one of the two principal islands in the Admiralties.

McGowen Team (consisting of McGowen, Technical Sergeant Ceasar

J. Rameriz, Sergeants Walter A. McDonald and J.A. Roberts, Private First Class John P. Legoud, and Private Paul V. Gomez) was selected to perform the mission. Lieutenant Barnes was to be the contact officer. McGowen and his team went in by Catalina flying boat (PBY). Their uniforms were jungle camouflage, soft caps, and green camouflage face paint. The majority carried carbines, grenades, two days' rations, and an SCR-300 radio.

The team went in on 27 February at a point on southern Los Negros, buried its rubber boat near the beach, and moved out. For the next several hours McGowen Team dodged a number of Japanese patrols. They spent the entire day scouting as far as an airstrip, then returned to their hiding place near the beach. The team remained there all night. In the morning McGowen contacted Barnes, on an inbound PBY, by radio. McGowen, concerned that his team might not be exfiltrated, reported to Barnes that the island was "lousy with Japs."

As a result of this reconnaissance naval gunfire was directed on the Japanese troop concentrations reported by McGowen Team, throttling their commitment during the assault phase of the landing. The invasion, termed a "reconnaissance in force," was eventually successful. The official after-action report credited the Alamo Scouts with timely last minute intelligence having a positive effect on the success of the landings.

As mentioned in the previous discussion of the missions of the Amphibious Scouts, two Alamo Scouts teams took part in operations with Amphibious Scouts teams. These teams were Thompson Team and Dove Team. Thompson Team, which graduated in Class One, included Lieutenant George S. Thompson, Sergeants Jack E. Bensen and Theodore T. Largo, Privates First Class Anthony Ortiz and Joshua Sunn, and Private Joseph A. Johnson. There were Scouts from Hobbs Team (Class Two) who accompanied Thompson Team on this mission; they were Sergeant Herman S. Chaney, Corporal Gordon H. Butler, and Private Joe Moon. Dove Team (Class Two) included Lieutenant John M. Dove, Staff Sergeant John G. Fisher, Tech/5s Irving G. Ray and James W. Roby, Tech/4 Denny M. Chapman, and Private Alton P. Bauer.

The end of the war came during the latter part of Class Nine. The training center was closed and most of the Alamo Scouts were returned to their units for further transfer back to the States and discharge. After the Japanese surrender, two teams of Alamo Scouts accompanied Sixth Army headquarters to Japan. There they conducted missions to identify and secure weapons dumps, and to continue personal security duty for General Krueger. In November 1945, without ceremony or fanfare, the last Alamo Scouts teams were disbanded. During the more than 130 Alamo Scouts missions, not one of the Scouts was killed or captured—indeed an incredibly impressive achievement.

Of all the stories from all the missions, probably the one that best demonstrates the close relationship between the Alamo Scouts and General Krueger, their founder, is from a mission that was canceled. In June 1944, Lieutenant Woodrow H. Hobbs and his team (Class Two) were told to plan the kidnapping of two Japanese generals. A Japanese prisoner who had worked at the camp where the generals lived had provided very detailed information about the camp layout and the daily habits of the generals, such as when they ate, when one of them went horseback riding, and so forth.

The Hobbs Team, working with training center operations officer, Lieutenant McGowen, briefed Krueger on their plan. McGowen stated that it could be done but that it would be extremely dangerous. The ways in were limited and always under observation. The generals were well guarded and it was likely the team would take serious casualties. Krueger canceled the operation with the terse statement: "I wouldn't take the whole damn Jap army for one Alamo Scout."

The Alamo Scouts served as the pattern for similar units in later wars. The Viet Nam Long Range Reconnaissance Patrols and today's Long Range Surveillance Units have many of their aspects drawn directly from the Alamo Scouts. Special Forces considers the Alamo Scouts as part of its heredity. The U.S. Army Ranger School adopted the ASTC principle of sending graduates back to their parent units to spread the benefits of their training.

CHAPTER FOURTEEN

ALAMO SCOUTS: SUMNER
TEAM AT PEGUN ISLAND

Four Alamo Scouts teams were formed from the graduates of Class Three. This class was conducted at Mangee Point, near Finschhafen, New Guinea. The four teams totaled 4 officers and 24 enlisted men. They were: Littlefield Team, led by Lieutenant Wilbur F. (Bill) Littlefield; Lutz Team, led by Lieutenant William B. (Bill) Lutz; Farkas Team, led by Lieutenant Arpad Farkas; and Sumner Team, led by Lieutenant Robert S. "Red" Sumner. Farkas Team conducted only one mission, a reconnaissance in the Manokwari area, before its leader was recalled by his unit and the team disbanded.

As soon as the graduation ceremony was finished, on 22 June, the Scouts and staff began breaking down the camp to move it further west to Hollandia, New Guinea. Class Three was the last class whose training was run by Lieutenant Colonel Bradshaw, the first director of the ASTC.

In July, Sumner Team went on two short missions, a two-day reconnaissance of Cape Oransbari in the Vogelkopf area of New Guinea, and a two-day recon of Manokwari. Both of these missions were in the fairly routine category—nothing out of the ordinary happened and they proceeded fairly much in line with the team's training.

By mid-August, Sumner and his men were working out of the Navy PT boat base at Woendi Island, also in New Guinea. Other members of the team included Staff Sergeant Lawrence E. Coleman, Corporals William F. Blaise and Robert Schermerhorn, and Privates First Class Paul B. Jones, Edward Renhols, and Harry D. Weiland. All of the Scouts on Sumner Team were from the 31st Infantry Division; most of them had graduated from the U.S. Navy Amphibious Beach Demolitions School at Fort Pierce, Florida before leaving the States. On the afternoon of 22 August, Sumner Team was alerted for a mission. It would be like no other mission that an Alamo Scouts team had conducted.

Three days earlier a PT boat had gone into the Mapia Group, consisting of the three tiny islands of Pegun, Bras, and Fanildo. These islands, located about 400 miles south of Morotai and almost 125 miles east of Biak, contained a pre-war agricultural experimental station. The PT boat was looking for a downed Australian Beaufighter aircraft and crew. When it passed Pegun, three enlisted men from Fifth Air Force decided to go ashore to look for souvenirs. The PT boat dropped them off and continued to look for the missing airplane. After a sweep through the islands the aircrew was found, on Bras. Mechanics on the PT boat went ashore, repaired the plane, and it was airborne in a few hours. Then the PT headed back to Pegun to pick up the three airmen.

As the boat approached the island, all those on board had their eyes glued to the shoreline of the small, fairly flat island. Without warning, one of the airmen came running out to the edge of the surf, gesturing for the PT boat to get out of the area. Several shots rang out and the airman fell face down into the water.

The PT boat left the area quickly and returned to its base at Woendi. There, the PT boat commander reported what had happened to the Navy and also to the Air Corps headquarters on Noemfoor Island. Included in the report was a request for someone to go in at Pegun and rescue the three airmen. Sumner Team was alerted and told they would depart sometime that night if the mission was approved.

Lieutenant Sumner wrote his mission plan from the sketchy details he obtained from the PT crew and the Air Corps passengers. He also had a recent aerial photograph of the area to help in the planning but it was of little real value. His order was short, just over two typewritten pages, and contained several courses of action for his team, depending on what they found.

His team's mission was twofold: "To reconnoiter PEGUN ISLAND of the MAPIA Group to determine the possibility of effecting the rescue of 3 Air Corps EM left ashore . . . [and to] further reconnoiter Island for possible estimate of enemy personnel stationed there." The decision to actually rescue the airmen was left to the team's discretion, depending on what the enemy situation was in the immediate vicinity. The team ashore would also include an officer from the Netherlands East Indies Forces, Lieutenant H. Swart.

The contact team consisted of Lieutenant McGowen and four members of the team formerly led by Lieutenant Farkas: Staff Sergeants Ray W. Wangrud and Harold N. Sparks, and Privates First Class Jack C. Bunt and Charley D. Hill. Their mission was to help Sumner Team prepare, get them ashore from the delivering PT boat, act as radio contact during the mission, and pick them up as they were finished. Just before Sumner Team departed, Lieutenant Swart elected not to go and Corporal Schermerhorn was left behind because of a malaria attack.

The Scouts took carbines as individual weapons, although Coleman carried a .45 caliber "grease gun" and Weiland a BAR. Each man carried 75 rounds as his basic load plus two hand grenades; those with automatic weapons carried 150 rounds as a basic load. Four smoke grenades were distributed among the team along with one SCR-300 radio for the scout team and another for the contact team on the PT boat. The SCR-300 was a line-of-sight UHF radio favored by the Alamo Scouts.

An estimate of the enemy situation on Pegun, provided by the Sixth Army G-2 staff, put the Japanese strength at about 350. Sumner, after briefing his plan and receiving approval to launch, was told by Brigadier General McNider, commanding Cyclone Task Force (a force subordinate to Sixth Army), that the Alamo Scouts were only to attempt a rescue if they had sufficient firepower to be sure they could get away safely with the airmen. McNider told Sumner that he could engage the enemy only as a last resort. "General Krueger simply will not permit the loss of a Scout team on an operation of this type," McNider said. Sumner Team was authorized to make the attempt as soon as possible.

Sumner and his team checked their equipment one last time and reviewed the assignments. Coleman and Jones were the boat security team, Renhols and Weiland were the beach security team, and Blaise would carry the radio. A sailor and one of the Scouts on McGowen's contact team would row Sumner Team ashore. When all was ready, the three PT boats in the party were loaded and departed Woendi Island at midnight. A Coast Guard frigate was also part of this sea convoy; its mission was to linger over the horizon, monitoring the PT radio net, and be on-call to assist in the event of trouble. Sumner was glad to have the firepower of the two extra PT boats and the frigate available in case anything went wrong while his team was ashore.

At about 0320, the PT boat carrying the Alamo Scouts slowed to a crawl. Sumner, who had been watching the boat's radar scope with the Navy skipper, moved on deck and told his team to get ready. A rubber boat was put over the side and inflated. Coleman, the team sergeant, supervised the loading of equipment and then the Scouts. As the rubber boat was ready to shove off, McGowen leaned over and reminded Sumner to turn on the team's radio. Sumner told the rowing party to head for shore. Forty minutes later, the Scouts were ashore and the rubber boat was on its way back out. Just after the contact team departed, two of the Scouts swept the landing beach clear of footprints. The landing had been smooth and now Sumner Team was in its perimeter defense, all lying prone with one-third of the team on alert, changing status every half-hour. First light was due at 0530 and dawn at just after 0600.

Just at first light, Sumner was startled to hear a "loud rustling sound" followed by a sharp noise to his rear, in the direction of Weiland. As he turned to see what happened he heard the rest of his team snickering. A large palm frond had fallen from the tree above Weiland, just missing him. Soon after, the Scouts stiffened to wide-awake alertness as they heard two raps on his rifle by Jones. A nine-man Japanese patrol was headed their way. The patrol moved along, rifles slung, chewing fruit and casually throwing away the rinds. The Japanese wore identical white jerseys with a large blue ball in the center of the shirt, blue shorts, and leather high-top campaign shoes, and carried *Arisaka* rifles. The patrol passed within 15 yards of the Alamo Scouts but kept going. This was obviously a routine patrol and not one out looking for the Scouts. The Scouts' infiltration onto the island had not been detected.

Off to the south, the Scouts could now see six small buildings in various stages of collapse. They remembered that they had been told during their intelligence briefing that the island was sometimes used as a target for bombing practice by the Air Corps. Smoke rose from one of the buildings. Sumner assumed it was probably a cooking fire but could not see any other movement. Just 70 yards away stood a single story house with a screened-in porch. Sumner directed his team, by hand signals, toward this lone house. The Scouts crawled forward, two at a time. When they came to a depression about 20 yards from the house, they crawled down inside and paused to listen for sounds of any activity. All they heard was the clucking of chickens. After 15 minutes and no movement, Sumner directed his men toward the group of six buildings.

Sumner remained in the depression as the Scouts moved to within 100 yards of the group of buildings. They could hear voices but were unable to be certain where they were coming from. Sumner moved to the edge of the depression and examined the area with his binoculars. He was able to see through two of the buildings and determined that they were not occupied.

He could plainly see laundry hanging outside several of the other buildings but none of it appeared to be American clothing. The Scouts continued to watch the area, looking for signs of the airmen.

Suddenly, Jones, on the right flank, spotted two Japanese heading in the direction where the Scouts were hidden. As he passed the word to the others, he could see two more Japanese soldiers further behind the first two. Sumner turned his binoculars to his right and watched the Japanese, figuring they were about 150 yards away. Then, just as suddenly as Jones had spotted them, the Japanese disappeared from view. Sumner was certain they had seen his team.

Using hand-and-arm signals, he directed the team to head back to its pick-up point, with Coleman and Weiland, both armed with automatic weapons, making up the rear guard. As the Alamo Scouts began to set off, Sumner glanced at his watch. He was surprised to see that it was 0900; they had been on patrol for just over three hours.

The return trip was uneventful, marked by the same maneuver-and-cover movements the team had used while reconnoitering the buildings. Wherever possible, they took advantage of the surrounding foliage and terrain to hide their movement. At last the entire team was reassembled at its pick-up point, with Jones and Renhols guarding the landward approach to their assembly point. Sumner was by now confident that there were no Americans being held alive on the island. He signaled Blaise to break the team radio out of its hiding place and tell the PT boats that the team was ready to be pulled out. While Blaise talked to McGowen, the rest of the Alamo Scouts listened to Japanese movement and talking. The sounds seemed to be coming from their right. Sumner now became concerned because he knew that the nine-man patrol they had spotted earlier was off to the team's left. Would they be able to hold off an attack from two directions? Blaise signaled to the team that the PT boats were on their way.

Sumner quickly calculated that the Scouts could probably hold off an attack from between 25 to 30 men, even if it came from two directions. He determined that it made good sense for the Scouts to wait for the Japanese to come at them rather that initiating any action. He remembered the general's caution in the final briefing, "You can put your team shore, lieutenant, but you will not make a fight out of it." He also knew that the Scouts would be most vulnerable once they were in the water.

Blaise crawled over to Sumner and whispered that the PT boats would need some visible sign from the team to determine its location. Sumner nodded and moved to the dune line and stood facing the lagoon. Renhols moved over and stood behind his lieutenant, facing inland. As he felt Renhols' back against his back, Sumner heard Blaise talking to McGowen on the radio. Blaise signaled Sumner that McGowen could see the standing Scouts. "Send in the boats—we're coming out," Blaise radioed. The Scouts did not know how much longer the Japanese would wait.

As before, McGowen sent in a sailor and one of the Alamo Scouts from his contact team to paddle the rubber boat to the waiting team. As soon as he saw the rubber boat emerge from behind the PT boat, Sumner dropped to one knee and felt Renhols do the same. He decided that he now had no choice but for his team to wade out to the incoming boat. He knew that the two men in the boat could become targets and the only way to attract fire from them was to give the Japanese another, closer target. He was still confident of his team's firepower and decided to put them in the water. He believed that this would, in the long run, bring the two elements (the Scouts in the water and the incoming boat) together quicker. Blaise passed on a report; the other two PT boats were on the way at full battle stations and an Australian Beaufighter was on station to give air support if needed.

Sumner spoke quietly to his men, telling them his plan to get in the water and move to the rubber boat. "We are going to walk out backwards—we haven't got a choice. Fan out and form a semi-circle." He sent Jones and Renhols out first. As they turned around in the water, facing the shore, he sent Blaise next, with an order to stay on the radio. Weiland and Coleman went next and finally Sumner, walking backwards to keep his eyes ready for any Japanese movement.

When the water reached Sumner's waist, the Japanese opened fire, first from the front and then from the right flank. The Alamo Scouts returned fire at the bushes in the dunes, aiming at what they hoped would be waist level. The two automatic weapons fired in bursts and the remaining Scouts fired single shots. Almost at once the Japanese fire slowed down, then new fire, the distinctive sound of an *Arisaka* rifle, came at the Scouts from their left. Sumner's worst calculations, incoming fire from two flanks, were now a reality. He directed Weiland, with the BAR, to return fire to the left. As the team continued to move backwards and shoot at the shore, the lieutenant glanced at Weiland again, watching him finish a magazine and quickly exchange it for a new one, putting the empty inside his fatigue jacket. Sumner described this later by saying, "Weiland was as cool as if he was on a KD range."

The Japanese fire picked up and continued to reach for the Scouts, zipping around them and ricocheting off the water as they moved closer to the incoming rubber boat. So far, no one had been hit. The loitering PT boat was unable to fire at the Japanese because the Alamo Scouts were in its line of fire. Then, at just about the same time, Blaise called for air support as McGowen was directing the Australian Beaufighter to help the struggling Scouts.

The first of the Scouts in the water reached the rubber boat as the Aussie pilot made his first run on the island, blasting away with all six of his .50 caliber guns and two of his 20mm cannons. The twin-engine plane came roaring in, tail high, some 90 feet off the ground. The Japanese fire died away very noticeably. The rest of the Scouts scrambled onto the rubber boat, which had taken several hits but was still afloat thanks to the compartmentation of its cells. The Scouts began paddling furiously and all three PTs now opened up on the island. One of the PT boats moved closer and soon hid the rubber boat from the beach fire. The Beaufighter made a second run on the Japanese positions.

The Scouts threw their equipment and weapons on board and quickly clambered onto the PT boat. As soon as his crew had hauled the rubber landing boat aboard, the PT commander pushed his engines to the limit, taking his boat and the Alamo Scouts team quickly to safety. The remaining PT boats kept up their fire, covering the other boat. McGowen described the action afterwards: "When Red came out, the patrol boat [the Coast Guard frigate] came up and shelled the holy hell out of the place with 20s, 40s, and 3-inch. It was a beautiful sight." Incredibly, in all the shooting, none of the Scouts had been wounded.

On the way back to Woendi Island, Sumner began preparing his afteraction report. He was very satisfied with the performance of his Scouts, confident that he had made the correct choice when he had voted for those he wanted on the team at the end of their training class just one month before. He concluded in his report that they had not found any evidence of the airmen and that they were probably dead. He noted later that virtually every contingency he had planned in his patrol order had happened except for the easy exfiltration.

Several nights later, Tokyo Rose gave the Japanese side of the fight in her broadcast over Radio Tokyo. "Imperial Marines have repulsed an Allied attack on the Mapia Islands with losses." The Scouts figured that, since none of them had been hit, the Japanese had suffered the losses.

Three months later, in November, elements of 2nd Battalion, 167th Infantry landed on Pegun Island and met no enemy resistance. The Japanese were gone. The commander, Lieutenant Colonel Leon L. Matthews, reported that his unit found the bodies of three enlisted men in a common grave. Two of them had their hands tied behind their backs and had been shot in the back of the head. Although none of them had dog tags, their uniforms bore markings of the Army Air Corps. The 2nd Battalion, 167th was Sumner's parent unit. He was, as were all of the Alamo Scouts, only on temporary duty status from this unit while in the Scouts. In September 1945, Sumner met Matthews, who told the Scout team leader what the unit had found on Pegun. Matthews said that he had heard of the Sumner Team operation but thought Sumner, despite the uniform markings, was one of the bodies found. Sumner said later that this last remark did not "show too much confidence in one of his long time platoon leaders, does it?"

On 1 January 1945, in a ceremony on Leyte to present awards to many Alamo Scouts for several missions, the men of Sumner Team received Bronze Stars for their part in the attempted rescue at Pegun Island. By the end of the war, Sumner Team was one of the few early teams that was still together, despite the fact that in June 1945 Sumner moved to the Special Intelligence Section of the G-2 staff. This section was created to control the activity of Alamo Scouts teams, particularly in their dealings with Philippine guerrilla units. Lieutenant Chester B. Vickery, a recent graduate from Class Seven, had taken Sumner's place as team leader.

CHAPTER FIFTEEN

ALAMO SCOUTS: NELLIST
AND ROUNSAVILLE TEAMS
AT CABANATUAN

In late January 1945, Sixth Army was pressing to the southwest, advancing steadily toward Manila. The liberation of this capital city was General MacArthur's highest priority. On the afternoon of the 26th the Sixth Army G-2, Colonel White, was updated on the situation at the Cabanatuan prison camp. This camp was located about 50 miles north of Manila and contained at least 300 Allied prisoners. Many among the prisoners were survivors of the infamous Bataan death march. That afternoon there was a new urgency to the briefing.

The Japanese had been increasing troop movements around the city of Cabanatuan since it was a major logistics and communications center in the area. The prisoner-of-war camp nearby, of necessity, was required to provide quarters for the large numbers of transient Japanese troops in the area. On several occasions in the past, general plans for a raid on this POW camp had been discussed but no plan was ever completed. As White and his special assistant, Major Frank Rowale, received the new information from Major Robert Lapham (an American officer who led a large Filipino guerrilla force), they became concerned for the safety of the prisoners at Cabanatuan. They decided that the time had come for action but, as White said, "It's too big a job for the Scouts to handle but they can sure help."

Three Alamo Scouts team leaders, Lieutenants Tom J. Rounsaville, William E. Nellist, and John M. Dove, were summoned and a planning session followed. Teams led by Rounsaville and Nellist had previously executed a prisoner release mission which had been planned by Dove, so all of them were logical choices to be involved in this mission.

Class Four of the Alamo Scouts Training Center was conducted from August to September 1944 at Hollandia, Dutch New Guinea. The teams led by Rounsaville and Nellist were the only ones from Class Four that were retained by the Alamo Scouts. Rounsaville's team included: Technical Sergeant Alfred Alfonso, Sergeant Harold Hard, and Privates First Class Franklin Fox, Francis Laquier, and Rufo Vaquilar. Nellist's team included: Staff Sergeant Tom Siason, Technical Sergeant Wilbert G. Wismer, Corporal Andrew Smith, and Privates First Class Sabas Asis, Gilbert Cox, and Galen C. Kittleson. Kittleson, the team's machine gunner, was the last of the Alamo Scouts on active duty when he retired in 1978. He also participated in Operation Ivory Coast, the Special Forces raid on Son Tay POW camp in North Viet Nam during November 1970.

Within three weeks of graduation both teams had already completed a warm up mission. "We spent our first couple of weeks conducting small patrols on the mainland and with the Navy, riding around in PT boats," recalled Nellist later. Sixth Army G-2 learned of a Japanese prison camp on the east coast of the Vogelkop or "the Bird's Head" part of the western end of New Guinea near Cape Oransbari. The prisoners at this camp included a prominent Dutch governor and his family.

After first conducting a reconnaissance of the camp area, Rounsaville and Nellist refined the plan to attack the camp and liberate the prisoners; the plan had been devised by Lieutenant Dove, who had already led his team on two harrowing missions behind Japanese lines. They decided that the most appropriate way into the camp was through a swamp on the one side of the camp that the Japanese had left unguarded, apparently believing that there was no danger from that side. Both teams wore soft caps and fatigue uniforms. Their weapons included shotguns, submachine guns, pistols, and grenades. Nellist, an expert marksman and the best shot in the Alamo Scouts, carried an M-1 Garand.

By 0400 on 5 October, after two false starts, the two teams were in place. Rounsaville Team plus two men were on the outskirts of the camp and the remainder of Nellist Team was at a secluded Japanese outpost near the planned exfiltration beach. Ten minutes later, Rounsaville fired a single shot from his pistol into one of the huts to signal the start of the attack. Within three minutes the entire Japanese garrison was dead. Rounsaville Team then set fire to the huts and began moving the freed prisoners to the beach. Andy Smith said later, "We were in there less than four minutes before we secured the area. In that short time we had all the prisoners released and had killed all the Japs. The raid went off like clockwork." Not one of the Alamo Scouts had even been wounded.

Meanwhile Nellist, who was supposed to coordinate his element's attack with Rounsaville's, did not begin shooting until almost 0530; no one had heard any shots at the camp. However, once they began shooting it did not take long to finish the job. One hour later Rounsaville Team and the recently freed prisoners arrived; shortly thereafter Nellist made contact with Lieutenant Dove. Soon the two teams with their former prisoners, 66 in all including former Dutch and Javanese citizens and one large French family, had been loaded onto the arriving PT boats and sped to freedom. Rounsaville said later, "It was a textbook operation. We hit the camp at the right time, at the right place, with the right men!" The entire mission lasted just about 12 hours.

The plan developed for the Cabanatuan mission called for a reinforced company of the 6th Ranger Battalion to conduct the raid on the POW camp, with reconnaissance support to be provided by the two Alamo Scouts teams, and reinforcement and local security provided by a force of Filipino guerrillas. General Krueger approved the plan and established a meeting for noon the next day to review the plan with all present plus Lieutenant Colonel Henry A. Mucci, commander, 6th Ranger Battalion.

At the planning meeting on the 27th, Lieutenant Dove was assigned to be liaison between the Rounsaville and Nellist Alamo Scouts teams and the 6th Rangers. The Alamo Scouts would depart that evening and spend the entire next day and night conducting reconnaissance on the POW camp. The teams would be escorted by Filipino guerrillas, who would also work closely with the local populace to insure that word did not get out about the mission. Weather for the next several days was to be warm and dry, with medium to high cloud cover and a full moon period for the nights of 29 and 30 January.

Lieutenant Colonel Mucci selected C Company and 2nd Platoon of F Company to comprise the raiding force. He would lead the 120 Rangers on a 30-mile cross-country march from their drop-off point, Guimba. The Rangers would link up with the Alamo Scouts on the morning of the 29th. The raid was scheduled for just after dark that night, which would give the entire force that whole night to move to a friendly area with the liberated prisoners. To add to the hazard of this mission, Mucci was told that friendly air units would not know about his force being in the area. The G-2 would arrange with friendly ground units to be expecting two green flares as a sign of friendly units preparing to move back through the front lines.

Late in the afternoon of the 27th, the two Alamo Scouts teams were taken by truck to Guimba. Their uniforms consisted of fatigues and soft caps; no rank or unit insignia were on the fatigues. Most carried M-1 rifles, although others carried M-1 carbines and Thompson sub-machine guns. The teams arrived safely at the headquarters of a Filipino guerrilla unit commanded by Captain Juan Pajota. The area around the POW camp was divided up and sectors assigned for reconnaissance. The main road which ran past the camp, all the small trails in the area, the many rice fields, and even the banks of the nearby Pampanga River were to be covered. Most important of all, the camp itself was to be scouted, but at a distance. Numbers and disposition of Japanese troops, the presence of tanks, weapons, and even the numbers of prisoners were all essential elements of information to be collected. Rounsaville and Nellist were due to link up with the Rangers at 0600 on the 29th.

When that rendezvous was made, the intelligence was discouraging. Mucci had been ready to attack as soon as it got dark that night but the Alamo Scouts team leaders convinced him that their reconnaissance was not complete. What they already knew, however, showed heavy concentrations of Japanese troops within three to four miles of the camp as well as many inside the camp. The terrain surrounding the camp was flat and open, making approach difficult. Captain Pajota reported that about 500 POWs were in the camp. Mucci agreed to put the raid on hold for 24 hours, hoping for some of the Japanese troops to leave and allowing time for more detailed reconnaissance by the two Alamo Scouts teams. A signal was sent to Sixth Army advising of the delay.

Just after midnight, several Alamo Scouts crossed the Pampanga River and crawled to the camp. Two hours later they reported their findings: the Japanese troops moving along the road were not entering the camp. Other sides of the camp were surveyed but still no one had been able to get close to the front gate. Nellist and Private First Class Vaquilar donned native clothes and walked through a nearby field, and entered what they hoped was an abandoned hut. Once inside they began sketching what they could see of the camp. They were joined later by Sergeant Hard and Privates First Class Cox and Fox, who had crawled all the way from the river. The Alamo Scouts who were watching the perimeter of the camp were farther away than the men in the hut.

By 1600 on the 30th, while the Rangers were reviewing aerial photos and sketch maps of the camp from the Alamo Scouts, a young Filipina woman approached the guards at the front gate and spoke with them. Nellist became nervous, fearing they had been given away. After a while, however, he could detect no unusual activity. He then sent Fox back to the Ranger position with the message that the remaining Alamo Scouts would stay where they were until after dark but would send someone back if the situation changed.

At 1700 the Rangers, with a force expanded to 375 by the Filipino guerrillas, departed their base area for the POW camp. When the force approached to within a mile of the camp, they dropped to the ground and crawled the remaining distance. This took almost an hour and a half. As they neared the camp, they were met by Alamo Scouts who helped guide them closer. Soon afterwards, at 1945, the attack was launched.

Within 45 minutes almost all of the Japanese in the camp had been killed and the raiders and former prisoners were approaching the Pampanga River. Violent execution had carried Mucci's plan. When all were across, the rear security element, including some Alamo Scouts, was signaled and fell in at the end of the march. As the force regrouped and moved the 513 liberated prisoners out, the Alamo Scouts were detailed to provide security for the medical detachment and the wounded. They would remain in place for a while.

At 2300 that night, the first message about the raid was sent to Sixth Army. It would not be until the following night before the Alamo Scouts returned to friendly lines. Sergeant Alfonso, with a serious groin wound, and Rounsaville, with a fragment wound in the buttock, were the only casualties among the Alamo Scouts.

The success of this raid had required secrecy and surprise. General Krueger praised the rescue as "carefully planned, effectively reconnoitered by Alamo Scouts, daringly executed by the Rangers and guerrillas, the surprise achieved . . . a brilliant success." The weekly Sixth Army G-2 report for the period described the operation as "an almost perfect example of prior reconnaissance and planning" demonstrating "what patrols can accomplish in enemy territory by following the basic principles of scouting and patrolling . . ."

Mission Critique

As with so many of the special operations forces of World War II, the Alamo Scouts were a child of necessity. General Krueger needed a force that was responsive to his command and would provide accurate and timely intelligence to his staff; this intelligence was to be the basis for effective operational plans for Sixth Army. Later the Scouts would perform additional missions, on an as-needed basis—missions such as prisoner rescues, and coordination and control of guerrilla activities. For a variety of reasons, most of them related to the evaluation criteria already established, the Alamo Scouts are America's quintessential special operations force of World War II. The short history discussed here really only touches on several high points of their history. Let's look at a few of the facts.

The Alamo Scouts established a training program that survived several wars nearly intact, a program that was created from bits and pieces of other programs but still highly original and pertinent to Sixth Army needs. Every member on a team was there because every other member believed he should be and wanted him there. Every member of a team had an important role in each operation and contributed to each operation's plan. Missions were of a basic type but flexible for each situation—there was no "school solution," no one right way to do things. The Scouts teams were available for short notice operations and had the luxury to conduct mid-term planning for other missions. Missions used a variety of infiltration and exfiltration methods. Perhaps one of the only methods not used was by parachute, although two of the teams, Nellist and Rounsaville, were both entirely composed of airborne-qualified men. None of the teams, however, was on jump status. Missions were marked by inter-service and inter-team cooperation, imagination in planning, and always with the idea of getting every man back alive. Unless operational necessity precluded it, each mission was rehearsed at least once; on-mission each of the Scouts remained cautious and ready to go beyond the plan if necessary. The Alamo Scouts conducted more than 130 missions and did not have a single man killed or taken prisoner. Above all, it is the team concept of organization and execution that sets the Alamo Scouts apart from the many reconnaissance organizations of the U.S. Army—in World War II and since.

Using first the Vandenbroucke criteria as a guide, although not all of the missions were a complete success or accomplished all pre-mission objectives, none was characterized by any negative aspects of these criteria. The Scouts used all *intelligence* available to plan the operation. *Coordination* with other organizations, which sometimes supplied additional members to the team and at other times supplied rides to and from target areas, was a routine mark of each mission. None of the remaining criteria (*faulty information to leader-*

ship, wishful thinking, or *inappropriate intervention*) entered the picture of any Alamo Scouts mission planning or execution. In one of the more arduous missions, the Cabanatuan raid, the overall mission leader, Lieutenant Colonel Mucci, was far-sighted enough to take the recommendation of the Scouts teams supporting him and delayed mission execution for 24 hours so he could get better target intelligence. Of the McRaven criteria, *simplicity, speed,* and *surprise* are most easily recognized in the Scouts operations. If each team could not always conduct sufficient rehearsals, one of the best ways they covered *repetition* was by working with classes in training to refresh their skills.

Even in this book, the Alamo Scouts are the exception in special operations forces—their missions were carefully planned and executed, and they all supported the overall plans for Sixth Army in particular and the Southwest Pacific theater in general. These missions were all justified and carefully reviewed before being approved for execution. Planners and higher headquarters staff worked together in this process, and not as adversaries. Immediate, even interim, and detailed after-action reports were submitted from which operational and training lessons learned were gleaned and applied. The Alamo Scouts were, without question, the "Pros from Dover."

SOURCES

Books, diaries, unpublished manuscripts:

Andrews, John; *Airborne Album—1943–1945—Normandy to Victory;* Phillips Publications; Williamstown, NJ; 1993

Black, Robert W.; *Rangers in World War II;* Ivy Books; New York; 1992

Breuer, William B.; *The Great Raid on Cabanatuan—Rescuing the Doomed Ghosts of Bataan and Corregidor;* New York; John Wiley & Sons; 1994

——————; *MacArthur's Undercover War—Spies, Saboteurs, Guerrillas, and Secret Missions;* New York; John Wiley & Sons; 1995

Burford, John; *LRRPs in Action;* Carrolltown, TX; Squadron/Signal Publications; 1994

Dwyer, John B.; *Scouts and Raiders—The Navy's First Special Warfare Commandos;* Westport, CT; Praeger; 1993

Finnegan, John P.; *Military Intelligence—A Picture History;* U.S. Army Intelligence and Security Command; date unknown but around 1986

General and Special Staff sections; *Report on the Luzon Campaign;* Sixth United States Army; undated

Grimes, Martin; *Turnip Greens and Sergeant Stripes;* New Rochelle, NY; Arlington House; 1972

Hochstrasser, Lewis B.; *They Were First—The True Story of the Alamo Scouts*; unpublished manuscript in author's collection; 1944

Hogan, David W., Jr.; *The Evolution of the Concept of the U.S. Army's Rangers, 1942–1983*; Duke University Doctoral Dissertation; 1986

—————; *U.S. Army Special Operations in World War II*; Government Printing Office; Washington, DC; 1992

Johnson, Forrest B.; *Hour of Redemption: The Ranger Raid on Cabanatuan*; New York; Manor Books; 1978

King, Michael J.; *Rangers: Selected Combat Operations in World War II*; Combat Studies Institute (Leavenworth Papers, USCGSC); Fort Leavenworth; 1985

Krueger, Walter F.; *From Down Under to Nippon*; Combat Forces Press; Washington, DC; 1953

Macksey, Kenneth; *Commando Strike—The Story of Amphibious Raiding in World War II;* London; Leo Cooper; 1985

McConnell, Zeke; *Diary—Alamo Scouts*; unpublished; 1944

McMillan, George; *The Old Breed—A History of the First Marine Division in World War II;* Infantry Journal Press; Washington, DC; 1953

Miller, John, Jr.; *Cartwheel: The Reduction of Rabaul;* Office of the Chief, Military History (United States Army in World War II—The War in the Pacific); Washington; 1959

Morison, Samuel E.; *Breaking the Bismarcks Barrier—22 July 1942–1 May 1944;* Boston; Little, Brown (History of the United States Naval Operations in World War II, Volume VI); 1950

Niles, Gibson; *The Operations of the Alamo Scouts (Sixth U.S. Army Special Reconnaissance Unit);* U.S. Army Infantry School; Fort Benning; 1948

Powe, M.B. and E.E. Wilson; *The Evolution of American Military Intelligence;* U.S. Army Intelligence Center and School; 1973

Ross, Bob; *Diary—Alamo Scouts, Sixth Army;* unpublished; 1945

Rottman, Gordon L.; *US Army Rangers & LRRP Units 1942–1987;* Osprey Publishing; London; 1987

Rounsaville, Tom J.; *The Operations of the Alamo Scouts (Sixth U.S. Army Special Reconnaissance Unit)*; U.S. Army Infantry School; Fort Benning; 1950

Smith, Robert R.; *The Approach to the Philippines;* Office of the Chief, Military History (United States Army in World War II—The War in the Pacific); Washington; 1953

—————; *Triumph in the Philippines*; Office of the Chief, Military History (United States Army in World War II—The War in the Pacific); Washington; 1963

Stanton, Shelby L.; *Order of Battle—U.S. Army, World War II;* Presidio Press; Novato, CA; 1984

Wright, Bertram C.; *The 1st Cavalry Division in World War II;* Tokyo; Toppan Printing; 1947

Zedric, Lance Q.; *The Alamo Scouts: Eyes Behind the Lines—Sixth Army's Special Re-*

connaissance Unit of World War II; Western Illinois University Master's Thesis; 1993

——————; *Silent Warriors of World War II—The Alamo Scouts Behind Japanese Lines;* Ventura, CA; Pathfinder Publishing; 1995

Articles, other papers:

Assistant Chief of Staff, G-3; "Combat Notes"; Headquarters Sixth Army; 21 March 1945

Author unknown; "Alamo Scouts Sixth Army"; date and source unknown

Author unknown; "Enemy on Luzon—An Intelligence Summary; Chapter IV, Special Reconnaissance Operations"; source unknown

Author unknown; "The Saga of Bill Nellist—Alamo Scout"; in *Airborne Quarterly;* Spring 1991

Chronis, Peter G.; "Alamo Scouts: Masters of Stealth"; in *The Denver Post;* October 5, 1993

Dilley, Michael F. and Lance Q. Zedric; "The Recon of Los Negros"; in *Behind The Lines;* May–June 1995

Garland, Al; "Alamo Scouts Played Vital Role in War"; in *The Benning Leader;* September 10, 1993

Hughes, Les; "The Alamo Scouts"; in *Trading Post;* April–June 1986

Johnson, Raymond and Alfred Hahn; "Alamo Scouts, U.S. 6th Army—1943–1945"; in *Company of Military Historians*; Plate 499

Lindsey, Beverly; "CSM Galen C. Kittelson Retires—Last of the Alamo Scouts"; in *Static Line*; probably September or October 1978

McCracken, W.W. and A. A. Littman; "The Alamo Scouts"; in *Trading Post;* April–June 1963

Mehle, Michael; "25 WWII Veterans Gather to Remember Their Alamo"; in *Rocky Mountain News*; October 2, 1993

Mucci, Henry A.; "We Swore We'd Die or Do It"; in *The Saturday Evening Post;* April 7, 1945

Nabbie, Eustace E. (pseud. Mayo S. Stuntz); "The Alamo Scouts"; in *Studies in Intelligence;* date unknown

Pames, George; "The Great Cabanatuan Raid"; in *Air Classics;* two issues, date unknown but probably 1981–1984

Raymond, Allen; "Team of Heroes: The Alamo Scouts"; in *The Saturday Evening Post*; June 30, 1945

Sackton, Frank J.; "Southwest Pacific Alamo Scouts"; in *Armored Cavalry Journal;* January-February 1947

Shelton, George R.; "The Alamo Scouts"; in *Armor;* September–October 1982

Spencer, Murlin; "Saga of the Alamo Scouts"; in *Detroit Free Press;* October 15, 1944

Wells, Billy E, Jr.; "The Alamo Scouts—Lessons for LRSUs"; in *Infantry;* May–June 1989

Zedric, Lance Q.; "Prelude to Victory—The Alamo Scouts"; in *Army;* July 1994
————— and Michael F. Dilley; "Raid on Oransbari"; in *Behind The Lines*, November–December 1995

Interviews and letters with:
Galen C. Kittleson (several interviews between 1992 and 1999)
William Nellist (several interviews in 1992 and 1995)
Tom J. Rounsaville (several interviews in 1992, 1995, and 1998)
Andy Smith (several interviews in 1992, 1995, and 1998)
Robert S. Sumner (several letters and interviews between 1992 and 1999)
Mayo S. Stuntz (several interviews in 1992, 1995, and 1998)

CHAPTER SIXTEEN

THE JEDBURGH PROJECT

As early as July 1942 the British Special Operations Executive (SOE)) was at work on a plan to send small teams of Allied soldiers into France secretly, to coordinate the activities of local resistance groups. The codename "Jumpers" was suggested for this project but was not accepted. Instead, "Jedburgh," the name of a small Scottish town on the English border, was selected from an approved list of codenames. The name was also appropriate because a Scottish group in the 12th century had conducted guerrilla warfare against British invaders in the Jedburgh area of Scotland. For the next two years, F Section, SOE and the Special Operations (SO) section of the Office of Strategic Services (OSS) worked together to put the Jedburgh Project into action.

The initial draft of the Jedburgh Project called for two- or three-man teams of British soldiers to contact local French resistance groups and supply them with weapons, establish radio contact between the groups and SOE, to arrange "dropping points and reception committees for further arms and equipment," and to act as guides for Allied units following the invasion of Europe. By the end of 1942, the basic concept had changed in several ways. British and American soldiers were to be included on the teams as well as at least one officer of the nationality of the country to which the team would deploy, that is, France, Holland, or Belgium. Everyone on the team, except the radio operator, had to speak the local language. The Jedburgh teams, or Jeds as they were called, would be dropped into areas controlled by local resistance groups; the idea that they would later act as guides was dropped from the basic concept.

In March 1943, the idea was tested during Exercise Spartan, conducted on the Salisbury plain southwest of London. Spartan was the first "practice

D-Day." SOE staff officers took the role of Jeds. They worked with local resistance groups and inserted individual agents behind enemy lines. The critical review by SOE for this operation concluded that the Jedburgh concept
was valid. One major lesson this review asserted was that the teams should
be dropped about 40 miles behind German lines to avoid detection. Two
other lessons were learned in Spartan: the Jeds could be very helpful by attacking enemy communications lines with small-scale guerrilla strikes and
by supporting advancing friendly forces with tactical operations. No thought,
however, was given to ways that these tactical operations could be coordinated, specifically because the review did not address direct communications
between the Jeds in the field and the advancing friendly forces. This problem
was never resolved.

One other long-range result of Spartan was the finalization, in March
1943, of a memo between SOE and SO/OSS with the cumbersome title
"Coordination of Activities of Resistance Groups Behind Enemy Lines with
Allied Military Operations in an Opposed Invasion of Northwest Europe."
In the memo, the two organizations outlined their intent to arm, equip, direct, plan, and coordinate actions and operations of these resistance groups.
In order to force the Germans to disperse their units instead of concentrat-
ing them at the point of invasion, SOE and SO/OSS decided to train the
resistance units in guerilla warfare, weapons, communications, demolitions,
fieldcraft, and security. Parachute drops would supply these units with
weapons, explosives, radios, and operational funds. Finally, a combined headquarters element from SOE and SO/OSS would operate under the control
of the Supreme Headquarters, Allied Expeditionary Force, to direct the Jedburgh teams. This element was referred to as Special Forces Headquarters
or SFHQ.

In July 1943, two separate memos, one sent in British channels and one
sent in American channels, outlined the concept for the Jedburgh Project.
These memos detailed the composition and missions of the Jedburgh teams:
the teams would consist of three men, two officers and a radio operator; and,
as had been decided in late 1942, at least one of the two officers would be a
native of the country where the team deployed. The missions were those that
had been outlined in April. Each of the memos was approved and one month
later the plan for implementing the concept was given initial approval by
OSS. Soon after, a joint decision was made to begin recruiting for the teams.
Initially, the planners envisioned that 70 teams would be necessary with an
additional 35 teams in reserve. This was soon revised to be a combined total

of 100 teams. Training would take two months, perhaps longer. It was now time to move beyond the planning and make the Jeds an actuality, instead of merely a paper force.

Recruiting began in October 1943. In the U.S., the Joint Chiefs of Staff gave OSS permission to recruit 100 officers and 50 enlisted men for the Jedburgh Project. The enlisted men were to be radio operators and were recruited at several signal training schools. Most of the officers were recruited from airborne units at Fort Bragg, Camp Mackall, and Fort Benning. Those who made it through the initial screening were sent to two OSS training sites, Area F in the Washington, DC area and Area B in the Catoctin Mountains of Maryland. Intensive psychological screening and courses in map reading and land navigation; communications; first aid; intelligence tradecraft; explosives and demolition; hand-to-hand combat including knife fighting; and weapons training were conducted at these sites.

At the completion of this screening period, those who were selected for assignment were sent to England. They arrived in mid-December to begin more training. British and French candidates were screened in a similar process, with French soldiers starting their training in Scotland in November. At the same time as the recruiting drive was on, SOE and SO/OSS were dropping agents, weapons, and supplies to the partisans in Western Europe, preparing them for the coming invasion and cautioning them not to precipitate operations but to wait for word from London. Remarkably, all of the cautions were heeded.

In late December, the "Basic Directive on Jedburghs" was approved. The teams were to be the "theater special operations reserve . . . intended to respond to 'last-minute' requirements" relayed to them from SFHQ. Once the Jeds had linked up with their partisan groups they would continue to operate with them until London directed a change in mission.

Training for the Jeds was conducted at several sites in England and Scotland. There was also continued assessment throughout this training, with one period of assessment particularly interesting. This was to evaluate the candidate's ability to operate under stress and included three components—the stress interview, the construction problem, and the brook test. The stress interview was essentially a hostile interrogation, designed to evaluate emotional stability under severe strain. Some interviewees were told they had failed just to study their reactions. The construction problem consisted of "a number of large wooden blocks, and dowels of various lengths that fit into circular holes in the blocks." The object was to build a cube of specific size with the assistance of two soldiers, who had been instructed to be as obstreperous as possible, hindering success at every turn. The brook test consisted of moving two heavy items over a water obstacle using ropes of varying lengths, several short boards (none long enough to reach all the way across the brook), and a pulley. Ten minutes were allowed to complete the brook test.

All Jeds, regardless of previous qualification, had to undergo three days of parachute training at an SOE school. This included three jumps: one each from a balloon at 700 feet, a plane at 500 feet, and a plane at night. As the last Jeds were completing this training, the Jedburgh School at Milton Hall, a large country estate 90 miles north of London, was opened and students began to report for their final phase of training.

This phase was run by a combined U.S.-British staff. Until the various teams were deployed on operational missions, the Milton Hall commandant was their commander. The emphasis during this phase was on practical field training exercises. Thus, few new skills were taught. Rather, the Jed trainees were drilled over and over on techniques to the point that they became second nature. New topics included the use of one-time cipher pads; forged documents; German counter-guerrilla tactics; and debriefing sessions with various agents who had already conducted operations in German-occupied areas.

The training emphasized the roles the Jeds would play in their missions with the local resistance groups: liaison, organization, and leadership. Several large-scale exercises were conducted to shake out the training. Whenever possible and practical, operational changes were made. In late March, the teams were formed. To this point, the training had been given to groups of trainees. In a technique similar to that also used by the Alamo Scouts in the Pacific, the Jeds decided on their own team composition. From 1 April onward, all training was done per team. If there was a breakdown in any team's organization, the members were allowed to re-form the team with different members. This formation and re-formation process was referred to among the teams as "marriage" and "divorce."

At about this same time, French soldiers in the Jeds were told to assume *noms-de-guerre*. They were to use these pseudonyms when operational to prevent any reprisals against their families in case they were captured and broke under interrogation. This practice led to several discussions on the legal status of guerrilla or partisan soldiers. The Germans held that such forces were illegal and forbidden by international law. On the other hand, the Allies obviously disagreed and acted accordingly. Tricolor arm bands were included in all supply drops as a minimum fulfillment of the 1907 Hague Convention requirement that partisans wear a distinctive emblem or uniform.

During May 1944, two specialized training blocks were given to some of the Jeds. Teams bound for Holland were sent to Scotland for a ten-day course in the use of two-man folboats or kayaks. Teams going into France spent time with air crews working out details of drop zone selection and marking as well as finding improvised landing fields for cargo planes.

On 2 May, 15 Jedburgh teams deployed to North Africa in preparation for their insertion. SFHQ had previously established a nine-man staff at a safe-house in the Baker Street section of London to conduct briefings for the Jeds deploying from England. The plan was for the teams to be briefed and then taken to a departure airfield right away.

On 3 June, the first team, codenamed HUGH, was sent through this safe-house and jumped into France on the night of 5 June. HUGH went in blind, meaning there was no reception committee on the ground. The Jeds were to go in to central France accompanied by an SAS team codenamed BULLBASKET. The SAS team was to conduct raids on German rail lines between Limoges and Chateauroux and between Bordeaux and Tours. The Jeds were to establish a base and "coordinate partisan support for the SAS team." HUGH was in France for three and one-half months. During that time they had over 9,000 resistance members in their area, a number beyond their capabilities to control. Eventually two other Jed teams, HAMISH and JULIAN, jumped in to take some of the training load from HUGH. As a result of HUGH's activity, German units retreating from southwest France had to be diverted around the Jed team's area of operations. HUGH did better than the SAS BULLBASKET team that accompanied it into France; the SAS operation was virtually destroyed by the Germans.

HAMISH jumped on the night of 12 June and could not find any Germans to fight, so instead concentrated on its training mission. About a month later, the resistance group that HAMISH was training decided to attack a battalion-size German element. Such a pitched battle was contrary to the direction of the Jeds, who had taught hit-and-run tactics. The Maquis attacked anyway and suffered more than 15 killed, which they could ill afford.

Team HARRY was sent in on the night of 6 June, with an SAS team, HOUNDSWORTH, to an area in the Morvan mountains. HARRY's mission was similar to HUGH's. Three nights later, also accompanied by SAS teams, Jed teams GEORGE and FREDERICK jumped into Brittany. These were the first of 14 Jed teams sent in to Brittany over a four-month period.

Six of these teams jumped in to work with resistance groups in the Finistere region, the western-most area in Brittany. In June and July, these six Jedburgh teams prepared the partisans to work with Allied units, gathered intelligence of value to Allied units moving into the area, ambushed fleeing German units, and established escape-and evasion nets for downed fliers. They also protected the flank of Patton's Third Army as it began its breakout in August. Their activity in support of Patton was so effective, according to one after-action report, that they released units of Third Army to take part in Patton's circling drive around German units in Normandy while the resistance completed mopping-up operations in Brittany.

HORACE was one of the teams that jumped into Finistere, arriving on the night of 17 July. The Germans quickly learned of the Jeds in the area and offered a reward of one million francs for their capture; no one ever collected this reward. HORACE began calling for resupply drops almost immediately. In mid August, the Jeds began ambushes of German units on the flanks of American units in the area. They also began conducting intelligence operations to support Allied units. HORACE was pulled out and sent back to England in mid September.

Jedburgh teams from Algiers began jumping into southern France as early as 8 June. VEGANIN and QUININE jumped that night and AMMONIA the following night. Their missions were to prevent the 2nd SS Panzer Division (*Das Reich*) from leaving its garrison areas and reinforcing the Normandy beachhead. This became an uphill fight for the Jeds because "the vast bulk of the people were scared stiff to help . . ." The radio operator of VEGANIN was killed on the jump and the team was reinforced by DODGE. Some members of this combined team were later captured but those who remained shifted their emphasis and moved Maquis units to support the Allied invasion of Southern France (Operation Dragoon), which began on 15 August.

On 29 June, CHLOROFORM jumped in to the Drome area. Later that summer, CHLOROFORM led a Maquis unit on a mission to destroy a bridge across the Durance River. They completed this operation on 16 August. Seven more teams from Algiers were dropped in to southern France during the period 12-15 August to support the Dragoon invasion but several arrived too late to contribute anything of substance to the Allied landings.

In the northeast area of France, 11 Jed teams from London were sent in to support the 12th (U.S.) Army Group. JACOB, the first team dropped, jumped in on the night of 12 August but resupply drops were canceled because of German activity in the team's area. In just over a month after its insertion, two of the team's three members had been killed. AUBREY, dropped the same night as JACOB, had a mission to support an SOE circuit named Spiritualist. The team spent the next ten days or so teaching the Maquis members various sabotage techniques and took an active part in an ambush conducted on 25 August. Within a week of the ambush, AUBREY had also returned to London. The Jeds in team AUGUSTUS were killed on their first operation, caught with false identity papers, the team radio, and weapons. Most of the other teams dropped into the northeast of France complained in their after-action reports that they had also been sent in too late to be of any effective use.

During their training, the Jeds had been told they would remain operational until overrun by Allied units unless they were pulled out (or compromised) earlier. Over four months (June to September 1944), 276 Jeds jumped into occupied France, Belgium, and Holland, completing 99 missions. Some of the Jeds served on more than one team. Although most teams were composed of three men, there were two two-man teams, five four-man teams, and two five-man teams. Jeds worked in southern France following the invasion there by Patch's Seventh Army, organizing partisans and performing missions similar to those in western and central France. During September, six teams (DUDLEY, EDWARD, DANIEL II, CLAUDE, CLARENCE, and STANLEY II) were dropped into Holland prior to Operation Market-Garden, the operation designed to lay an airborne carpet, capturing bridges for an armor force to cross the Rhine at Arnhem. Their mission was to coordinate support of the Dutch underground for the paratroopers and armor units in Market-Garden.

As the Jedburgh teams were withdrawn, the Americans were sent on other missions, some of them for OSS. Many of them went to China to work with OSS in the Far East. These other missions were *not* Jedburgh missions, despite being labeled as such by several histories. Following the last team extraction, the Jedburgh Project was shut down.

The Jedburghs are the only example in this book of a multi-country organization that was used for special operations. Others from World War II that come to mind include the First Special Service Force, made up of U.S. and Canadian soldiers; the Special Air Service Brigade, which had units of French (3rd and 4th regiments) and Belgian (5th regiment) soldiers; and SAARF, the Special Allied Airborne Reconnaissance Force, a U.S.-British-French-Belgian-Polish organization that was deployed near German prisoner of war camps to make early contact with both captors and prisoners in order to prevent possible problems surrounding the end of the war operations. In addition, the discussion of the SAS jeep raid at Sidi Haneish refers to Stirling's early inclusion of French paratroopers in the original SAS organization, although they were not used on that operation. After reviewing the process to get the Jedburghs approved, it is understandable why there weren't more such multi-national units.

After World War II, President Truman dissolved the OSS, thus creating a vacuum in the area of guerrilla or partisan warfare expertise in the military. An examination of American special operations history shows that this was perfectly in character—we seem to create special units only *when we need them* instead of planning ahead.

Three men who would have an impact on the later development and use of special operations forces served on Jedburgh teams. They were: William E. Colby of Team BRUCE, later leader of the Norwegian Special Operations Group or NORSO, and, much later, Director of the Central Intelligence Agency, the successor of OSS; John K. Singlaub of Team JAMES, later involved in special operations during the Korean War as part of the CIA, and, much later, commander of MACV-SOG during the Viet Nam War; and Aaron Bank of Team PACKARD, later the organizer and first commander of 10th Special Forces Group (Airborne), the U.S. Army's first special forces unit.

Mission Critique

What did the Jeds accomplish? Opinions are mixed and it often depends on the position of whoever expresses it. Eisenhower said that the worth of the French Resistance in the fighting following D-Day was equivalent to 12 divisions. Since there were other groups working with the various Resistance units besides the Jeds, this 12 division credit does not belong to the Jeds alone. In their after-action reports, the Jeds were critical of the radio equipment they used because they broke easily on jumps. Team after-action reports reveal two other criticisms: earlier insertion was needed and the team's effectiveness would have been greater if they had been dropped deeper behind enemy lines. As it was, some of the teams were overrun by friendly units before they could be really effective. Another area of criticism involves the Special Forces Detachments, from SOE and SO/OSS resources, attached to each army headquarters. These detachments served as liaison for SFHQ and their respective army headquarters with the Jed teams in the field. The Jeds and SF Dets were not in direct communication, however. All messages, each way, had to go through SFHQ in London. Both the Jeds and SF Det personnel said in their respective after-action reports that this was cumbersome and made the Jeds less responsive in support of the armies headed their way. Maybe, as one writer has said, the Jedburgh Project was just years ahead of its time.

Maybe—but there were still problems to fix. As always, communications caused many *coordination* problems, some that could have been fixed in a way that the supported units would have wanted but were not. Communications were also convoluted because the units that really should have talked with one another, the Jed teams and the SF dets, did not; this same problem also existed between the Jed teams in the field and the advancing units that they were supposed to support. This direct communications would have provided better *intelligence* and operational data to the supported units. *Intelligence* was a mixed affair as applied to target areas where Jed teams were sent; sometimes the German *intelligence* of the presence of Jed teams was better than what SFHQ had of the area before any team was sent in. This is always a hazard in special operations as it is for *any* military operation. The other Vanden-broucke criteria don't apply to the Jedburghs.

Of the McRaven criteria, the ones that seem to apply here are *simplicity* and *security*. *Simplicity* applies to the target intelligence, mentioned above. *Security* has some bearing on this, because some of the Jed teams had reception teams they didn't expect. This had more to do with poor security on the receiving end than in the dispatch area, again a problem common but not peculiar to special operations.

All things considered, the Jeds were an excellent idea executed with great care, skill, and good results. Aaron Bank was so impressed with the idea and the team training that he used them as the basis for the 10th Group at Fort Bragg and, eventually, all of U.S. Army Special Forces units. The SAS emulated the Jedburgh idea in France and Italy. Later, during the Korean War, the basic Jedburgh idea was used in the formation of the United Nations Partisan Forces Korea units. It was a good idea that just needed a little fixing.

SOURCES

Books, papers, and official documents:
"Basic Directive on Jedburghs, Prepared Jointly by SOE/SO"; dated 20 December 1943

Crawford, Steve; *The SAS Encyclopedia*; Miami, FL; Lewis International; 1998

Dear, Ian; *Subservion & Sabotage—Tales From the Files of the SOE and OSS*; London; Arms and Armour Press; 1996

Gutjahr, Robert G.; *The Role of Jedburgh Teams in Operation Market Garden;* Master's Thesis for U.S. Army Command and General Staff College; Fort Leavenworth, KS; 1990

Hogan, David W., Jr.; *U.S. Army Special Operations in World War II;* Washington; Center of Military History; 1992

Irwin, Wyman W.; *A Special Force: Origin and Development of the Jedburgh Project in Support of Operation Overlord;* Master's Thesis for U.S. Army Command and General Staff College; Fort Leavenworth; 1991

Lewis, S.J.; *Jedburgh Team Operations in Support of the 12th Army Group, August 1944;* Fort Leavenworth; Combat Studies Institute; 1990

Mendelsohn, John (editor); *OSS Jedburgh Teams, Volumes I and II;* New York; Garland Publishing; 1989

Rosner, Elliot J.; *THE JEDBURGHS: Combat Operations Conducted in the Finistere Region of Brittany, France from July–September 1944;* Master's Thesis for U.S. Army Command and General Staff College; Fort Leavenworth; 1990

Articles:

Bruske, Ed; "The Spirit of the Jeds"; in *Washington Post*; 14 May 1988; Style Section, pages C1-C2

Hughes, Les; "The Special Force Wing"; in *Trading Post*; July–September 1988, pages 4–15

————; "The Special Allied Airborne Reconnaissance Force"; in *Trading Post*; July–September 1991, pages 7–20

CHAPTER SEVENTEEN

BATTLE AT MERVILLE BATTERY

M any stories of bravery and intrepidity have been told about the air- borne invasion supporting D-Day, 6 June 1944—and for good reason. It has been said that much of the task of the paratroopers in the pre-invasion darkness was in the nature of a roving commission. In fulfilling this, the sky soldiers were performing the classic duties of airborne troops: to harass the enemy, disrupt his communications, and create a condition of alarm and de- spondency in those areas behind his forward troops. One of the finest exam- ples of this is found in the battle for Merville Battery.

The Merville Battery was a strongpoint containing what was thought to be four 150mm guns. Based on overhead photography, Allied intelligence determined that these guns were sighted to enfilade the beaches which the British 3rd Infantry Division would storm at 0600. The battery was some 400 meters square, surrounded on the outer perimeter by barbed wire fencing. Inside this was a 100-meter deep minefield and an inner perimeter of con- certina wire 15 feet deep and 5 feet high. The battery was believed to be manned by between 180 and 200 men.

The task of taking the Merville Battery was given to Lieutenant Colonel Terence B.H. Otway and his 9th Battalion, 3rd Parachute Brigade, 6th British Airborne Division. The guns had to be taken by ground troops be- cause they were completely encased in concrete emplacements that were covered by over ten feet of earth. This protection made them virtually im- pregnable to air bombardment. Lieutenant Colonel Otway went to great lengths to prepare his unit. He requisitioned an area similar to Merville near Newbury and had a duplicate of the battery constructed. His 635-man bat- talion then spent two months rehearsing. The rehearsals included five day- time and four nighttime live fire run-throughs. After five more days of thorough briefings, each man in the battalion was required to prepare a sketch of the plan. Finally, Otway considered that his men were ready.

As any paratrooper fully knows, plans are one thing and execution is another. Instead of being dropped into an area one by one-half mile, the 9th Battalion was scattered over a 50 *square mile* area, a common occurrence for all of the paratroopers jumping that night. The official after-action report best describes what happened next: "By 0250 hours the battalion had grown to 150 strong with twenty lengths of Bangalore Torpedo. Each company was approximately 30 strong . . . no three inch mortars—one machine-gun—one-half of one sniping party—no six-pounder guns—no jeeps or trailers or any glider stores—no sappers—no field ambulance but six medical orderlies—no mine detectors—one company commander missing . . ." Crouching in the dark and seeing his time run out, Otway decided he could wait no longer and ordered his unit to its mission.

Just before 0430, as they reached the outer perimeter of the battery, Otway's party met up with the only portion of the battalion that had been dropped correctly, the battery recon party. In a small, cramped area members of the recon party briefed their commander. This small unit had wasted no time. They reported that a raid by 100 Lancaster heavy bombers dropping 4,000- and 8,000-pound bombs designed to soften the objective had completely missed the target. Despite having no equipment or tape to mark the lanes through the minefield, the recon party had penetrated the entire battery area to the inner perimeter. They had spent over half-an-hour next to the concertina spotting the German locations by listening to their talking and other noises inside the perimeter. Although German sentries walked within *two feet* of where they lay, no member of the recon party was detected.

After this briefing, Otway began to move his unit toward the battery. At that moment, two things happened almost at once. Six German machine-guns opened up on the approaching paratroopers and two of the three gliders which were to land atop the battery appeared overhead. The one British machine-gun with the assault force quickly silenced three of the German machine-guns. A diversion party of seven men took out the other machine-guns as they made their way to the main gate of the battery. One of the gliders, lost in the fog, overshot the area by more than three miles. The second glider landed 200 meters from Merville Battery. As the crew emerged from the crashed glider they encountered a German relief force bound for the battery. They immediately brought the relief force under fire and stopped it.

Meanwhile, the main assault force blew two paths through the inner perimeter with Bangalore Torpedoes. Otway and his men ran screaming and shooting into the battery. Bomb craters, wire, and mines slowed their progress, but nothing could stop them. Within a few minutes they had reached the guns and engaged the Germans in hand-to-hand combat. The German resistance was stiff until one of the defenders caught sight of the badge on the jacket of the paratroopers. His shouted cry of "*Fallschirmjaeger!*" ["Paratroopers!"] caused his comrades to lose heart and they quickly surrendered. The main battery guns, discovered to be only 75mm, were quickly spiked.

Just before 0500, Otway sent the signal that the battery had been taken. The back-up plan had been for one of the battleships at sea to fire on the battery if Otway's paratroopers had not eliminated it by 0530. British casualties in the assault on the battery were 68 killed or wounded. Otway's battalion had taken its objective with less than one-quarter of the force intended to accomplish the mission and had captured the battery just in the nick of time.

The battle at the Merville Battery would eventually take its place among the finest actions ever undertaken against a specific objective.

Mission Critique

Of the single missions discussed in this book, there are only a handful that seem to deserve special mention. This does not imply that all went well on the operation but that, once in place for the mission to begin, the men involved carried out their operation as nearly perfectly as possible. The principal reason for the high regard for the Merville Battery operation is because Otway and his men were able to bring it off with less than 25% of the original force. This operation's execution demonstrates the value of teamwork and cross-training for a mission, a condition that is so absolutely essential in special operations that these two qualities are among the hallmarks of what special operations forces are.

Otway's problems were both compounded and assisted by a situation that plagued most of the airborne operations in support of the D-Day invasion—dispersal. The wide dispersal of the paratroopers was caused by the troop carriers either missing the drop zones completely or avoiding antiaircraft fire and then dropping their troops.

Accounts of the action at Merville Battery all show that the Germans never really understood the strategic potential or importance that the Allies placed on the battery. This was probably because the prevailing German expectation was for an invasion at Calais rather than at Normandy.

There is almost no criticism, Vandenbroucke or McRaven, for this operation except *coordination*. In this particular operation the airborne troops were widely scattered (more widely than planned) by the air carriers. The D-Day jumps were probably the culmination of this problem during World War II. This should have been an easier task than it was in the various events leading up to and including D-Day. What was missing was command emphasis at high levels. The jumps after D-Day got better in terms of putting the paratroopers on the correct drop zone. In the case of D-Day, the dispersion of paratroopers turned out to be a blessing in disguise because it confused the Germans even more about the strength of the invading paratroopers, leading to the problem of where to send sufficient opposing forces to fight them. This, however, is a victory for the paratroopers and not a left-handed compliment to the air carriers, because this result was purely serendipitous.

SOURCES

By Air to Battle—The Official Account of the British Airborne Divisions; London; His Majesty's Stationery Office; 1945

Crookenden, Napier; *Dropzone Normandy*; New York; Charles Scribner's Sons; 1976

Gale, Richard N.; *With the 6th Airborne Division in Normandy;* London; Sampson, Low, Marston; 1948

Galvin, John R.; *Air Assault—The Development of Airmobile Warfare;* New York; Hawthorn Books; 1969

Gregory, Barry; *British Airborne Troops;* New York; Doubleday; 1974

MacDonald, Charles; *Airborne;* New York; Ballantine Books; 1970

Norton, G.G.; *The Red Devils—The Story of the British Airborne Forces*; Harrisburg, PA; Stackpole Books; 1971

Ryan, Cornelius; *The Longest Day—June 6, 1944;* New York; Simon and Schuster; 1959

Saunders, Hilary St. G.; *The Red Beret—The Story of the Parachute Regiment 1940–1945;* London; Michael Joseph; 1950

Tugwell, Maurice; *Airborne to Battle—A History of Airborne Warfare 1918–1971;* London; William Kimber; 1971

CHAPTER EIGHTEEN

OSS Operations Groups

Perhaps the idea for ethnic units to train partisan units started with the Army's attempts to create special "ethnic" infantry battalions. At least two such battalions *were* created, the 99th and the 122nd. The 99th was composed of Norwegians while the 122nd was known as the "Greek Battalion." By June 1943, the Army had given up on most of its ethnic units and had turned over control of the 122nd to the OSS. The Special Operations branch of OSS had recently formed a new section, designated Operations Groups, and it was to this section that control of the 122nd was passed. The OSS Operations Groups form part of the historical mosaic that led to the later formation of Army Special Forces and upon which much of the operational doctrine of today's Special Forces is based.

From its beginning, OSS had been developing plans to energize partisan forces throughout German-occupied Europe. By early 1943 these plans were ready to be put into action. Brigadier General William J. "Wild Bill" Donovan, Director of OSS, believed that commando-type operational groups could best fulfill that part of his mission to supply men to the military who were "trained to carry out sabotage operations and guerrilla warfare in enemy-occupied territory." The plan for these operations groups, or OGs as they were soon called, was to form units composed of parachute and language qualified military specialists to jump into behind-the-lines areas, make contact with partisan groups, train the partisans in guerrilla techniques, and then work with the trained partisan units to execute ambushes, large-scale raids, and sabotage operations. Because they were on strictly military missions, the men of the OGs were to wear their uniforms at all times.

The OGs were originally authorized by a specific directive of the Joint Chiefs of Staff on 23 December 1942. This directive told OSS to organize teams that would serve as the nucleus for training indigenous forces in enemy and enemy-occupied territory.

OG Branch, which would control the field groups, was established on 13 May 1943 within OSS headquarters. Field forces subordinate to the branch were to number about 540 soldiers. Branch personnel began work by refining an already active OSS recruiting program. This program assumed that all those soldiers in each OG would already have had basic combat training and specialty training, and that the operational training would build on this base. Line units, therefore, were the logical pool from which to recruit. Four branches were targeted: Infantry, Engineer, Signal, and Medical. Physical capability and language ability were the initial requirements each recruit had to meet. They also had to volunteer for hazardous duty behind enemy lines.

Recruiters from OG Branch began their wide-spread manhunt in the spring of 1943, some of it before the branch was formally established. They fanned out to the bases that were training men in the needed specialties. Additionally, the recruiters went to three bases that were homes to some specialties they considered essential—Fort Bragg for parachutists, and camps Carson and Hale for military skiers. Sometimes the recruiters were approached by soldiers who were anxious to join them but whose unit had not been visited by the recruiters. Personal interviews explored each candidate's abilities and motivation. The interviews were carefully configured to maintain basic operations security by not telling candidates any specific details of potential missions. About 10% of those interviewed were considered suitable and selected for training.

At Camp Carson, so many men from the 122nd Infantry Battalion volunteered for the OGs that the battalion commander offered the entire unit. Such a move was entirely unprecedented and required the eventual approval of the War Department before OSS could act on the offer. In the end, 17 officers and 205 enlisted men were picked by the recruiters for training. Only 32 of those chosen failed to complete the operational selection training. In a similar action, 10 officers and 69 enlisted men from the 99th Infantry Battalion, stationed at Camp Hale, volunteered and were transferred to OSS. All of them completed the rigorous five-month training process.

Organization of field units and training were the next steps in the formation of the various OGs for deployment overseas. The pattern of organization was to recruit for specific target countries. Thus, initial recruiting was for units destined for Italy and France, then Norway, Yugoslavia, and finally, Greece. OSS decided that the basic size of an OG would be 4 officers and

30 enlisted men. Each group was to be commanded by a captain with a first lieutenant as executive officer. This organizational structure was flexible enough to split into two sections and each section could split into two squads. In actual experience, OGs varied from 3-man liaison teams (one officer, and two enlisted men, one of whom was a radio operator) to some units larger than the projected 34-man group. In France, captains were in command of sections, which were the basic OG unit. At least one French OG, UNION II, was composed almost entirely of U.S. Marines and led by a Marine Corps legend, Peter Ortiz. However, the OGs were usually Army units.

In April 1943, the recruiting teams sent their first volunteers to training. The group was 19 officers and about 181 enlisted men, to be used in Italy. In July and August, the first group destined for France, 13 officers and 83 enlisted men, went through training. The first OG to be used in Yugoslavia completed its training by late October 1943; others finished in late January 1944. The Yugoslavia OG totaled 15 officers and 110 enlisted men. During the winter of 1943–44, six more OGs (two for Italy and four headed to France) were formed. A German OG was formed in the spring of 1944 and arrived in North Africa by July.

OSS training was generally conducted at several sites, northern Virginia and the mountains of Maryland in particular; some training was conducted overseas. Volunteers for the OGs were not the only group receiving training at these sites. Others included those going to Jedburgh teams, those who were to be "case officers" or "agent handlers," and even those destined for either analytical or psychological operations positions on various OSS staffs. As was true for many of the special operations units put together during World War II, OGs received training that both capitalized on the basic combat and specialty training the volunteers already had, but also kept an eye on skills they would need once they went operational.

Much of the OSS training covered ground similar to that of other special operations units. First and foremost, it included very healthy doses of physical training. Not the least of the training, however, included many hours on such diverse subjects as: demolitions; American and foreign small arms; scouting; patrolling; field medicine; compass and map reading; hand-to-hand combat (including use of knives and improvised weapons); camouflage techniques; security in the field; living off the land; raiding; and methods and equipment of insertion and extraction. Among these insertion/extraction methods were mountain and ski training, parachuting, and amphibious operations.

Other operational techniques included radio and continuous wave communications, and fire support coordination. One OSS document noted, "Aggressiveness of spirit and willingness to close with the enemy was [sic] stressed." The same document noted, probably unnecessarily, that, "A large percentage of the tactical exercises were coordinated at night."

Based on the OG's mission, emphasis in the training was two-fold. First, the candidate must be able to absorb the training. Second, and equally important, the candidate must be able to use the training to teach it to others. One was no good without the other, at least as far as the OGs were concerned.

Every attempt was made to train as units those who would be deploying to the same place. As time passed, the training contingents were formed as companies, based on destination. In this manner, A Company consisted of OGs bound for Italy and the German OG, B Company of those headed for France, and C Company of those headed for the Balkans. A separate OG to be sent to Norway was not given a letter designation but was simply referred to as NORSO, an obvious acronym of Norwegian Special Operations Group. In the early summer of 1943, the Greek government requested that OSS send an OG to Greece. It was as a result of this request that the 122nd was turned over to the control of OSS. There was a Polish OG that was based in Warnham, England along with some French and the Norwegian OGs. These groups in England were directly subordinate to Special Forces Headquarters (referred to as SFHQ), an arm of OSS' Special Operations Branch in London. Except for its location, no other mention of the Polish OG has so far been found in OSS records.

Focusing on the operations of two specific groups will best illustrate the larger picture of OG operations during the war. These two groups are the Italian OG and NORSO.

Soon after the liberation of Corsica in October 1943, the Italian OG established a base area at Ile Rousse. This base was used to provide further unit training and as a staging area for missions. The initial operations of this OG consisted of establishing observation posts on islands astride German ship lanes. Ship movement and plane spotting reports were sent back to OSS regional headquarters on Corsica. Small scale reconnaissance and raiding missions were carried out on other Mediterranean islands as well as against several coast installations on the Italian mainland. The area around Spezia was the target of an amphibious raid by an OG section in late March 1944. The section was discovered by the Germans and, following several hours of very hostile interrogations, shot, even though its members were in uniform and therefore legitimate prisoners of war.

At the end of June 1944, the Italian OG moved to the mainland of Italy. From then until the end of the war, this OG worked principally with the various partisan elements in northern Italy, a responsibility shared with other OSS elements as well as with various British organizations, including SOE and the SAS. The OG sent sections in to contact partisan units, trained and supplied these units, and then led them on missions, usually reconnaissance or sabotage missions. The Italian OG was used occasionally to attempt rescues of downed aircrews, a mission that met with limited success.

In April 1945, as the war was nearing its end, Italian OG sections, working with their partisan groups, concentrated on two types of operations: moving aggressively to cut enemy escape routes out of Italy and conducting counter-scorch operations. The latter type of operation attempted to seek out and stop German attempts to scorch the Italian countryside as they were retreating. A particularly successful counter-scorch mission was carried out near Genoa that prevented the demolition of the city's road network and resulted in 3,000 German POWs. The official OSS history cites "the most spectacular counter-scorch operation" as preventing the virtual destruction of Venice and its harbor.

SFHQ in London controlled virtually all intelligence and special operations in Scandinavia. SFHQ had promised the Norwegian government, for almost a year, that an OG would be formed and deployed. Plans as early as July 1944 called for selective sabotage in Norway.

What was lacking was authorization to execute the plans. The authorization had been withheld in an attempt to avoid German reprisals against the civilian population, particularly since the success of recent SOE operations conducted in Norway that were targeted against the German heavy water production facility in the Telemark region. When the Allied offensive in the west ground to a halt in December 1944 because of the German counter-thrust at the Bulge, SFHQ received a request to prevent or retard the movement of German forces in Norway from reinforcing German units engaged at the Bulge.

Late 1944, coincidentally, marked the end of OSS authorization to recruit candidates from the 99th Infantry Battalion. The unit had taken a high number of casualties in France and was eventually absorbed by the recently activated 474th Infantry Regiment. The 474th also included the Americans in the First Special Service Force and the survivors of Darby's three Ranger battalions. Recruiting to fill out NORSO was authorized and suggestions pointed to using former Jedburgh team members. Major William E. Colby,

from Jedburgh Team BRUCE, was selected to lead NORSO. After his selection, Colby was asked, almost as an afterthought, "By the way, can you
ski?"

Colby moved his OG to Blairgowrie, Scotland where he initiated a training schedule that emphasized skiing and various field problems. He also continued to recruit soldiers for his OG. In January 1945, following intense
negotiations between the U.S. and China, OSS was authorized to train 20
Chinese commando units, using the OG concept as its basis. NORSO was
asked for volunteers and 29 members stepped forward. Despite this draw-
down in his unit's strength, Colby continued to plan. NORSO would deploy
in two groups: the advance party, consisting of Colby and 11 soldiers, including a radio operator, would jump in during January and establish a base camp;
the main party of 24 men would jump in during February. This plan was
modified and delayed several times, the last time on the night when NORSO
was to be dispatched. On 24 March, only four of the planned nine aircraft
showed up to take Colby and his men to Norway. A last minute scramble
juggled men and equipment onto the four planes. The drop zone was the
frozen Lake Jaevsjo, cushioned by a layer of snow. Five Norwegian skiers were
the reception committee. Only 16 members of the team were able to jump.
Their equipment was scattered over a wide area. Five other team members
were dropped in Sweden.

Despite all the planning, Colby and his men were isolated. There were
about 4,000 Germans within a 25-mile radius of their base camp and, based
on intelligence reports, the Germans were aware that NORSO was in the
vicinity. Resupply missions for NORSO were canceled several times, mostly
due to bad weather.

Colby began planning an attack on a railroad bridge. After considering
several targets, he settled on a bridge near Tangen, since most of the other
targets he considered were heavily guarded. On 13 April, NORSO and six
others, including four from an SOE mission in the area, set out for their target. Colby had hoped to blow the bridge as a German troop train was crossing
it but had to settle for just taking out the bridge. NORSO team members
left U.S. flag shoulder patches behind, hoping the Germans would not take
reprisals against local civilians. By 18 April, everyone on the mission had
made it back successfully to the base camp, after avoiding several German
ski patrols that had been looking for them. The five men who had jumped
into Sweden joined the team this same day.

Planning began in earnest for the rest of NORSO to join Colby and his men. On 25 April, NORSO attacked and destroyed two and one-half kilometers of railroad track near Skartnes. When they returned, some of the men were sent to find an overdue resupply plane. After some searching, they found the plane's crash site. There were no survivors. The NORSO team conducted a short burial service and took pictures of the site for the families of the aircrew.

NORSO did not conduct any further missions. Colby and his men eventually accepted the surrender of a German unit. On 20 May, the rest of NORSO arrived from Scotland to assist in various garrison duties and in late June the entire group sailed for home on a British aircraft carrier.

The Norwegian OG was one of several that had supplied men for the OSS mission to China. Various OG and Jedburgh teams had members sent to the Far East but their missions there did not fall under the mantle of their previous organizational names. The OG concept, using language-qualified American soldiers in uniform to conduct military training for partisan forces, was revised in the early 1950s when the Army created the first Special Forces Group, the 10th, at Fort Bragg.

A brief clarification needs to be made concerning organization and insignia of the OGs. In August 1944, all of the OG companies, groups, and contingents in the Mediterranean Theater of Operations were placed under the operational command of the 2671st Special Reconnaissance Battalion, Separate (Provisional), with its headquarters in Caserta, Italy. In some documents, the 2671st's designation is given as (Provisional) (Separate). By the time the 2671st was activated, the unit strength was over 1,100.

There is some minor confusion about OG composition because there existed in Italy at this same time a D Company, under the OSS' 2677th Regiment. Its mission, however, was not as an OG and it was not connected to the 2671st. There were also OSS teams assigned to various Corps or Army headquarters but, once again, these were not part of the Ops Groups; generally, these teams reported back to OSS headquarters in London or to SFHQ.

Many of the OGs wore a red-on-black shoulder tab or arc with the wording "SPECIAL RECON. BN." on the top of their left shoulder sleeve. As is typical with many special units of World War II, this insignia was never officially approved by the Army, though it appears that OSS may have ordered the insignia to be made anyway. Another insignia, the Special Force or SF wing, was worn by OGs stationed in England, though it was originally designed to be worn by members of the Jedburgh teams. Those OGs subordinate to the 2671st appear not to have worn the SF wing. Later in the war, when B and C Companies were sent to the China-Burma-India theater, they continued to wear the "SPECIAL RECON. BN." tab.

Mission Critique

With the OSS Ops Groups, we conclude the organizational study of units that were the basis for the formation of the U.S. Army Special Forces (there is one operational background that will be discussed in the Triple Nickel chapter that is still to come). There are some aspects not covered in this book but were alluded to, such as the Alamo Scouts' work with guerrilla units. Even that had its basis in the work of many of the Americans who stayed behind in the Philippines and organized and led many of these same guerrilla units. Additionally, the Jeds did many of the same things the Alamo Scouts and the American stay-behinds did. At this point in time, it is easy to see where and how the Army Special Forces developed its roots.

The ultimate accomplishment of the OGs was when NORSO accepted the surrender of a German unit, and it did so because it was there, behind the lines where the Germans were. One of the things that caused so many other special operations forces problems, but did not seem to be a problem for the OGs, was communications. One possible explanation is that the OGs were not deployed as far from friendly lines as other units were. Whatever the reason, good communications definitely worked in the OG's favor.

As with the Jeds, only a sampling of the different OGs is used in this chapter to give the flavor of the OG experience in World War II. One of the keys to success for the OGs was to require that soldiers in the various groups be language-qualified. For many of those recruited the language was, in fact, their native tongue. This characteristic is still alive in Special Forces units of today.

The question still remains, "Was it worth it to raise and deploy the various Ops Groups?" The answer is yes and further, it was one of the better efforts made by OSS. There is little to criticize about the OGs. While the original idea seemed to some to be *wishful thinking*, later operations showed this not to be so. As with any mid- to large-size special operations force, *speed* and *surprise* were lost but not enough to cause major disruptions of any particular OG. *Repetition* didn't play a part in the operations but did come into play in training, and later operations showed the benefits of this training.

One of the things not mentioned in source material was the results of lessons learned from previous operations applied to later missions. Because this is so inbred in U.S. Army doctrine, it was likely taken for granted, though it is certain that it did happen. It would have been helpful to see where and when these "lessons learned" were applied.

SOURCES

Books:

Bergen, Howard R.; *History of 99th Infantry Battalion—U.S. Army;* Oslo, Norway; Emil Moestue A-S; 1945

Brown, Anthony C. (editor); *The Secret War Report of the OSS*; New York; Berkley Publishing; 1976

Ford, Kirk, Jr.; *OSS and the Yugoslav Resistance;* Westport, CT; Praeger; 1992

Giannaris, John with McKinely C. Olson; *Yannis;* Tarrytown, NY; Pilgrimage Publishing; 1988

Haney, Ken; *U.S. Marine Corps Paratroopers, 1940–1945;* Jackson, TN; privately published; 1990

Heimark, Bruce H.; *The OSS Norwegian Special Operations Group in World War II;* Westport, CT; Praeger; 1994

Mattingly, Robert E.; *Herringbone Cloak—G.I. Dagger: Marines of the OSS*; Quantico, VA; Marine Corps Command and Staff College; 1979

Smith, Bradley F.; *The Shadow Warriors—O.S.S. and the Origins of the C.I.A.;* New York; Basic Books; 1983

Smith, R. Harris; *OSS—The Secret History of America's First Central Intelligence Agency;* Berkeley; University of California Press; 1972

War Report of the OSS, Volume 2—The Overseas Targets; New York; Walker Publishing; 1976

Articles:

Hughes, Les; "Insignia of the OSS"; in *The Trading Post;* April–June 1993; pages 2–19

——————; "The Special Force Wing"; in *The Trading Post;* July–September 1988; pages 4–15

CHAPTER NINETEEN

RAID ON LOS BANOS

When the 82nd Airborne Division was alerted to jump into Zaire in the spring of 1978 on a rescue mission to secure the safety of Americans trapped by the Cuban-led terrorists there, few troopers realized that they were filling a role initiated by paratroopers a generation before by one of the units of the Sixth Army fighting in the Philippines, the 11th Airborne Division.

The 11th, commanded by Major General Joseph M. Swing, was the only U.S. airborne division to serve in the Pacific theater during World War II. The only other U.S. airborne unit in the Pacific area was the 503rd Parachute Infantry Regiment. The 11th was initially composed of two glider regiments (the 187th and 188th) and one parachute regiment (the 511th). Before and after deployment from the States, jump training was given to as many of the members of the glider regiments as possible. This was done to make the 11th more flexible in its capabilities.

Prior to the Los Banos operation, the 11th Airborne had been alerted for several jump missions. Just as with the airborne divisions in Europe, most of these operations had been canceled. Two were not. The first came during the fighting on Leyte. A Battery, 457th Parachute Field Artillery Battalion jumped onto the area near Manarawat on 4 December 1944 to provide close-in support to units in the area. This site was a table-top plateau chosen as the most suitable area for a base after a thorough area search by the Division Reconnaissance Platoon, which had spent about ten days behind the lines scouting several areas. The next day, B Company, 1st Battalion, 187th and a platoon of C Company, 127th Engineer Battalion jumped onto the same site. The infantry was to secure the artillery position while the engineers were to clear a plateau to facilitate landings by L-4 aircraft.

The second combat jump occurred on Luzon, on 3 February 1945. The 511th jumped onto Tagaytay Ridge to reinforce the other two regiments of the 11th in their attacks against Japanese positions. This ridge was also selected after scouting by the Recon Platoon.

On 6 December 1944, in an action that occurred only twice during World War II, paratroopers jumped onto an area held by enemy airborne units. In the first incident, British paratroopers of the 1st Para Brigade, during the invasion of Sicily in July 1943, jumped onto a drop zone near the Primasole Bridge in order to secure the bridge. The British did not know until after they jumped that the bridge was held by units from the 3rd *Fallschirmjaeger* Regiment, which had jumped there earlier. In the 1944 action, 750 Japanese paratroopers from the Katori Shimoei Force jumped onto San Pablo airfield on Leyte; an airfield being held by paratroopers of the 187th Glider Infantry Regiment.

On 3 February 1945, the 11th Airborne Division was alerted to prepare plans for a raid to release more than 2,100 Allied prisoners being held at Los Banos, a Japanese POW camp about 50 miles south and east of Manila. But the rapid advance of U.S. forces on Luzon raised other fears. The recent success of the raid on the Cabanatuan POW camp, only the week before, hatched fears that the Japanese would kill their prisoners rather than allow the Allies to rescue them. Lieutenant General Oscar Griswold, commander of XIV Corps, kept a close watch on the planning. In order to affect the complete rescue of the internees, it would be necessary to move them quickly through almost 30 miles of enemy held territory. The fact that the shores of Laguna de Bay ran close to the prison compound simplified planning for this phase.

The plan of attack developed by the 11th Airborne Division headquarters consisted of five phases:

1) Infiltration of the Division Reconnaissance Platoon reinforced by Filipino guerrillas across Laguna de Bay to mark the beaches and drop zone, to act as guides for the attack forces, and to silently destroy as many sentries as possible.

2) Destruction of the Japanese garrison at the prison by forces parachuted near the camp.

3) Establishment of a beachhead at Laguna de Bay for the evacuation of the internees using amphibious vehicles.

4) Launching an attack at a distance from the camp to create a diversion

that would tie down Japanese troops in the area and prevent reinforcement of the prison staff.

5) Preparation of a reception area for housing and hospitalizing the remaining internees.

The division G-2 staff began preparing a map of the target area based
on interrogation reports, aerial photographs, and two scouting patrols by the
Recon Platoon. On 18 February a guerrilla unit brought in three engineers
(Peter Miles, Ben Edwards, and Fred Zervoulakis) who had recently escaped
from Los Banos. Miles reviewed the division's intelligence information and
provided an update. He also reviewed the area map, made corrections, and
added details. His debriefing provided current details as to the number, location, and condition of the camp internees. A Recon Platoon patrol that
night confirmed Miles' information. Thirty-six hours before the operation,
the troopers who were to execute it were withdrawn from action and, under
the cover of darkness, moved to staging areas. Here they received detailed
briefings on the operations plan.

On 22 February commanders of the major units involved in the raid conducted their pre-operation reconnaissance. That evening the 1st Battalion,
511th Parachute Infantry Regiment and the amphibious vehicles they would
ride on the following morning moved to the vicinity of Mamatid on the western shore of Laguna de Bay. A near-by beach would be their launch point. A
report detailing heavy truck traffic at the Los Banos camp came to the division headquarters late that night; after some consideration, the staff decided
to ignore the report.

The Division Reconnaissance Platoon, composed of one officer and 22
men, and an 80-man guerrilla detachment, were given three missions in the
plan: infiltrate the camp area and mark the drop zone at the appropriate time;
mark the landing beach for the amphibious force; and, at H-Hour, attack
and kill the camp sentries, silently if possible. On the night of the 21st, the
recon force crossed Laguna de Bay in small boats and landed about five miles
east of the POW camp. One part of this force was becalmed during the trip
and didn't arrive until late the following day. Those who did make it hid during the day. On the evening of the 22nd, the recon force moved to its designated place, taking almost ten hours to cross flooded rice paddies on the way.
One of the members of the Recon force was Corporal Terry R. Santos, who
had graduated in Class Four from the Alamo Scouts Training Center.

The men of B Company of the 1/511th spent the night of the 22nd sleeping under the wings of their C-47 transports. At daybreak of the 23rd, they donned their parachutes and equipment, and loaded onto the C-47s that would take them to their target. The amphibious force departed Mamatid beach early in the morning, heading for Los Banos. Just before H-Hour, members of the Recon Platoon prepared columns of smoke to mark the drop zone and the beach landing sites.

The pilots of the approaching C-47s corrected their flight paths based on the smoke columns and began their jump run onto the drop zone, a small field surrounded on three sides by trees and on the fourth by railroad tracks. A high tension wire ran across the field.

At exactly 0700, the green light went on inside the first of nine C-47s approaching the prison camp. Lieutenant John M. Ringler, B Company commander, led his unit into the swirling prop blast. The opening of Ringler's parachute 450 feet over the drop zone signaled the opening of the attack. The sky immediately overhead the drop zone was filled with parachutes. Every member of B Company landed on the small drop zone, without injury, and headed for the camp. Also at 0700, the remainder of the 1/511th stormed from amphibious vehicles onto the beach near the prison camp and the recon elements began destroying strategic machine gun points inside the compound.

Acting with near-perfect coordination, the three elements overwhelmed the Japanese garrison at the prison compound, killing all 247 defenders. They set fire to all of the buildings that housed Japanese troops and alerted the internees to prepare to leave the camp. Only one prisoner suffered a slight wound, while two of the rescue force were killed and four were wounded. All of the rescue force casualties were members of Corporal Santos' party from the Recon Platoon. The internees were quickly rounded up, accounted for, and moved to the beach area for evacuation. At this point the entire operation had taken just under 40 minutes.

The internees were loaded onto the amphibious vehicles which departed for a return trip to Mamatid beach. It took two trips to evacuate all of the internees plus the entire attacking force, including the Recon Platoon and B Company. At Mamatid, the freed prisoners were quickly loaded onto trucks and taken to a site where a hot meal, beds, cigarettes, and chocolate waited for them.

One of the stories told about the freed prisoners concerns a little old lady who dragged her heels when the paratroopers told her to pack her personal items and prepare to leave the camp. When she was questioned about why she was moving so slowly she told the paratroopers, "Night after night I've dreamed of this day, and in all my dreams of rescue, I was rescued by Marines. You're not Marines."

After the operation General MacArthur radioed General Swing, "An operation such as that performed today will gladden the hearts of soldiers throughout the world." The 11th Airborne Division had also earned its nickname from this operation. The religious internees of Los Banos referred to the descending paratroopers as "the Angels." This was eventually adopted as the official division name. The division song includes the lines:

> "Down from heaven comes Eleven
> And there's hell to pay below . . ."

Mission Critique

The 11th Airborne Division was the first U.S. unit to arrive in Japan, handpicked by General MacArthur to spearhead American occupation forces. In one form or another, airborne units from this division would remain in Japan for at least the next 10 years. Its operation at Los Banos was a well-run mission, one that included forces that were deployed by water, air, and land.

It is obvious that this mission was necessary and is another example of a small but very well executed mission, one totally appropriate for a special operations force. What makes this raid so interesting is the "tri-phibious" execution, demonstrating that the troopers of the 11th Airborne understood how to perform both conventional and special operations missions. It is possible that this operation *could* have been executed without a parachute element, infiltrating a ground force in with the reconnaissance unit, similar to how the Rangers and Alamo Scouts and Philippine guerrillas did at Cabanatuan. However, in this case, the planners determined that parachute insertion was a faster means of entering the battlefield.

Normally *coordination* among such widely separated forces, especially considering that they were scattered and had differing roles in such a tight time schedule, could have been a problem. In this case it was not. Each force played its part well, which led to an almost perfect execution of the operations plan. Although there were a number of different objectives, the *simplicity* of the plan is that it was broken into several component parts which were then distributed to the various units involved. This allowed each unit to concentrate on its part yet remain aware of what each other unit needed to do in case they needed assistance. Virtually every element in McRaven's formula for a good special operation is present and none of Vandenbroucke's negatives are. The appropriate level of force was used at each point in the execution, ensuring success.

SOURCES

Books:

Flanagan, Edward M., Jr.; *The Angels—A History of the 11th Airborne Division 1943–1946*; Washington; Infantry Journal Press; 1948

————; *The Los Banos Raid—The 11th Airborne Jumps at Dawn*; New York; Jove Books; 1986

Galvin, John R.; *Air Assault—The Development of Airmobile Warfare;* New York; Hawthorn Books; 1969

Smith, Robert R.; *United States Army in World War II—The War in the Pacific-Triumph in the Philippines;* Washington; Office of the Chief of Military History; 1963

Tugwell, Maurice; *Airborne to Battle—A History of Airborne Warfare 1918–1971;* London; William Kimber; 1971

Articles:

Foss, Peter J.; "'Angels' at Los Banos"; *Infantry*; unknown issue

Interviews and letters with:

Terry Santos (several letters and interviews between 1992 and 2001)

CHAPTER TWENTY

Operation Dracula

The Japanese Army was retreating in much of Southeast Asia. The battle of Imphal swayed back and forth across great stretches of the wild country of Burma. In Meiktila, north of Rangoon, a Japanese counterattack ground Lieutenant General William Slim's 14th Army to a halt. It was the last week of March 1945 and Rangoon had to be in Allied hands before the mid-May monsoons or the fighting would grind even slower. Slim depended very heavily on air resupply from planes based in India, planes that would be grounded in the monsoon.

With the northern, overland, route to Rangoon seemingly blocked, a plan for an amphibious assault of Rangoon up 24 miles of the Rangoon River was prepared and approved. Soon after the approval, the planners discovered several problems with the plan as written: the river was mined; coastal guns, especially on the west bank of the Rangoon River at Elephant Point, would hamper minesweeping operations; and a seaborne assault on the guns was out of the question because the coastal waters were too shallow to allow any ship with large enough guns to come within range. Already short of transport aircraft and not really wanting to jeopardize the scanty resupply missions, Slim's staff reviewed other methods of assaulting these guns, which were at the mouth of the Rangoon River and the Gulf of Martaban.

The staff decided that an airborne assault was necessary but initially could not decide whether the assault should be by parachute or gliders. For a variety of weather and drop zone reasons the staff eventually ruled out using gliders so Slim reluctantly approved the parachute operation. The weather experts picked 2 May as the date for the amphibious assault. The paratroopers would have to go in the day before in order to secure the guns and the waterway entrance. The mission was code-named Operation Dracula.

Parachute forces in the Indian Army had been formed in October 1941 when British Army and RAF jump instructors established an Air Landing School in Delhi and the 50th Indian Parachute Brigade was activated, also in Delhi. The first brigade commander was Brigadier W.H.G. Gough, who was already jump qualified; he was later replaced by Brigadier M.R.J. Thompson. The 50th Brigade included three national Parachute Battalions: 151st (British), 152nd (Indian), and 153rd (Gurkha). The Air Landing School was later moved to Campbellpore and Chaklala (now in Pakistan). In October 1942 the 151st (British) Para Battalion was redesignated as the 156th Para Battalion and transferred to the Middle East. Two months later the 3/7th Gurkha Regiment, recently returned from fighting in Burma, was converted to a parachute unit and designated the 154th Gurkha Para Battalion.

Early training had the same problem in India as it did in many other countries—lack of transport aircraft and a limited supply of parachutes. Because India was at the far end of the priority logistics chain the only aircraft available for jump training was the Vickers Valencia, a twin-engine biplane with a troop carrying capacity of 20. The pilot and observer sat in the Valencia's open cockpit in the nose of the plane. The Valencias, known affectionately to the Indian paras as "Flying Pigs," had a cruising speed of about 85 miles per hour and could take off and land on short runways. An exit hole was cut in the floor of the plane for the jumpers.

In April 1942, Leslie L. Irvin, the American parachute manufacturer, visited India. Irvin soon established a local factory in Kanpur to make parachutes for the Indian Army. By June the supply of parachutes had improved and continued to improve throughout the war.

When it was first established, the jump school required all prospective students to pass a color blindness test. This test produced a high failure rate. When official requests were made to dilute this requirement, they were turned down. The problem was solved by an inventive method. Since many of the RAF medical examiners did not speak any of the local dialects, it was necessary to administer the test using an Indian Army officer as an interpreter. The failure rate plummeted. Eventually the test requirement was dropped.

Jump training lasted for three weeks with five jumps required for qualification: on the first jump, the jumpers exited one at a time; then came slow pairs, then quick pairs, then the entire stick; by the fifth jump the students jumped with weapons and equipment, and conducted a simple tactical exercise after landing and assembling. Equipment containers were attached to bomb racks which were located just forward of the exit hole. These containers were usually released halfway through the exiting stick by the jumpmaster. Timing the release of the equipment containers was absolutely critical to avoid injuries. The first Indian to make a parachute jump was Lieutenant A.G. Rangaraj of the 152nd Para Battalion.

By the spring of 1945 plans were already in effect to split up the 50th Indian Parachute Brigade to form the cadre of the newly-created 44th Indian Airborne Division. A composite battalion group from the many units of 50 Brigade was formed to implement Operation Dracula. The battalion group was under the command of Major G.E.C. (Jack) Newland and was composed almost entirely of members of the Gurkha parachute units.

The battalion group was formed as follows: staff and A and B companies of 153rd, C and D companies of 154th, and special personnel for battalion headquarters and support companies from both battalions as necessary. In addition, a section of combat engineers from 411th Parachute Squadron Indian Engineers, a section of the 80th Parachute Field Ambulance, two pathfinder teams, and detachments from the brigade signal and intelligence units were attached. By mid April the battalion group was assembled at Chaklala for training; it was joined there by the support attachments. A reserve force was designated, and briefings and rehearsals began. The force was then moved to Midnapore, where it remained for ten days, until 29 April.

In Midnapore, the air support linked up with the paratroopers. Air support was American C-47s; the pilots had no previous experience dropping parachute troops. Special racks for equipment bundles had to be constructed. Canadian jumpmasters, who had worked with the Gurkhas before, were pressed into service. One full dress-rehearsal jump was conducted and went well. On 29 April, the battalion group was moved to Akyab, its staging base (or 'perching area'), where it was joined by the reserve element. The reserve was to be dropped in a separate operation. Final briefings were conducted—intelligence reports estimated that opposition at the target would be light.

The battalion group was to be flown to its target area in 40 C-47s manned by the 1st and 2nd Air Commandos, American Air Corps units with no experience in parachute drops. The 1st Air Commandos was the unit that had towed gliders for Brigadier Orde Wingate's second Chindit expedition into Burma when it went behind Japanese lines in March 1944.

At 0230 on 1 May, the pathfinder aircraft, two C-47s, took off. Forty minutes later, the main body departed. The 400 mile approach flight was marked by incredibly bad visibility and deteriorating flying conditions. The fighter escort had to turn back. At 0545, the green light came on as the first planes reached the leading edge of the drop zone, five miles west of Elephant Point, and the Gurkha paratroopers jumped. The drop was absolutely perfect. Everyone landed on the drop zone. There was no opposition on the ground and the Gurkhas assembled quickly. There had been only five minor jump casualties.

The paratroopers moved west for two-and-one-half miles. A stop was called to wait for their target to be engaged by air support. Despite being almost 3,000 meters from the target, some of the bombs fell short and one of the Gurkha companies suffered 15 killed and 30 wounded. At 1530, the reserve force jumped in, another perfect drop. At 1600 a pre-arranged supply drop was also perfect.

Also at 1600, the leading company reached Elephant Point. By now it was raining steadily as it had been for most of the day; the rain became heavier by 2000 that night.

The Japanese troops in the bunkers immediately opened up with machine-gun fire. Small ships at the mouth of the river also opened up. Air support was directed to suppress the fire coming from the ships and the paratroopers began their assault on the bunkers. Japanese opposition was light but stubborn. Hand-to-hand fighting followed and then the paratroopers attacked the bunkers with flame throwers, soon overcoming stiff resistance. A flare indicating success was fired and the Gurkhas began to consolidate their position. It rained heavily for three days. The battalion area was eventually covered by three feet of water.

The next day, 2 May, the amphibious landing was conducted. The paratroopers watched the minesweepers enter Rangoon River, followed by the amphibious assault force as it headed north. On 3 May, Rangoon fell. On 8 May, the monsoons began, two weeks early.

On 5 May, the paratroopers moved from Elephant Point to the university area in Rangoon and conducted anti-looting patrols in the area. Ten days later, the paratroopers left for India where they would join other units that were forming the 44th Indian Airborne Division.

Mission Critique

Of what are considered the minor airborne operations of World War II, Operation Dracula is thought by some military experts to be one of the finest examples of the economical and effective use of paratroopers. As always, in this mission the Gurkhas delivered when the time came. Weather, one of those factors that cannot always be counted on in military operations, especially special operations, played a small part in this operation's execution. It was a factor in planning because it determined the timing of the operations and it was a factor in the execution because it hampered movement of the paratroopers in the objective area, but as it turned out, it was only a minor factor in the execution phase. The major factors here were *speed, surprise,* and *purpose,* just as McRaven advocates in the criteria for a successful execution. In the planning phase, both Vandenbroucke and McRaven would be pleased with this mission because it involved *coordination* of several elements, including two by air (aerial delivery of the paratroopers and, later, air support against the ships at the mouth of the river), and *simplicity.* It is interesting that even though the pilots of 1st and 2nd Air Commandos had no previous experience dropping paratroopers, they were dead-on at Elephant Point.

This operation was another of those special operations, like the Amphibious Scouts setting up lights for the Leyte channel, which was very important to larger operations that depended on them. There is little doubt that early capture of Rangoon, before the monsoons, put the Japanese off-balance instead of giving them the upper-hand for several more months.

SOURCES

Karim, Afsir; *The Story of the Indian Airborne Troops*; New Delhi; Lancer International; 1993

Neild, Eric; *With Pegasus in India—The Story of 153 Gurkha Parachute Battalion;* Singapore; privately published by Jay Birch; undated

Norton, G.G.; *The Red Devils—The Story of the British Airborne Forces;* Harrisburg, PA; Stackpole Books; 1971

Praval, K.C.; *India's Paratroopers—A History of the Parachute Regiment of India;* London; Leo Cooper; 1975

Tugwell, Maurice; *Airborne to Battle—A History of Airborne Warfare 1918–1971;* London; William Kimber; 1971

PART 2

BEHIND FRIENDLY LINES

OVERVIEW

B ehind *their own* lines is usually the last place special purpose, special
mission organizations expect to fight. However, it has happened. U.S.
parachute units in World War II dropped into or just behind friendly front
lines to reinforce units on the ground in Italy and on Noemfoor Island in the
Pacific. This technique has been used several times since, notably by the
French in 1954 to reinforce embattled Dien Bien Phu and by the U.S. 173rd
Airborne Brigade in Viet Nam during Operation Junction City in February
1967.

Friendly lines tend to bring their own set of problems for special operators, which is why missions there can be as hazardous as those in enemy-
controlled territory. There is always the danger that friendly forces didn't get
the word that special operators will be in their area of responsibility. This
could cause them to mistake the special units for enemy forces; this is a problem also faced by reconnaissance forces when returning to friendly areas.
Good planning and communications can usually minimize this problem.

What prompts commanders to use special units in friendly areas? Often
it is the same basic reason that prompts them to use them in enemy areas—
these units have a *capability* the commander can or needs to use. Occasionally
the commander interprets this capability broadly; that is, this unit has some
special skill that demonstrates its members' ability to learn another special
skill and combine the two in operations within friendly areas. This was particularly the case for one of the units discussed in this section, the 555th Parachute Infantry Battalion. Members of this specialized unit received explosive
ordnance disposal training and some refined jump training by the U.S. Forest
Service to qualify them as Smokejumpers, a fairly new technique at the time
(1945).

Another reason causing special units to operate in friendly areas is a commander's decision based on the rationale that this force may be the only organization available on which the commander can depend, even if the mission is purely a conventional one. The use of GALAHAD as part of the static defense force at Myitkyina airfield was just such a decision. Stilwell knew he could rely on GALAHAD to perform the mission and, deep down, he probably wanted a U.S. unit as part of the defensive force; after all, GALAHAD had *captured* the airfield.

Rarer is the instance where the unit itself will suggest an operation. Rare as it may be, the first case study demonstrates just exactly that situation—an intelligence operator who devises a concept quite unique in the annals of special operations forces and then puts the plan into operation, again and again.

Intelligence organizations have their own versions of special operations. Usually these involve people who recruit others to commit espionage or, sometimes, sabotage. Counterintelligence special operations include using double agents or what are euphemistically called dangle operations—holding agents out hoping they will be recruited by the opposition. The U.S. Army used to have several specialized fields of expertise for counterintelligence agents involving use of polygraph, of clandestine listening devices, lock bypass techniques, or cameras (hidden or over a long distance or in subdued light).

During World War II, intelligence organizations conducted a wide variety of operations. Some organizations dealing with different OSS or SOE teams were detailed in Part 1. There were also many intelligence deceptions that were used by all the various countries during the war. The U.S. Office of Naval Intelligence (ONI) may not be willing to admit that it sponsored the missions in the case study used here, principally because of the dubious legal techniques used. However, this assumes that ONI knew about the details of these missions—and there seems to be some doubt how high up the chain of command that knowledge went. Willis George, the leader of the surreptitious entry team, reported the results of the various jobs by claiming that he had a confidential informant who had taken the photographs or had access to the information. There is no clear way to know if ONI was aware who George's informants really were.

Notwithstanding this, the team of ONI agents that George led for almost two years in New York City displayed its share of daring and had more than a few close calls. It is unlikely that these operations would have been pulled off outside the country. By operating in a friendly area, the ONI agents had the advantage of being on the same side as any police or military force that might respond if they were caught. Even so, they relied on bluff on those few occasions when things did not always go according to plan—and the bluffs worked every time.

There are other examples of friendly area missions assigned to special operations forces. One of the earliest, in World War II, was in the Southwest Pacific. Alamo Scouts teams served as personal security detail for the Sixth Army commander, General Walter Krueger, when they were not conducting reconnaissance missions. Similarly, in Europe, select members of the First Special Service Force performed the same duties for their commander, Colonel Robert T. Frederick. Ever since, up to and including the war in Iraq, special operations forces have performed personal security duties for commanders at various levels. Notwithstanding the occasional stretches in rationale to justify the use of special operations forces in friendly lines, the fact that they have been used that way and continue to be used thus to this day is ample proof of the versatility of the operations that planners assign to these forces—versatility at least in the minds of the planners.

Missions behind friendly lines will continue to be an option that commanders consider for special operations forces. The Gulf War provides another example of such a use, this time not one directed at the Iraqis, but probably just as important in winning the war. U.S. Special Forces personnel who were qualified in the language of the various allied countries of the coalition forces were used as interpreters/translators assigned to coalition units. This provided a mechanism for adjoining units to communicate with each other easier and faster, with less likelihood of error based on language. By their presence, they also used one of their other skills, as trainers, to teach coalition units standard tactics and even some basic military subjects. A common base in tactics meant that similar military actions would be carried out in a uniform manner. Finally, by using all these skills from a pool of soldiers from units of the same country as the overall commander, a common goal— one combined operations plan—could be fostered. These Special Forces soldiers are credited with helping to keep the fragile coalition together.

SOURCES

Dilley, Michael F.; *GALAHAD—A History of the 5307th Composite Unit (Provisional)*; Bennington, Vermont; Merriam Press; 1996
Kagan, Donald; *On the Origins of War and the Preservation of Peace*; New York; Doubleday; 1995

CHAPTER TWENTY-ONE

BREAKING AND ENTERING

The seven-man team set about the job quietly, efficiently, and quickly. They took off their shoes as soon as they got inside the entry door, then, each holding a sketch of the office's floor plan, moved to their individual tasks. The agent-in-charge and the evaluator went to a central area in the office suite to be on-call wherever needed. The photographer began putting curtains over the windows to keep light from leaking out. Each man checked the area he was working to see what the dust layer looked like.

The two search groups, desks and safes, began working. The desk man opened each desk, sketched the contents of the individual drawers, and examined the documents inside. The manipulation man sat in front of a safe and began spinning the dial, determining how many wheels were in the dial pack and finding the drop-in point. Then he began maneuvering the wheel pack around, measuring any changes in the gap of the drop-in point, alert for the tell-tale signs that would give him the combination.

In a short while, the safe manipulator let out a quiet noise that told those nearby he had opened the safe. He, too, sketched the contents first. The evaluator moved from team to team, looking at documents they offered him and telling them which were of interest. Those were taken to the photographer, who snapped pictures of each page with a microfilm camera with an infrared flash.

One of the security men, in the team's truck outside the building, recognized an office worker as he walked down the street toward the entry to the building. His radio man called the agent-in-charge while he signaled one of the inside security men. Upstairs, work stopped momentarily so the team could be briefed on what was happening. They went back to work, a little more quickly and with some apprehension, knowing they could be discovered at any minute now. The office worker approached the building elevator but stopped when he saw a man in overalls approaching him.

The man, whose overalls had the name *Longman's Building Survey Engineering Company* stitched over the upper left pocket, explained that the building was closed, even to occupants, for several hours and the elevators shut off while they measured the structure for "sway stress cracks." The test would be finished by morning and the office worker could get in then. The engineer even produced a carbon copy of a letter from the building superintendent notifying the various occupants of the test; the letter was dated the previous week. The office worker sighed and left. The radio man passed the message to the entry team.

The agent-in-charge reported the all-clear. In five hours, when everyone was finished, several team members used "dustguns," filled with talcum powder and charcoal, to cover their presence at desks, filing cabinets, and safes. Others dusted floors and swept carpets to cover their foot tracks. When everything was secure, they put their shoes back on and departed, locking the office behind them. No one in the office ever found out that the team had been there.

What you have just read is a typical description of one of the strangest-ever special operations during World War II, conducted by the surreptitious entry team of the Third District, Office of Naval Intelligence. It was stranger still because it was conducted in New York City in the behind-the-lines area inside a foreign consulate. The agent-in-charge of the surreptitious entry team was Willis D. George, a civilian special agent of ONI, who later took a similar operation on the road into Germany for the OSS.

George had come to ONI by a roundabout route. He was a World War I artillery veteran. He later worked on several stock exchanges and for the Chicago Board of Trade. From 1935 to 1937 he was an investigator for the Customs Bureau, operating mostly in Cuba on drug and alcohol smuggling cases. These cases were usually coordinated with the ONI and FBI. George also worked briefly for Canada, investigating German sabotage and espionage in the aircraft industry.

In August 1941, ONI hired him to conduct background investigations on people who needed security clearances. Part of his job included surveillance of foreign diplomats. George said later, "Much of this surveillance work was unbelievably dull, but all of it was good training . . ."

The training that George meant had nothing to do with following people. Rather, he learned both how unobservant and how gullible people were.

He also learned how an effective disguise and a well-played part could lead to mission success.

George described mission success this way: "Surreptitious entry, carefully prepared and brilliantly executed." George proposed to his superior that an ONI team break into foreign consulates in the New York City area, open safes, and copy or photograph the contents. His boss did not tell him not to do it but only reminded George that getting caught "would be extremely embarrassing to the Navy Department."

George's first chance came almost immediately. While on duty one night in mid 1942, he received a message that reported activity at an embassy in Washington. The embassy staff had spent most of the previous day burning papers. The message asked if the country's consulate in New York had also been burning papers.

Borrowing a set of overalls and a pass-key from the building superintendent, George spent an anxious hour or so walking through the consulate that very night. He could plainly smell that papers had been recently burned. He also noticed several safes and filing cabinets, all locked. George was determined to come back and find out what was inside the locked containers. He reported what he had found to his boss and received permission to go back—with the admonition against getting caught.

George decided he needed a skilled crew to go back inside with him. He would need a locksmith or two (one for locks, one for safes), a photographer who could operate a microfilm camera, a linguist who could tell the team which papers were important, and a team of searchers. His team had sixteen men on it. With no more than a vague notion of what they would do and instructions to two of the team to keep consulate members out if they showed up, George and his team set out on their first job.

Once inside, the team scattered to several rooms. Soon, the lock experts had several safes open and the photographer was busy clicking away. One packet inside a safe was heavily sealed and marked on the outside: "Secret, only to be opened in case of war." The team photographed the package but wisely put it back without tampering with it further. They rubbed a few doorknobs and left. Their report attributed the photographs to a confidential informant. Needless to say, ONI Headquarters in Washington wanted to know more from this informant, especially what was inside the sealed package.

George was not certain how he would be able to do that. Within a few days, however, he had his answer. The British Security Service loaned the team a 50-year-old woman for an indefinite period. She was a flaps-and-seals expert. She could open whatever they needed; she had been doing this for years, all over the world. The team worked out and practiced a set of signals to keep everyone informed of any danger. If all else failed, one of the security men was to knock down and tie up any consulate member who could not be persuaded to leave or remain outside. Several nights later, the team went back to the consulate, lugging an assortment of pots, pans, steam-kettles and packages. The British expert, whose name George never learned, opened the package and the contents were photographed, then she re-sealed it, leaving hardly a trace of her activity. George described the contents as diplomatic dynamite.

The team went back several more times, eventually finding and copying sensitive code material. A few nights after finding the codes, as George and the team were ready to go in again, he decided to take a precaution and go up first, alone. Putting on his building cleaner overalls, he went upstairs to the consulate. As soon as he was inside an overhead light snapped on and he was staring at two pistols! The overalls saved the day; the consul believed George was a cleaner, not the burglar he was expecting, and sent him on his way.

Because of the close call, the team examined how it was operating and instituted several significant changes. From then on they took blackout curtains with them for all windows and doors where they worked. They also cleaned up thoroughly after they were finished, including sweeping all carpets and replacing dust where it was when they entered. The most important change they implemented was to sketch the inside of desks and safes before they disturbed anything. This would guide them when they had to put things away, leaving them as they found them and making their presence less likely to be discovered. When the team finally finished with this consulate, after *ten weeks* of surreptitious entries, they had discovered a wealth of information, including a list of contacts that German agents, working out of the consulate, had made with American residents.

George and his team next used their entry techniques on a number of cases that led nowhere. At the same time, they perfected their operation and began extensive training and cross-training sessions. The office set up an elaborate photo developing laboratory and purchased several mobile radios. George also refined the membership needed for a successful entry. They now had 11 agents: an agent-in-charge; two locksmiths (as before, one for locks and one to manipulate safes open); a photographer; a flaps-and-seals expert; an evaluator, who was a linguist and would review documents to determine what should be photographed; three men as outside security; and two radio operators. All of those on the inside team had multiple duties.

The team was then sent to Chicago, where it was targeted against a man suspected of espionage activity. They spent a month following him everywhere he went and uncovered nothing. Next, they began to go through his trash, looking at every piece of paper he threw away. They still found nothing, even after three months on the case. George decided they needed to go in. The team eventually spent one night in the man's offices, leaving no trace of the entry. What they found was evidence of an extensive German espionage operation. To avoid giving away how they found out about it, ONI spent the next month arresting those in the spy ring one at a time instead of all at once, eventually getting every one of them.

It was during the Chicago operation that the team developed a cover story that allowed it to operate more openly in a building and which it used thereafter, wherever it operated. They called themselves stress engineers and told everyone who asked that they were checking the building for cracks caused by swaying. They told people that the elevators had to be shut off so their operation would not interfere with the engineer's delicate testing instruments. They even rented empty office space and listed a telephone as belonging to the "*Northwest Engineering Company.*" This provided a backup to the name on the team's truck, which was usually parked outside whatever building they were testing. The truck was a stake-out point for one of the security men and a radio operator. When they returned to New York, the team established the Longman's cover.

In the first year of the team's operations, it performed almost 100 surreptitious entries. By this time, what they had done in Chicago—going through all the offices in one night—became standard procedure. Despite apparent haste, the team was thorough and left nothing to chance. Before the team actually made its one entry, George had conducted at least one reconnaissance visit of the target to make a diagram of the layout, check for alarms or cameras or hidden recording equipment, determine what kind of locks or combinations would have to be bypassed, and where security posts should be established. All of this information served as the basis for more detailed research by the team before attempting an entry. Then they went to work on the building managers, arranging to set up their stress test equipment.

George and his security men would spend several days before an entry; working in the building as cleaners, giving the occupants plenty of time to get accustomed to their faces. This helped later on if, while an entry was in progress and someone from the target consulate showed up, he would be more willing to believe a man whose face he recognized.

In February 1944, having completed 200 successful surreptitious entries since August 1942, George transferred to the OSS. He completed the basic agent training course and expected to go overseas immediately. However, his harsh comments on the end-of-course critique alerted the school faculty to his talents and he was retained as an instructor. During the next nine months he completely revised the surreptitious entry part of the course, even writing a manual on "Picks, clicks, flaps, and seals." In mid-January 1945, George finally got his wish and was transferred to OSS London where he began training a team to conduct surreptitious entries in Europe. Two months later the team began operations.

George soon learned that his team did not need to go in surreptitiously since they were employed in areas already controlled by the Allies. He also found that they did not have the luxury of spending time manipulating the safes and vaults they were asked to open. The team quickly learned how to blow safes open with the wonder explosive—C-2 plastic. A short period of trial-and-error was all the team needed to learn how to quickly open a safe without destroying the contents. The team also became expert at peeling open huge vault doors that were not persuaded by the C-2. In all, George's team opened 79 safes and vaults in five weeks.

After the war, George had trouble finding a job. When prospective employers found out what he did during the war, they were usually less than enthusiastic about hiring him. But George was optimistic, saying, "I could always go back to the Stock Exchange, where robbery, although no longer strictly legal, is still considered genteel."

Mission Critique

If there was ever a case where audacity carried the day in special operations it was certainly in the ONI operations described here, that of the enemy from an unexpected direction. Generally, there was no major opposition by those in charge of George's operations except being told by one superior not to get caught or embarrass the Navy.

The Naval Intelligence surreptitious entry teams should only be classified as a special purpose, special mission organization *as a result* of their operations; they certainly were not that before the missions began. Later, when Willis George trained his OSS team for their operations in Germany, he had almost two years' experience as his basis for training the men and planning the operations. This does not imply that anyone could have conducted these operations; however, George could have done it with *any* of the agents in his Naval Intelligence unit. At the time of the ONI operations no special training was available or needed, except for the flaps and seals techniques. Everyone else on the team was there because of an individual skill he already possessed, either language or locks.

The Naval Intelligence agents and their support team made their plans as they went along; many of the individual plans were a reaction to the situation at the moment, with little foresight to hazards, especially the early missions. Only after they made errors did they incorporate changes into their method of operation, including the cover story they eventually developed to explain their presence in the buildings. This team actually used *two* covers: one to explain their presence on site and one they used on reports. They referred to their surreptitious entries as a source on their reports, implying (or lying, depending on how harsh one wants to be in describing this action) to their superiors, who would get their intelligence reports, that *someone else* had access to the information and was passing it on to the Navy. While this would protect the Navy from embarrassment, it did not give their superiors or analysts reading and evaluating their reports the true story of how they obtained the information, i.e., committing an illegal act against a sovereign country.

There is a need to separate the earlier comments about the necessity of these operations and whether they needed special operators to execute them from any critical comments about the operations themselves. The operations are examined critically, based on the established criteria.

George and his teams seemed to improve with time, especially if you consider each prior operation as simply the *repetition* phase in the preparation for the next mission. As they went along the ONI operators got a little more elaborate, as well as more *secure*, in their covers and also did not try to get everything in one night. They spread the take out for as long as needed but didn't spend a lot of time on any given entry. This helped to cut down on the stress and tension they must all have been under when inside, which can become almost unbearable if done over an extended period of time. This is not to say that they didn't make mistakes, only that any mistake they did make went unnoticed by those who owned the places George and his team penetrated.

The major unknown about these operations is their value. George is the only person who has written about them and he doesn't go into much detail on what Naval Intelligence learned as a result of these break-ins. He does refer to several espionage operations that were detected and broken up but he is not specific in the details. We can assume that his immediate superiors, who *did* know where the information came from, were pleased with what his team found. However, that really doesn't allow for an objective evaluation. After all, many of these operations could have produced diplomatic problems for the U.S.

There is some second hand objective judgment of these operations. It is certain that OSS would have been able to learn whatever it needed to know about George's operations. The fact that OSS brought George into the organization, then later allowed him to be an instructor at one of its schools and an author of at least one of its publications, and still later let him form another safecracking unit and deploy it operationally, seems to establish that OSS made a good assessment of the work he did for ONI.

The overall assessment of these operations is that they were pretty good, based on the one-sided version that we know, and that, as in many special operations, good planning and a healthy dose of luck played large parts in their execution. And, of course, audacity.

SOURCES

George, Willis D.; *Surreptitious Entry;* Boulder, CO; Paladin Press; 1990

CHAPTER TWENTY-TWO

RESCUE AT GRAN SASSO

Perhaps the most daring use of special operations forces behind friendly lines was conducted in September 1943 in Italy.

On 24 July, the Italian government revolted against Benito Mussolini as part of secret negotiations with the Allies. Victor Emmanuel III, the King of Italy, dismissed Mussolini and ordered him imprisoned by the new government, headed by General Pietro Badoglio, and held in a secret location. Although word of the negotiations was withheld from the general public, the Germans found out. Hitler was furious. He considered the actions of the Italian government to be traitorous. Mussolini was his friend and Hitler wanted something done—immediately. Two days later, six officers were summoned to the Wolf's Lair to be quizzed by Hitler; one of them would be chosen to find and rescue Mussolini. As it turned out, only one of them was familiar with Italy, having twice traveled to Naples on a motorcycle. The fact that this same officer was Austrian and was the commander of *Friedenthaler Jadgverbaende* (Friedenthal Hunting Groups, Germany's first special forces, patterned after the British Commandos) made the choice easier. The man chosen was SS Captain Otto Skorzeny, 6'4" tall, weighing 220 pounds, and with a face scarred by dueling swords from his student days.

Captain Skorzeny was placed under the nominal command of General Kurt Student, founder of the German Parachute Corps. The two officers spent most of the night discussing plans and forces available to them. The 1st Parachute Division was stationed in Rome and would, Student decided, be available to supplement Skorzeny's Friedenthal special force. Skorzeny called his second-in-command, Lieutenant Karl Radl, and told him to arrange to move 50 of their best men to the Pratica di Mare Airfield at Frascati, the German headquarters located about 30 miles south-east of Rome.

Radl was to equip the force with two machine guns for every ten men, machine pistols for each man, grenades, plastic explosive, tropical uniforms and helmets, rations for six days and emergency rations for three additional days, Very pistols, and civilian clothes for the officers.

During the night Skorzeny awoke abruptly. As he wrote later, "I remembered the fact that I was the father of a family. Was I to throw myself into the great adventure without drawing up my will? I turned on the light again and drew up my 'last will and testament.'"

The next day, Student and Skorzeny, posing as an aide to the general, flew to Rome in a *Heinkel* 111. That evening they dined with Field Marshal Albert von Kesselring, the commander-in-chief of German troops in Italy. Hitler had specifically instructed Skorzeny that von Kesselring was not to be told about the rescue operation. The field marshal briefed Student and Skorzeny on the latest developments in Italy and introduced them to two other dinner guests—Kappler, the German police attaché in Rome, and Dollmann, a German who had lived in Italy for many years and was supposed to have some good local contacts. Skorzeny learned that none of the dinner guests knew anything that could be of much help to him.

On 29 July, Radl and the Friedenthal special force he had picked arrived. By this time, rumors about Mussolini's whereabouts had him in Switzerland on vacation, a suicide, and in a medical sanatorium suffering from a serious disease. Since the 29th was Mussolini's 60th birthday, the Germans attempted a ruse to locate him. Hitler arranged for a deluxe edition of the collected works of Nietzsche, the German philosopher, to be delivered to von Kesselring. The field marshal was given specific instructions that the books must be delivered to Mussolini personally. Badoglio was polite but firm—the books would be delivered to the prisoner but no German would be allowed to visit him, wherever he was.

Kappler, the police attaché, provided the next item of information. Following his dismissal by the king, Mussolini had been driven to a police barracks in Rome in an ambulance. Here the trail ended again, until the proprietor of a restaurant in Rome talked about a letter. It seems that the maid of a customer was the fiancé of a soldier at the penal island of Ponza—located 25 miles offshore, between Rome and Naples. The letter mentioned "a very high ranking prisoner" who had recently arrived at Ponza. On 7 August, a Navy officer mentioned to Skorzeny that Mussolini had been moved, by cruiser, to Spezia. The Italian government was apparently playing a shell game with the prisoner.

Hitler ordered Skorzeny to raid the cruiser. Before he could conduct the operation, information from a German naval liaison officer on Sardinia reported that Mussolini had left the cruiser and had been moved to a villa on the tiny island of La Maddelena after having spent only a short time on Sardinia. Skorzeny and Lieutenant Warger, one of his officers who spoke Italian, went to the port on La Maddelena and confirmed that Mussolini was there. Skorzeny returned to Rome and arranged to conduct an aerial reconnaissance of Sardinia, La Maddelena, and Corsica; the route was to mislead anyone who might be watching for a reconnaissance. On 18 August, Skorzeny left Rome in a *Heinkel* 111. The plane landed on Sardinia for refueling, which allowed Skorzeny time to conduct an on-the-ground reconnaissance. At 1500 the He-111 took off on its return trip but never arrived. It was attacked by two British pursuit planes and shot down. Although Skorzeny survived the crash, he had broken three ribs.

Two days later, on his return to Frascati airfield, Skorzeny received a shock. A message from Führer Headquarters ordered him to launch a parachute attack on the island of Elba where, Admiral Canaris reported, Mussolini was being held prisoner. Neither Skorzeny nor Radl believed this bit of intelligence and, through General Student, received permission to go to Führer Headquarters and conduct a briefing. This briefing convinced Hitler to cancel the parachute attack on Elba and, instead, he approved the plan Skorzeny preferred, which was to raid the villa at La Maddelena. Hitler added a caution, "You must understand, Captain Skorzeny, if the enterprise fails for any reason, it may be that I shall have publicly to disavow your action. I should then say that you had concocted an insane plan with the commanders on the spot and acted without authority."

However, the attack never happened. Several days after the briefing, on 26 August, Skorzeny and Warger, wearing the uniforms of German sailors, conducted a final pre-raid reconnaissance of the villa. They learned that Mussolini had been removed earlier that morning, flown out in a white airplane. Skorzeny was back to where he started. But, in his own words, "Once again chance, that great patron of those who dare, came to our help."

While accompanying Student on an inspection trip, Skorzeny learned about a white airplane flying in the Apennines. Several days later, Skorzeny was given an intercepted radio message from the Italian Ministry of the Interior. The message read "Security measures around Gran Sasso completed" and was signed "Cueli," the general responsible for Mussolini's security. For several days, Skorzeny and Radl tried to learn about Gran Sasso. The best information they found was from a travel agency brochure which described the Hotel Campo Imperatore, a winter sports center built on a plateau of the Gran Sasso peak, 6,000 feet high in the Apennines, about 100 miles northeast of Rome. The hotel was connected to the valley below only by a cable car. Skorzeny and Radl also learned that the roads leading into the valley were heavily guarded by the *Carabinieri.*

Once more, Skorzeny believed that an aerial reconnaissance was needed. He and Radl arranged to fly on an He-111 equipped with an automatic camera. On the morning of 8 September, dressed in light-weight *Afrika Korps* uniforms, Skorzeny and Radl flew from Pratica di Mare Airfield, at an altitude of 15,000 feet to take pictures of their target. On the way the crew told them that the automatic camera had malfunctioned. Despite the bitter cold, Skorzeny cut a hole through the perspex of the belly gunner's position and, with Radl holding his legs, hung outside the plane, head first, and took three pictures with his own small camera. Immediately after taking the second picture, Skorzeny "noticed a little meadow, virtually triangular in shape, just behind the hotel. In a flash came the thought—this is our landing ground!"

On the return pass at the hotel, Skorzeny and Radl changed places, with Radl now hanging outside the plane. When he was pulled back inside Radl muttered, "I'll strangle the next fellow who ever tells me again about the beautiful blue Italian sky!" On the flight into Frascati, Skorzeny and Radl watched an Allied bombing of the airfield, landing only minutes after the last bomb had been dropped. They learned the reason for the raid; it was in celebration of an Allied radio announcement declaring the Italian surrender. Early the next morning, 9 September, the Allies landed at Salerno. In the region around Rome, there was sporadic fighting between German and Italian units.

Over the next two days, Skorzeny learned that the whole valley below the Gran Sasso had been sealed and that local trade unionists were complaining about the civilian staff of the hotel being expelled "simply to accommodate that Fascist Mussolini." Skorzeny had his reconnaissance pictures developed. These confirmed that the grassy field he had spotted was the only possible landing ground available. He and Radl discussed two options—a parachute assault and a glider landing. Common to both options was to have a battalion from the 1st Parachute Division, commanded by Major Mors, jump into the valley the night before and seize the cable car station at the base of the mountain at the designated zero hour. After further discussion with General Student and several of his staff officers, Skorzeny decided that the main assault would be by gliders. Student fixed zero hour as 0600 on 12

September. It would take until then to assemble the necessary 12 DFS-230 gliders, which would have to be flown in from France. One other change to the plan was made as well—Major Mors and his paratroopers would leave Rome by trucks on the morning of the raid and drive to their target.

On 11 September, Skorzeny addressed his assembled forces. "The long waiting-time is over. We have an important job to do tomorrow. Adolf Hitler has ordered it personally. Serious losses must be anticipated and, unfortunately, cannot be avoided. I shall of course lead you and can promise you that I will do my utmost. If we all stick together the assault will and must succeed. Anyone prepared to volunteer take one step forward." Not one man wanted to be left behind. Soon after, while the members of the raiding party were being picked and equipped, Skorzeny heard an Allied broadcast that Mussolini had arrived as a prisoner in Africa on an Italian man-of-war. After recovering from the initial shock, he examined his maps carefully. He decided, based on his knowledge of the exact time of the Italian fleet's departure, that "even the fastest ship could not possibly have reached Africa so soon. The wireless message must, therefore, be a hoax." All preparations continued.

The following morning, a bright and windless Sunday, Skorzeny's raiders marched to the airfield and were ready to go at 0500. But the gliders had not yet arrived. Zero hour was re-set for 1000. At 0800 Skorzeny sent Radl to Rome; he was to bring back General Ferdinando Soleti, who had recently sent troops to Gran Sasso. Skorzeny believed that the Italians on the ground at the resort would be less likely to open fire if they recognized one of their own officers in the glider party. At 1000, zero hour was re-set again, this time for 1400. By noon, the gliders began to land at Frascati. Skorzeny conducted a final inspection of his men and their equipment. The 12 gliders were each to carry 9 raiders and a pilot. The pilot of the lead tow plane was the same one who had flown Skorzeny and Radl on their photo reconnaissance.

While the tow planes were being refueled, General Student and Skorzeny reviewed the attack plan for the tow plane and glider pilots. When he heard all of the details, Soleti said he would not take part in the operation. Skorzeny forced the Italian general to the back of the briefing room and said quietly to him, "You will ride in the third glider with me, General, or the Italian army will be short one general." At 1230 Skorzeny's men were about to board the gliders when the wailing of sirens announced an air raid. The raiders ran to the nearest shelters. Fate had once again stepped in. The Allied bombers were part of a large raid on Rome; they had been diverted at the last moment and bombed Frascati.

The air raid lasted less than half-an-hour. When he approached the gliders Skorzeny was relieved to see that they were all undamaged. He grabbed General Soleti and pulled him into the third glider in line, placing the Italian on the floor between his legs. Radl was in the fourth glider. At 1300 the gliders began taking off. Skorzeny's plan called for the men in the first two gliders to secure the landing zone at the resort and cover the landing of the remaining ten gliders. As the tow planes leveled out for their one-hour flight, they entered a heavy cloud bank.

It was not until they emerged from the clouds that Skorzeny received more bad news. The two lead planes were nowhere in sight. In addition, two of the later planes had run into bomb craters on the runway and were still on the ground. Now missing one-third of his raiding force, Skorzeny nonetheless gave the order to continue with the operation. In a short time, the Gran Sasso came into view. Skorzeny confirmed it was their target by the triangular patch of green that was their landing zone. "Helmets on!" he shouted. "Slip the tow rope!"

The world around the raiders in number three glider went suddenly quiet. Skorzeny looked out a slit he had cut in the fabric floor. He could see Major Mors and his paratroopers moving toward the cable car station. Then he looked through the glider's windshield and got the shock of his life. His landing zone was severely sloped, not flat, and it was strewn with rocks and boulders. He called out to the pilot, "Crash landing! As near to the hotel as you can get!"

The pilot immediately tilted the starboard wing and the glider entered a steep dive and rushed toward the ground. Skorzeny heard the corporal behind him throw up. When they were still a few feet above the ground, Skorzeny yelled, "Release the parachute" and Lieutenant Meyer yanked on the release and the drogue parachute blossomed behind the glider. The tail lifted and the nose went down. Skorzeny closed his eyes and felt a crash and heard the noise of shattering wood. With one last heave, the glider came to a stop, just a few feet short of a large boulder.

Skorzeny looked outside. They were less than 50 feet from the hotel. Realizing he was alive, his first thought was "three minutes." This was the time he had allotted to find and secure Mussolini. Skorzeny jumped out of the wrecked glider and urged his men on. "Don't fire until I fire," he told them.

Immediately ahead, an Italian policeman stood blocking a doorway. Skorzeny knocked him out of the way and pushed through the door. A radio operator sat at his transmitter. Skorzeny kicked the chair from under him and smashed the radio with his machine pistol. He looked around the room and saw no other exit. He and his men went back outside through the same door they had entered and raced along the front of the building and around a corner. Skorzeny looked up at the windows on the second floor as he and his men ran toward a door. He saw Mussolini looking down at him. *His target was now in sight!* Skorzeny swept his arm in a signal to tell Mussolini to get away from the window.

The German raiders rushed into an entranceway, colliding with several Italian policemen. Skorzeny leaped over two machine guns mounted on the floor and headed for a staircase. Behind him he heard his men knocking the *Carabinieri* down with their weapons; he also heard the yell *"mani in alto"* ["hands up"]. Skorzeny dashed up the stairs three at a time, turned left, and kicked open the first door he saw. Inside the room stood Mussolini and two Italian officers. Skorzeny signaled with his weapon for the officers to move away from Mussolini and stand with their backs to the door.

Lieutenant Schwerdt burst into the room and took charge of the Italian officers. Skorzeny turned to face Mussolini as the door to the room closed behind the departing Schwerdt. "Duce," the German captain said to the startled Mussolini, "the Führer has sent me to set you free." Skorzeny glanced out a window and saw Radl leading his men toward the hotel as the number five glider was landing. He had accomplished his mission within two minutes of leaving his glider, without a shot being fired, and before most of his gliders had landed!

Once an area had been cleared of rocks and other hazards, Skorzeny radioed for a Storch aircraft to land in the same area as his gliders had, then escorted Mussolini to the small airplane. When Skorzeny told the pilot, Captain Gerlach, that all three of them would be flying out, the pilot strenuously objected. Skorzeny had "to take him aside for a short but tense discussion" and the pilot was convinced. Following a harrowing take-off, the Storch flew to Rome, where Skorzeny and Mussolini transferred to a Heinkel He-111 for a further flight to Vienna.

For his daring operation, Hitler personally awarded Otto Skorzeny the Knight's Cross of the Iron Cross and promoted him to major the following day. Skorzeny would soon be put in charge of all German special forces and his units would have several more incredible successes; none, however, as incredible as the rescue of Mussolini.

Mission Critique

For this operation, Hitler, as the ruler of Germany, decided that Mussolini *had* to be rescued and he commissioned SS-Captain Otto Skorzeny to perform the mission. Hitler, early in his reign, had developed a friendship with Mussolini. This alliance was helpful to Germany because it split Italy from its World War I ally, France. Later, when Hitler was about to annex Austria in the *Anschluss*, he sent a representative to Mussolini to be certain that the Italian dictator would not oppose his plans. After his representative told him that Mussolini would not interfere with him, Hitler pledged his support, saying "I will never forget, whatever may happen. If he should need any help or be in danger, he can be convinced that I shall stick to him, whatever may happen, even if the whole world were against him." Hitler's decision, therefore, to attempt a rescue settled the question of necessity.

As far as the necessity of using special operations forces to execute this mission, Captain Skorzeny's special force was the correct decision for the Mussolini rescue mission. At the time the mission was assigned, and even until it was actually executed, no one knew for certain where Mussolini was being held or under what circumstances. As the mission progressed, several different options had to be considered as intelligence was gathered, including the possibility of coming in from the sea. When the Germans thought they knew where Mussolini was being held, they still had to decide how to get to him, whether by truck, parachute, or glider. Only a special force would have the variety of skills and the flexibility to successfully complete the mission, even if this meant learning a skill before going in or co-opting someone who already had the needed skill. Thus, Captain Skorzeny's unit was the ideal choice for this mission.

From start to finish the rescue of Mussolini may be one of the most convoluted special operations in World War II. From inception to execution it took about six weeks; six weeks of starting and stopping with several planned operations cancelled for one reason or another, but mostly cancelled because Mussolini's whereabouts were in doubt. In strict terms the operation itself was fairly short—the afternoon of 12 September. The period from late July to the morning of the raid was spent avoiding Vandenbroucke's first criteria, *inadequate intelligence*. The very basic question of any rescue mission is where is the person or group to be rescued? Those weeks were spent trying to find the answer.

Earlier we have seen examples of special operations where the rescuees were medium to large groups. In this operation the rescuee was a single man. The task of locating him was complicated by the fact that he was a high-profile individual whom the Italian government was as anxious to conceal as Skorzeny was to find and rescue. The several false starts in this mission are reminiscent of some of the missions that were planned and later canceled for airborne units in the European and Pacific theaters; this can be a very frustrating period for special operators because of the stress associated with pre-launch preparations and subsequent let-down. Additionally, plans must be changed and updated, and rehearsals for the new plan conducted. Finally, transportation, equipment, and logistics have to at least be re-examined and probably changed. In this case, success was due in large part to the organization Skorzeny assembled to assist in planning and executing this mission

All of the steps Skorzeny and his men took prior to mission launch are excellent examples of the absence of any of Vandenbroucke's criteria for failed missions. Right in the middle is a good example of *faulty information being provided to national leadership* when Mussolini was reported to be on Elba and Skorzeny was ordered to go get him. This plan was scuttled when Skorzeny, with General Student's blessing, appealed directly to Hitler based on more accurate *intelligence.*

Although Skorzeny was the leader of the raiders who would execute the rescue raid on Gran Sasso, the entire effort was under the direction of General Kurt Student, the father of the German airborne effort. Student's presence during the entire mission was no accident and not cosmetic in nature. He was in charge.

When examining this operation from the McRaven criteria, the special operators had planned, prepared, and executed thoroughly and professionally. The result was mission success. *Surprise, speed,* and *purpose* carried the day.

SOURCES

Books:

Beaumont, Roger A.; *Military Elites;* Indianapolis, IN; Bobbs-Merrill; 1974

Blacker, Irwin R. (editor); *Irregulars, Partisans, Guerrillas—Great Stories From Rogers' Rangers to the Haganah;* New York; Simon and Schuster; 1954

Brown, Ashley and Jonathan Reed (editors); *The Commandos*; Harrisburg, PA; National Historical Society; 1986 (The Elite—The World's Crack Fighting Men, volume 2)

Farrar-Hockley, Arthur H.; *Student;* New York; Ballantine Books; 1973 (Ballantine's Illustrated History of the Violent Century, War Leader book number 15)

Foley, Charles; *Commando Extraordinary;* London; Longmans, Green; 1954

Garrett, Richard; *The Raiders—The Elite Strike Forces that Altered the Course of War and History;* New York; Van Norstrand Reinhold; 1980

Infield, Glenn B.; *Skorzeny—Hitler's Commando;* New York; St. Martin's Press; 1981

Lucas, James E.; *Kommando—German Special Forces of World War Two;* London; Arms and Armour Press; 1985

Mrazek, James E.; *Fighting Gliders of World War II;* London; Robert Hale; 1977

Nowarra, Heinz J.; *German Gliders in World War II;* translated from German by Ed Force; West Chester, PA; Schiffer Publishing; 1991 (originally published as *Deutsche Lastensegler* by Podzun-Pallas Verlag, Friedberg)

Rosignoli, Guido; *Army Badges and Insignia of World War 2;* New York; MacMillan; 1972

Skorzeny, Otto; *Skorzeny's Secret Missions—War Memoirs of the Most Dangerous Man in Europe;* translated from French by Jacques Le Clercq; New York; E.P. Dutton; 1950

—————; *Skorzeny's Special Missions;* London; Robert Hale; 1957

Whiting, Charles; *Skorzeny;* New York; Ballantine Books; 1972 (Ballantine's Illustrated History of the Violent Century, War Leader book number 11)

—————; *The War in the Shadows;* New York; Ballantine Books; 1973

Wood, Alan; *History of the World's Glider Forces;* Wellingborough, UK; Patrick Stephens; 1990

Articles:

Author unknown; "The Execution of Il Duce"; *World War II;* April 1976

Johnson, Thomas M.; "The Most Dangerous Man in Europe"; *Reader's Digest;* March, 1949

Taylor, Blaine; "Skorzeny—Germany's Classic Commando"; *Soldier of Fortune;* two-part series, June and July 1985

CHAPTER TWENTY-THREE

THE TRIPLE NICKEL

The formation, organization, and operation of the U.S. Army Parachute Test Platoon in June 1940 is a well-known story in the annals of special purpose, special mission organizations. This was, however, the first of *two* test platoons at the Army's Parachute School at Fort Benning. The second was activated on 30 December 1943 and originally contained 20 enlisted men and 6 officers, the majority transferring from the 92nd Infantry Division, then stationed at Fort Huachuca, Arizona. The unit designation for the second Test Platoon was 555th Parachute Infantry Company. The 555th was the Army's first and only all-black airborne unit. During its major action in World War II, Operation Firefly, the 555th (or "Triple Nickel") would initiate and refine special operations techniques still in use today.

On 18 February 1944, 16 of the 20 enlisted men completed airborne training and received their coveted jump wings. Two weeks later, on 4 March, the six officers followed suit. These men formed the company cadre. As new members of the company reported for training, the cadre rotated through specialized training courses, such as jumpmaster, pathfinder, rigger, demolitions, and communications. Many of the early noncommissioned officers attended Infantry Officer Candidate School and, once commissioned, returned to the 555th. When the company reached a strength of 7 officers and 119 enlisted men, it shifted from individual to unit training. The progression of training was typical for parachute units at the time, although in most other units soldiers went through the training as individual fillers and not as a group or unit.

Another significant difference in training that the 555th initiated was in moving the men through leadership positions. On virtually every training jump, a different tactical objective was included. Enlisted soldiers were rotated through as platoon and squad leaders as well as on weapons crews. Bradley Biggs, a platoon leader of the 555th, wrote later, "Over the period of these exercises each trooper had the opportunity to lead and command, and to learn each assignment in a crew-served weapons team. This leadership development made it possible for so many to be promoted." On 17 July, the company transferred to Camp Mackall, where it was assigned to the Army's Airborne Command. The size of the company continued to grow. On 9 November, the company was redesignated Company A, 555th Parachute Infantry Battalion, commanded by Captain James H. Porter. The battalion was authorized a strength of 29 officers and 600 enlisted men. Everyone in a leadership position moved up, squad leaders became platoon sergeants, platoon leaders and sergeants became company commanders and first sergeants, and so on.

Two events, separated by almost three years, came to bear on the history of the Triple Nickel. In Japan, the Doolittle raid on Tokyo and other cities in the home islands in April 1942 shocked the Japanese. Until then, they had believed the U.S. was not capable of invading the home islands. They began to make plans to avenge the insult committed by Doolittle and his raiders. They called this the "Fu Go weapons project."

Meanwhile, in Europe, Hitler launched his last fateful offensive, cutting through the American and British lines in the Ardennes Forest. The 82d and 101st Airborne divisions were badly chewed up by this battle and needed many replacements. The 555th was alerted for duty in Europe but only as a reinforced company with a strength of 8 officers and 160 enlisted men. This downgrading action was necessary because the 555th was below its authorized battalion strength and had not yet begun its battalion training. In April 1945, just as the skeletonized company was completing almost three solid months of training in the field and was ready to rotate to Europe, the German Army collapsed. By this time, however, another threat had developed. Later that month, the Triple Nickel was transferred to Pendleton, Oregon on a highly classified mission, Operation Firefly. Having already made its mark in airborne history, the 555th was about to stamp that mark in indelible ink. It would accomplish this by fighting behind the lines in the U.S. northwest.

Beginning in November 1944, the Japanese had started their campaign to make the United States pay for Doolittle's raid. This campaign consisted of sending balloons with incendiary bombs aloft so they would be carried by the prevailing upper winds (what we now call the jet stream) to America. Once over land the balloons would descend and drop their incendiary clusters. The Japanese believed most of these incendiaries would land in large

West Coast cities and cause great havoc. In reality, most of those that made it to the West Coast landed in uninhabited areas and became a serious problem for the U.S. Forest Service, whose job included fighting forest fires in National Parks and Forests.

The Forest Service had been created in 1905 by President Theodore Roosevelt and had begun fighting fires almost immediately. By 1925 it was using planes to spot fires and within four years was able to drop supplies from planes to fire fighters on the ground. In 1940, the first parachute jump was made on a forest fire. The following year, the U.S. Forest Service Smoke-jumpers were organized.

When the balloon bombs were first discovered, military intelligence officers noticed that the ballast bags contained sand. Samples of this sand were delivered in secret to scientists of the U.S. Geological Survey to see if it was possible for them to pinpoint either the balloon launch sites or, at least, the origin of the sand. Four scientists, Clarence S. Ross, Julia Gardner, Kenneth Lohmann, and Kathryn Lohmann, examined the sand. These scientists were able, based on unique mineralogical and paleontological assemblages, to confirm two likely sites on the east coast of Japan. Later aerial reconnaissance corroborated the exact location of the second site and it was subsequently bombed.

Working with the War Department, the Forest Service had been able to prevent any widespread reports about the balloon bombs, although some articles had appeared without attributing any cause to the fires. The Chief of the Forest Service, Lyle F. Watts, was interviewed on radio in late May 1945, describing the balloon bombs in some detail. What was not mentioned was the fear that the balloon bombs would be used to carry chemical or biological weapons. The presence of the Triple Nickel was also not mentioned.

The 555th initially set up its main camp at an inactive B-29 Army Air Corps Base outside Pendleton, located in northeastern Oregon, and immediately established a strenuous three-week training program for the battalion's soldiers with the Forest Service Smokejumpers. As the training progressed the men of the Triple Nickel modified their uniforms to make them more functional—and safer. A 50-foot length of nylon rope was added to assist them down from trees, a common hazard in forest jumps. The heavy, fleece-lined jacket and trousers of the Army Air Corps bomber crews were added next to provide padding for rough landings. Finally, they modified football helmets by adding wire mesh grills to the front to protect their face and eyes. Once on the ground, they donned gloves.

The major modification the paratroopers used was one designed by Frank Derry, one of the very first Smokejumpers. Derry had cut several panels out of the standard parachute and replaced one of the olive drab suspension lines with one made of white material. By pulling on the white shroud line, a jumper could turn in the air, to take advantage of the wind or nullify it. It was thus easier to pick out a place to land instead of being completely at the mercy of the wind. This is the first example of military use of steerable parachutes.

Within six weeks the entire battalion had qualified as Smokejumpers. During the training with their new chutes and modified clothing and equipment, the men of the 555th also worked with explosive ordnance disposal trainers to become familiar with disposal and disarming techniques. In mid July, about one-third of the battalion moved to an Army Air Corps Base at Chico, California. Splitting the unit provided wider coverage of forest area (for both fire and balloon bomb response) and better use of the skills of the paratroopers. Within a week of the move, each group had conducted its first jump into a fire area.

Once on the ground after a jump, the Triple Nickel took off the fleece-lined uniforms and picked up whatever gear was needed, either to fight a fire or work on a balloon bomb. Discarded uniforms, parachutes, and unneeded equipment were left on the drop zone to be picked up on the way back to camp.

One former member of the battalion described a fire operation this way: "Digging a fire break or clearing a zone to either isolate the fire or keep it from jumping is smoky business. We stank of smoke and fought to keep upwind of it. Team work was the key. Watching out for your team members, keeping together and not losing anyone in the smoke or darkness was the top priority. We worked hard and ate like horses, often five big meals a day. The forest rangers furnished most of our meals and water. We saved ours for emergency or exit use."

After a team arrived back at camp following a mission, battalion officers and NCOs conducted detailed debriefings of each member and filed after-action reports. The average mission was four to six days long. On several occasions the paratroopers jumped into Canada, trying to limit the fire from spreading to the U.S. Captain Bradley Biggs stated that, in the case of balloon bombs, "We blew up only those bombs that represented a danger." Those not blown in place were eventually turned over to an intelligence unit for exploitation.

One of the most interesting missions the Triple Nickel conducted during this period was to help train a group of U.S. Navy pilots who were preparing to go overseas. Captain Biggs and 54 paratroopers from his company were to jump before dawn onto a small drop zone and attack along a 15-mile route, calling in air support on a series of widely-separated targets and then assaulting each target with live ammunition. It was a mission that would task the hardiest paratrooper, lasting all day and with little room for error. Biggs said that "It had all the features of a combat mission except for a real enemy. There was the low altitude jump, full combat load, no ground support, and no DZ markers or pathfinders." For the Triple Nickel, it was yet another chance to excel.

Biggs and his executive officer, Jesse J. Mayes, spent one full day reviewing the plan and reconnoitering the route the men of the Triple Nickel would cover. The drop zone was 400 yards long and 50 yards wide, and located in the mountains. The route to the various targets was up and down hill the entire way. There was great potential that heat and terrain could take a heavy toll. Each man carried a double ammunition load, two canteens, medical supplies, a compass, and two C-ration meals along with his combat pack. Jump altitude was 800 feet, allowing little time to react to a problem or a malfunctioning chute, "under conditions as close to combat as we might see." Each plane would make two passes, with nine paratroopers exiting per plane on each pass.

The pre-dawn flight was very rough. Many of the paratroopers became sick before they felt the planes slowing down and descending as they neared the drop zone. Only one man was injured on the jump and had to be evacuated. The remainder headed for their first target, which they had to reach before the sun came up. They were in position and radioed the planes in as the dawn broke. For the rest of the day, the operation went according to plan.

Just prior to the eighth and final target, the Navy dropped a resupply of ammunition and water. This final target was within view of an observation post where several senior Navy officers watched the demonstration. Short of the target, the paratroopers laid out their two-feet by four-feet red marker panels and called in an air strike with rockets and napalm. In the follow-on ground attack, the men of the 555th fired off all their remaining ammunition.

Before the paratroopers departed the exercise area the Navy officers thanked them for their realistic support. "The commander of the naval fighter squadron was extremely complimentary. A job well done."

Between 14 July and 6 October, the Triple Nickel fought 36 fires (19 from Pendleton and 17 from Chico) and disarmed or destroyed an unknown number of Japanese balloon bombs. In all, the missions included over 1,200 individual jumps with only 30 jump-related injuries and 1 fatality. They conducted at least one demonstration jump, on 4 July in Pendleton. Operation Firefly was an unqualified success. Because the Japanese balloon bomb operation was classified, it was not until many years after the war that the real mission for this operation was known and the 555th Parachute Infantry Battalion could receive full credit. The contributions the battalion made to special operations rugged terrain jumping is obvious to anyone who conducts even a cursory review of today's techniques.

On 14 January 1946, by specific invitation of Major General James M. Gavin, commander of the 82d Airborne Division and of the parade ceremonies, the Triple Nickel took part in the World War II victory parade in New York City. The 555th marched as part of the 82d and was authorized by Gavin to wear unit decorations awarded to the "All-American" airborne division during the war, including the Belgian *forragère* and the Netherlands lanyard. Just prior to the parade, the 555th had been attached (not assigned) to the 82d for admin and training purposes, physically locating back to Fort Bragg.

By September 1947, the 555th was assigned to the 82d and redesignated as the 3rd Battalion, 505th Airborne Infantry Regiment, the regiment Gavin commanded during the combat parachute assaults in Sicily and mainland Italy in 1943. Gavin believed it was only right for his former unit to lead the division in setting the example for integration.

On 9 December 1947, Gavin took the final step, a full 7½ months before President Truman signed Executive Order 9981, ordering "equality of treatment and opportunity" for all members of the military forces, irrespective of race, color, religion, or national origin. On that day, Gavin signed an order integrating the 82d Airborne Division and moving the men of the Triple Nickel to various units within the division and division headquarters.

Mission Critique

While planning Operation Firefly, the Army had no choice but to conduct the mission, if for no other reason than to prevent panic in the public at large. If the Japanese balloon bombs could be rendered harmless and their existence kept quiet from the American and Canadian public, the operation would be a success.

The U.S. planners had two choices for Operation Firefly. They could use

Forest Service Smokejumpers to do it or a military parachute force. Using the Smokejumpers had at least two major problems: these civilian firefighters would have to receive extensive explosive ordnance disposal training and would, potentially, have to spend an unknown amount of time on the mission, time when they would not be available for fighting forest fires. This latter would require the Forest Service to hire additional people to take their place on the fire lines.

Using military parachute infantry forces, who already had training and experience in employing explosive ordnance was a more sensible choice for Firefly. These paratroopers would require training in disarming ordnance but their ramp up time would be a lot shorter than using Forest Service personnel. Additionally, their cover as Smokejumpers was perfect for their Firefly operations and was successful in preventing widespread knowledge of the existence of the balloon bombs. As shown, they helped develop a jump technique that is still used by special operations forces today, known as rugged terrain jumping.

Although the main discussion stresses the Triple Nickel's contribution to rugged terrain operations there is another contribution that this unit made. This one was not unique to the 555th; in fact, most of the better special operations units in World War II made a similar contribution to special operations doctrine. The 555th, however, did it better than anyone else. This contribution is the method of cross-training unit members in a variety of skills and in different leadership positions. This is one of the best methods for building unit cohesion. Without this kind of cohesion the members of the unit don't work as well together, don't reach the ultimate, at least in special operations, of working as a team. The two best examples of the team concept are the Alamo Scouts and the Triple Nickel; the SAS, Popski's Private Army, and the Jeds also demonstrate this quality well.

With this unit there are few examples from Vandenbroucke's criteria and most from McRaven's. One of the criteria from Vandenbroucke's list, *coordination*, is present in several positive aspects here since the Triple Nickel dealt with some interesting organizations, such as the U.S. Forest Service and its Smokejumpers, and the U.S. Navy. *Security*, one of McRaven's key criteria, was the hallmark of Operation Firefly; it was kept so secret that not until many years after the end of World War II was the role of the 555th revealed to the public at large. This same *security* prevented the Japanese from knowing how many of their balloons made it to North America, where they landed, and what damage they had done.

All things considered, the Triple Nickel was typical of the other special operations units in this study. They did the things that the best special operations units did—they got good people, planned good operations, and executed with skill and style. Both Vandenbroucke and McRaven would happily give high marks to this unit and its operations.

SOURCES

Books:

Biggs, Bradley; *The Triple Nickels—America's First All-black Paratroop Unit;* Archon Books; Hamden, CT; 1986

Hurst, Randle M.; *The Smokejumpers;* Caldwell, ID; Caxton Printers; 1966

Lee, Ulysses; *The Employment of Negro Troops;* from The U.S. Army in World War II series; Office, Chief of Military History, U.S. Army; Washington, DC; 1966; pages 160–161

Maclean, Norman; *Young Men and Fire;* Chicago; University of Chicago Press; 1992

Articles:

Author unknown; "555th Reunites at Bragg"; in *The Paraglide;* October 4, 1979

Author unknown; "Green Berets Up a Tree"; in *Soldier;* date unknown, page 27

Author unknown; "Old and New"; in *The Paraglide;* October 18, 1979; page 6A

Gidlund, Carl; "African-American Smokejumpers Help Celebrate Smokey's 50th"; in *Fire Management News*, a publication of the U.S. Forest Service, Department of Agriculture

McGee, Deidra L.; "Triple Nickels Help Smokey Bear Celebrate 50th"; in *Pentagram;* August 12, 1994; page 12

Morris, Boyd F.; 'Addendum to "The Triple Nickle [sic]"'; in *The Trading Post;* the publication of the American Society of Military Insignia Collectors; Winter (January–March 1993); page 72

Nakashima, Ellen; "'Triple Nickel' Adds Up To Respect—Black Paratroopers Recall WWII"; in *Washington Post;* August 17, 1995; pages B1 and B5

Ross, Daphne R.; "The 'Fu-Go' Project"; in Letters, *Washington Post;* date unknown

Whyte, Pauline T.; "The Triple Nickel—An All-black Parachute Infantry"; in *Chicago Defender*, a six part series published in September 1981

Plus numerous articles over the years appearing in "The Static Line," College Park, GA

EVALUATION CRITERIA

PRELIMINARY:
- Is the operation *necessary*?
- Does the operation fit in with the *objectives of the major area command*?
- Should *special operations forces be used* to conduct this mission or is it better executed by conventional forces?

VANDENBROUCKE:
- *Inadequate intelligence*, including of the objective and enemy forces defending it.
- *Poor coordination*, including lack of compatible equipment; getting one agency or service to be fully alert and responsive to the needs of another; difficulties by planners in understanding one another's standard operating procedures; and outright confusion and mutual mistrust.
- *Provision of faulty information to the national leadership*, including deliberately misleading information or one-sided information.
- *Wishful thinking*, including missions designed or evaluated on assumptions that had limited basis in fact; rejecting information that runs counter to hopes for success by the planners or decision makers; and the blind desire to see a proposed mission proceed and succeed.
- *Inappropriate intervention in mission execution*, including by the national leadership or higher military headquarters. This is a factor that I label as "the President as squad leader."

McRaven:

Planning phase:
- *Simplicity*: limiting the number of objectives; good intelligence; and innovation.

Preparation phase:
- *Security*: preventing the enemy from gaining an advantage through foreknowledge of the mission by concealing the timing and means of insertion.
- *Repetition*: honing routine skills to a degree that allows quick reaction to a threat, provided that threat fits within the standard scenario the unit has developed and practiced. Because special operations vary enough from the standard, new equipment and tactics must be employed. This necessitates at least one (but preferably two) full dress rehearsals prior to insertion.

Execution phase:
- *Surprise*: catching the enemy off guard through deception, timing, and taking advantage of his vulnerabilities.
- *Speed*: getting to the objective as fast as possible to prevent expanding ones area of vulnerability and decreasing ones opportunity to achieve relative superiority.
- *Purpose*: understanding and executing the prime objective of a mission regardless of emerging obstacles or opportunities.

OPERATIONS DESERVING SPECIAL RECOGNITION

Operation	Unit conducting	Date(s) of operation
Bruneval Raid	C Co, 2nd Para Bn (Br)	27–28 February 1942
Sidi Haneish Raid	1 SAS (Br.)	26–27 July 1942
Gran Sasso Raid	Elements of *Friedenthaler Jadgverbaende* (Ger)	12 September 1943
Merville Battery Raid	9th Bn, 3rd Para Bde (Br)	5–6 June 1944
Los Banos Raid	Several elements of 11th Abn Div (U.S.)	23 February 1945
Operation Firefly	555th Para Inf Bn (U.S.)	April–October 1945
Elephant Point Jump	Several elements of 44th Abn Div (India)	1 May 1945

UNITS DESERVING SPECIAL RECOGNITION
• Popski's Private Army (Br.), operating in Africa, Italy, Europe, 1942–45
• The Alamo Scouts (U.S.), operating in the Southwest
Pacific Theater, 1944–45

BIBLIOGRAPHY

Books, diaries, unpublished manuscripts:
Andrews, John; *Airborne Album—1943–1945—Normandy to Victory*; Phillips Publications; Williamstown, NJ; 1993
Autry, Jerry; *General William C. Lee—Father of the Airborne;* Raleigh, NC; Airborne Press; 1995
Baker, Alan D.; *Merrill's Marauders*; New York; Ballantine Books; 1972
"Basic Directive on Jedburghs, Prepared Jointly by SOE/SO"; dated 20 December 1943
Barbey, Daniel E.; *MacArthur's Amphibious Navy—Seventh Amphibious Force Operations 1943–1945*; Annapolis, MD; United States Naval Institute; 1969
Beaumont, Roger A.; *Military Elites—Special Fighting Units in the Modern World;* New York; Bobbs-Merrill; 1974
Bergen, Howard R.; *History of 99th Infantry Battalion—U.S. Army*; Oslo, Norway; Emil Moestue A-S; 1945
Biggs, Bradley; *The Triple Nickels—America's First All-black Paratroop Unit;* Archon Books; Hamden, CT; 1986
Black, Robert W.; *Rangers in World War II*; Ivy Books; New York; 1992
Blacker, Irwin R. (editor); *Irregulars, Partisans, Guerrillas—Great Stories From Rogers' Rangers to the Haganah;* New York; Simon and Schuster; 1954
Bonham, Frank; *Burma Rifles*; New York; Berkley Highland Books; 1960
Breuer, William B.; *The Great Raid on Cabanatuan—Rescuing the Doomed Ghosts of Bataan and Corregidor;* New York; John Wiley & Sons; 1994
————; *MacArthur's Undercover War—Spies, Saboteurs, Guerrillas, and Secret Missions*; New York; John Wiley & Sons; 1995
Brown, Anthony C. (editor); *The Secret War Report of the OSS*; New York; Berkley Publishing; 1976
Brown, Ashley and Jonathan Reed (editors); *The Commandos*; Harrisburg, PA; National Historical Society; 1986 (The Elite—The World's Crack Fighting Men, volume 2)
————; *Desert and Air Services*; Harrisburg, PA; National Historical Society;

1986 (The Elite—The World's Crack Fighting Men, volume 14)

—————; *The Unique Units*; Harrisburg, PA; National Historical Society; 1986 (The Elite—The World's Crack Fighting Men, volume 10)

Burford, John; *LRRPs in Action*; Carrolltown, TX; Squadron/Signal Publications; 1994

By Air to Battle—The Official Account of the British First and Sixth Airborne Divisions; London; His Majesty's Stationery Office; 1945

Calvert, Michael; *Fighting Mad*; New York; Bantam Books; 1964

Canon, M. Hamlin; *Leyte: The Return to the Philippines*; Washington DC; Office of the Chief of Military History (in the United States Army in World War II series); 1954

Chapman, F. Spencer; *The Jungle is Neutral;* New York; W.W. Norton; 1949

Cohen, Eliot A.; *Commandos and Politicians—Elite Military Units in Modern Democracies*; Harvard University (Harvard Studies in International Affairs, Number 40); 1978

Connell, Brian; *Return of the Tiger*; Garden City; Doubleday; 1960

Cook, Graeme; *Commandos in Action*; London; Hart-Davis MacGibbon; 1973

Cowles, Virginia; *The Phantom Major—The Story of David Stirling and the S.A.S. Regiment*; London; Collins; 1958

Crawford, Steve; *The SAS Encyclopedia*; Miami, FL; Lewis International; 1998

Crookenden, Napier; *Dropzone Normandy*; New York; Charles Scribner's Sons; 1976

Davis, Howard P.; *British Parachute Forces 1940–45*; New York; Arco Publishing; 1974

Deane-Drummond, Anthony; *Return Ticket;* London; Collins; 1952

Dear, Ian; *Subservion & Sabotage—Tales From the Files of the SOE and OSS*; London; Arms and Armour Press; 1996

Dilley, Michael F.; *GALAHAD—A History of the 5307th Composite Unit (Provisional);* Bennington, Vermont; Merriam Press; 1996

Dwyer, John B.; *Scouts and Raiders—The Navy's First Special Warfare Commandos*; Westport, CT; Praeger; 1993

Farrar-Hockley, Arthur H.; *Student*; New York; Ballantine Books; 1973 (Ballantine's Illustrated History of the Violent Century, War Leader book number 15)

Feldt, Eric A.; *The Coastwatchers*; Melbourne; Oxford University Press; 1946

Ferguson, Gregor; *The Paras—British Airborne Forces 1940–1989*; London; Osprey Publishing; 1984

Finnegan, John P.; *Military Intelligence—A Picture History*; U.S. Army Intelligence and Security Command; date unknown but around 1986

Flanagan, Edward M., Jr.; *The Angels—A History of the 11th Airborne Division 1943–1946*; Washington; Infantry Journal Press; 1948

—————; *The Los Banos Raid—The 11th Airborne Jumps at Dawn*; New York; Jove Books; 1986

Foley, Charles; *Commando Extraordinary*; London; Longmans, Green; 1954

Ford, Kirk, Jr.; *OSS and the Yugoslav Resistance*; Westport, CT; Praeger; 1992

Foxall, Raymond; *The Guinea Pigs—Britain's First Paratroop Raid;* London; Robert Hale; 1983

Frost, John; *A Drop Too Many*; London; Buchan & Enright; 1982

Gale, Richard N.; *With the 6th Airborne Division in Normandy;* London; Sampson, Low, Marston; 1948

Galvin, John R.; *Air Assault—The Development of Airmobile Warfare*; New York; Hawthorn Books; 1969

Garrett, Richard; *The Raiders—The Elite Strike Forces that Altered the Course of War and History*; New York; Van Norstrand Reinhold; 1980

George, Willis D.; *Surreptitious Entry;* Boulder, CO; Paladin Press; 1990

Geraghty, Tony; *This is the SAS—A Pictorial History of the Special Air Service Regiment*; London; Arms and Armour Press; 1982

General and Special Staff sections; *Report on the Luzon Campaign*; Sixth United States Army; undated

Giannaris, John with McKinely C. Olson; *Yannis*; Tarrytown, NY; Pilgrimage Publishing; 1988

Glantz, David M.; *The Soviet Airborne Experience*; Fort Leavenworth; U.S. Army Command and General Staff College; 1984

Gordon, John W.; *The Other Desert War—British Special Forces in North Africa, 1940–1943*; New York; Greenwood Press; 1987

Gregory, Howard; *Parachuting's Unforgettable Jumps*; La Mirada, CA; Howard Gregory Associates; 1974

Gregory, Barry; *British Airborne Troops 1940–45*; Garden City, NY; Doubleday; 1974

Grimes, Martin; *Turnip Greens and Sergeant Stripes*; New Rochelle, NY; Arlington House; 1972

Guthrie, Bennett M; *Three Winds of Death—The Saga of the 503rd Parachute Regimental Combat Team in the South Pacific*; Chicago; Adams Press; 1985

Gutjahr, Robert G.; *The Role of Jedburgh Teams in Operation Market Garden*; Master's Thesis for U.S. Army Command and General Staff College; Fort Leavenworth, KS; 1990

Haney, Ken; *U.S. Marine Corps Paratroopers, 1940–1945;* Jackson, TN; privately published; 1990

Harclerode, Peter; *Para! Fifty Years of the Parachute Regiment;* London; Arms and Armour Press; 1992

Heimark, Bruce H.; *The OSS Norwegian Special Operations Group in World War II*; Westport, CT; Praeger; 1994

Historical Branch, G-2, War Department; *Merrill's Marauders*; Washington; American Forces in Action Series; 1945 (reprinted in 1968 by Normount Armament Company, Forest Grove, OR, and edited by Donald B. McLean)

Hoare, Mike; *Mercenary*; New York; Bantam Books; 1967

Hochstrasser, Lewis B.; *They Were First—The True Story of the Alamo Scouts*; unpublished manuscript in author's collection; 1944

Hogan, David W., Jr.; *The Evolution of the Concept of the U.S. Army's Rangers, 1942–1983*; Duke University Doctoral Dissertation; 1986

——————; *U.S. Army Special Operations in World War II*; Washington; Center of Military History; 1992

Hoyt, Edwin P.; *Merrill's Marauders*; Los Angeles; Pinnacle Books; 1986

Hunter, Charles N.; *Galahad*; San Antonio, TX; Naylor; 1963

Hurst, Randle M.; *The Smokejumpers*; Caldwell, ID; Caxton Printers; 1966

Huston, James A.; *Out of the Blue—US Army Airborne Operations in World War II*; West Lafayette, IN; Purdue University Studies; 1972

Infield, Glenn B.; *Skorzeny—Hitler's Commando*; New York; St. Martin's Press; 1981

Ind, Allison; *Allied Intelligence Bureau—Our Secret Weapon in the War Against Japan*; New York; Curtis Books; 1958

Irwin, Wyman W.; *Special Force: Origin and Development of the Jedburgh Project in Support of Operation Overlord*; Master's Thesis for U.S. Army Command and General Staff College; Fort Leavenworth; 1991

James, Malcolm; *Born of the Desert;* London; Collins; 1945

Johnson, Forrest B.; *Hour of Redemption: The Ranger Raid on Cabanatuan*; New York; Manor Books; 1978

Kagan, Donald; *On the Origins of War and the Preservation of Peace;* New York; Doubleday; 1995

Karim, Afsir; *The Story of the Indian Airborne Troops*; New Delhi; Lancer International; 1993

Kay, R.L.; *Long Range Desert Group in the Mediterranean*; Wellington, NZ; War History Branch, Department of Internal Affairs; 1950 (New Zealand in the Second World War Official History)

King, Michael J.; *Rangers: Selected Combat Operations in World War II*; Combat Studies Institute (Leavenworth Papers, USCGSC); Fort Leavenworth; 1985

Krueger, Walter F.; *From Down Under to Nippon*; Combat Forces Press; Washington, DC; 1953

Kuhn, Volkmar; *German Paratroops in World War II*; London; Ian Allen; 1978 (translated from the German by H.A. and A.J. Barker)

Ladd, James; *Commandos and Rangers of World War II*; London; Macdonald and Jane's; 1978

——————; *SAS Operations*; London; Robert Hale; 1986

Lassen, Don and Richard K. Schrader; *Pride of America—An Illustrated History of the U.S. Army Airborne Forces*; Missoula MT; Pictorial Histories Publishing; 1991

Lee, Ulysses; *The Employment of Negro Troops*; from The U.S. Army in World War II series; Office, Chief of Military History, U.S. Army; Washington, DC; 1966; pages 160–161

Lewis, S.J.; *Jedburgh Team Operations in Support of the 12th Army Group, August 1944;*

Fort Leavenworth; Combat Studies Institute; 1990

Lucas, James E.; *Kommando—German Special Forces of World War Two*; London; Arms and Armour Press; 1985

MacDonald, Charles; *Airborne;* New York; Ballantine Books; 1970

Maclean, Norman; *Young Men and Fire*; Chicago; University of Chicago Press; 1992

Macksey, Kenneth; *Commando Strike—The Story of Amphibious Raiding in World War II*; London; Leo Cooper; 1985

Mason, Herbert M.; *The Commandos*; New York; Duell, Sloan and Pearce; 1966

Mattingly, Robert E.; *Herringbone Cloak—G.I. Dagger: Marines of the OSS*; Quantico, VA; Marine Corps Command and Staff College; 1979

McConnell, Zeke; *Diary—Alamo Scouts*; unpublished; 1944

McLean, Donald B. (ed.); *Japanese Parachute Troops*; Wickenburg, AZ; Normount Technical Publications; 1973

McMichael, Scott R.; *A Historical Perspective on Light Infantry*; Fort Leavenworth; Combat Studies Institute (Research Survey No. 6); 1987

McMillan, George; *The Old Breed—A History of the First Marine Division in World War II*; Infantry Journal Press; Washington, DC; 1953

McRaven, William H.; *Spec Ops—Case Studies in Special Operations Warfare: Theory and Practice*; Novato, Ca; Presidio Press; 1995

Mendelsohn, John (editor); *OSS Jedburgh Teams, Volumes I and II*; New York; Garland Publishing; 1989

Merrill's Marauders Association (ed.); *The Legacy of Merrill's Marauders*; Atlanta, GA; Turner Publishing; 1987

Messenger, Charles; *The Commandos, 1940–1946*; London; William Kimber; 1985
—————, George Young, and Stephen Rose; *The Middle East Commandos*; London; William Kimber; 1988

Millar, George; *The Bruneval Raid—Flashpoint in the Radar War*; London; The Bodley Head; 1974

Miller, John, Jr.; *Cartwheel: The Reduction of Rabaul;* Office of the Chief, Military History (United States Army in World War II—The War in the Pacific); Washington; 1959

Morison, Samuel E.; *Breaking the Bismarcks Barrier—22 July 1942–1 May 1944*; Boston; Little, Brown (History of the United States Naval Operations in World War II, Volume VI); 1950

Morris, Eric; *Churchill's Private Armies*; London; Hutchinson; 1986

Moser, Don; *China-Burma-India*; Alexandria, VA; Time-Life Books (World War II); 1978

Mrazek, James E.; *Fighting Gliders of World War II*; London; Robert Hale; 1977

Newnham, Maurice; *Prelude to Glory—The Story of the Creation of Britain's Parachute Army*; London; Sampson Low, Marston; 1946

Neild, Eric; *With Pegasus in India—The Story of 153 Gurkha Parachute Battalion*; Singapore; privately published by Jay Birch; undated

Niles, Gibson; *The Operations of the Alamo Scouts (Sixth U.S. Army Special Reconnaissance Unit)*; U.S. Army Infantry School; Fort Benning; 1948

Norton, G.G.; *The Red Devils—The Story of the British Airborne Forces*; Harrisburg, PA; Stackpole Books; 1971

Nowarra, Heinz J.; *German Gliders in World War II*; translated from German by Ed Force; West Chester, PA; Schiffer Publishing; 1991 (originally published as *Deutsche Lastensegler* by Podzun-Pallas Verlag, Friedberg)

Ogburn, Charlton; *The Marauders*; New York; Harper and Bros.; 1956 (reprinted in 1960 by The Quality Book Club, London)

Otway, Terence B.H.; *Airborne Forces*; London; Imperial War Museum Books (reprint of a volume in The Second World War, 1939–1945, Army series); 1990

——————— (unattributed); *By Air to Battle—The Official Account of the British Airborne Divisions*; London; His Majesty's Stationery Office; 1945

Padden, Ian; *U.S. Rangers*; New York; Bantam Books; 1985

Peniakoff, Vladimir; *Private Army*; London; Jonathan Cape; 1950

Powe, M.B. and E.E. Wilson; *The Evolution of American Military Intelligence;* U.S. Army Intelligence Center and School; 1973

Praval, K.C.; *India's Paratroopers—A History of the Parachute Regiment of India;* London; Leo Cooper; 1975

Pugh, Harry; *Rangers—United States Army—1756 to 1974;* unpublished manuscript

Raff, Edson D.; *We Jumped to Fight;* New York; Eagle Books; 1944

Randolph, John H.; *Marsmen in Burma*; Houston, TX; John H. Randolph; 1946

Reinhardt, Hellmuth et al; *Russian Airborne Operations*; Historical Division, HQ, USAREUR; 1952

Romanus, Charles F. and Riley Sunderland; *Stilwell's Command Problems*; Washington; Office of the Chief of Military History, Department of the Army (United States Army in World War II, China-Burma-India Theater); 1956

Rosignoli, Guido; *Army Badges and Insignia of World War 2*; New York; MacMillan; 1972

Rosner, Elliot J.; *THE JEDBURGHS: Combat Operations Conducted in the Finistere Region of Brittany, France from July–September 1944*; Master's Thesis for U.S. Army Command and General Staff College; Fort Leavenworth;

Ross, Bob; *Diary—Alamo Scouts, Sixth Army*; unpublished; 1945

Rottman, Gordon L.; *US Army Rangers & LRRP Units 1942–1987*; Osprey Publishing; London; 1987

——————— and Akira Takizawa; *Japanese Paratroop Forces in World War II*; New York; Osprey Publishing; 2005

Rounsaville, Tom J.; *The Operations of the Alamo Scouts (Sixth U.S. Army Special Reconnaissance Unit)*; U.S. Army Infantry School; Fort Benning; 1950

Ryan, Cornelius; *The Longest Day—June 6, 1944*; New York; Simon and Schuster; 1959

Sanderson, James Dean; *Behind Enemy Lines*; New York; Pyramid Books; 1959

Saunders, Hilary St. G.; *The Green Beret—The Story of the Commandos 1940–1945*; London; Michael Joseph; 1949

——————; *The Red Beret—The Story of the Parachute Regiment 1940–1945*; London; Michael Joseph; 1950

—————— (unattributed); *Combined Operations—The Official Story of the Commandos;* New York; MacMillan; 1943

Saunders, Pete; *Special Air Service;* London; Outline Publications; 1983

Short, James G.; *The Paras—The British Parachute Regiment;* London; Arms and Armour Press; 1985

——————; *The Special Air Service and Royal Marines Special Boat Squadron*; London; Osprey Publishing; 1981

Silver, Lynette R. and Tom Hall; *The Heroes of Rimau—Unraveling the Mystery of One of World War II's Most Daring Raids*; London; Leo Cooper; 1990

Sinclair, William B.; *Jungle, Paddy, and Mud—Heroes, Awarded and Unrewarded—Mud, Gravel, Ruts, and Rocks*; Coeur d'Alene, ID; Joe F. Whitley, Publisher; 1986

——————; *Under Wraps For Eyes Alone*; Coeur d'Alene, ID; Joe F. Whitley, Publisher; 1990

Skorzeny, Otto; *Skorzeny's Secret Missions—War Memoirs of the Most Dangerous Man in Europe;* translated from French by Jacques Le Clercq; New York; E.P. Dutton; 1950

——————; *Skorzeny's Special Missions*; London; Robert Hale; 1957

Smith, Bradley F.; *The Shadow Warriors—O.S.S. and the Origins of the C.I.A.*; New York; Basic Books; 1983

Smith, R. Harris; *OSS—The Secret History of America's First Central Intelligence Agency*; Berkeley; University of California Press; 1972

Smith, Robert R.; *The Approach to the Philippines*; Office of the Chief, Military History (United States Army in World War II—The War in the Pacific); Washington; 1953

——————; *Triumph in the Philippines*; Office of the Chief, Military History (United States Army in World War II—The War in the Pacific); Washington; 1963

Stanton, Shelby L.; *Order of Battle—U.S. Army, World War II*; Presidio Press; Novato, CA; 1984

——————; *Rangers at War—Combat Recon in Vietnam*; New York; Orion Books; 1992

Stone, James H. (editor); *Crisis Fleeting: Original Reports on Military Medicine in India and Burma in the Second World War;* Washington, DC; Office of the Surgeon General, Department of the Army; 1969

Swinson, Arthur; *The Raiders: Desert Strike Force*; New York; Ballantine Books; 1968

Thompson, Leroy; *British Paratroops in Action*; Carrollton, TX; Signal/Squadron Publications; 1989

—————; *Unfulfilled Promise—The Soviet Airborne Forces 1928–1945*; Bennington, VT; Merriam Press; 1988

Tugwell, Maurice; *Airborne to Battle—A History of Airborne Warfare 1918–1971*; London; William Kimber; 1971

Vandenbroucke, Lucien S.; *Perilous Options—Special Operations as an Instrument of U.S. Foreign Policy*; New York; Oxford University Press; 1993

War Report of the OSS, Volume 2—The Overseas Targets; New York; Walker Publishing; 1976

Warner, Philip; *The Special Air Service*; London; William Kimber; 1971

Whiting, Charles; *Skorzeny*; New York; Ballantine Books; 1972 (Ballantine's Illustrated History of the Violent Century, War Leader book number 11)

—————; *The War in the Shadows*; New York; Ballantine Books; 1973

Whittaker, Len; *Some Talk of Private Armies*; Harpenden, UK; Albanium Publishing; 1984

Wiggan, Richard; *Operation Freshman—The Rjukan Heavy Water Raid 1942*; London; William Kimber; 1986

Willett, John; *Popski—A Life of Vladimir Peniakoff*; London; MacGibbon & Kee; 1954

Wood, Alan; *History of the World's Glider Forces*; Wellingborough, UK; Patrick Stephens; 1990

Wright, Bertram C.; *The 1st Cavalry Division in World War II;* Tokyo; Toppan Printing; 1947

Yunnie, Park; *Warriors on Wheels*; London; Hutchinson; 1959

Zaloga, Steven J.; *Inside the Blue Berets—A Combat History of Soviet and Russian Airborne Forces, 1930–1995*; Novato, CA; Presidio Press; 1995

Zedric, Lance Q.; *The Alamo Scouts: Eyes Behind the Lines—Sixth Army's Special Reconnaissance Unit of World War II*; Western Illinois University Master's Thesis; 1993

—————; *Silent Warriors of World War II—The Alamo Scouts Behind Japanese Lines*; Ventura, CA; Pathfinder Publishing; 1995

————— and Michael F. Dilley; *Elite Warriors—300 Years of America's Best Fighting Troops*; Ventura, CA; Pathfinder Publishing; 1996

Articles, other papers:

Assistant Chief of Staff, G-3; "Combat Notes"; Headquarters Sixth Army; 21 March 1945

Author unknown; "555th Reunites at Bragg"; in *The Paraglide;* October 4, 1979

Author unknown; "Alamo Scouts Sixth Army"; date and source unknown

Author unknown; "British Airborne Assaults 1940–45"; in *WWII* magazine; July 1976; pages 14–21

Author unknown; "Enemy on Luzon—An Intelligence Summary; Chapter IV, Special Reconnaissance Operations"; source unknown

Author unknown; "The Execution of Il Duce"; *World War II*; April 1976

Author unknown; "The History of the American Ranger"; *The Static Line*; August 1979

Author unknown; "Green Berets Up a Tree"; in *Soldier;* date unknown, page 27

Author unknown; "Marauder—NCO Helped Clear Burma Trail"; *The Fayetteville Times*; September 16, 1974

Author unknown; "Merrill's Marauders"; *Infantry School Quarterly;* no date

Author unknown; "Old and New"; in *The Paraglide*; October 18, 1979; page 6A

Author unknown; "Ranger"; U.S. Army Infantry School; 1964

Author unknown; "Ranger Units' Lineage, Honors Go To 75th Ranger Regiment"; *Army* magazine; June 1986

Author unknown; "The Saga of Bill Nellist—Alamo Scout"; in *Airborne Quarterly*; Spring 1991

Author unknown; *Trading Post* magazine (American Society of Military Insignia Collectors); issues of April–June 1975 and January–March 1979

Brumfield, Ruby G.; "Rodriquez Recalls Burma Mission"; *Army Reserve* magazine; Fall 1981

Bruske, Ed; "The Spirit of the Jeds"; *The Washington Post*; 14 May 1988; Style Section, pages C1–C2

Chronis, Peter G.; "Alamo Scouts: Masters of Stealth"; in *The Denver Post*; October 5, 1993

Connery, George; "The Inside Story of Merrill's Marauders in the Burma Jungle"; *The Washington Post*; eight part article appearing September 14–21, 1944

Dilley, Michael F. and Lance Q. Zedric; "The Recon of Los Negros"; in *Behind The Lines;* May–June 1995

Donaldson, Graham; "The Japanese paratroopers in the Dutch East Indies, 1941–1942"

Dontsov, I. and P. Livotov; "Soviet Airborne Tactics"; in *Military Review*; October 1964

Evans, Hoyte; "Popski's Private Army Cap Badge"; *Trading Post* magazine; date unknown

Foss, Peter J.; "'Angels' at Los Banos"; *Infantry*; unknown issue

Fugelman; "Beyond the Last Blue Mountain"; *Combat Illustrated* magazine; April 1981

Gabbett, Michael; "The Merrill's Marauders Patch"; *The Static Line*; November 1993

Garland, Al; "Alamo Scouts Played Vital Role in War"; in *The Benning Leader;* September 10, 1993

Gately, Matthew J.; "Soviet Airborne Operations in World War II"; in *Military Review*; January 1967

Gidlund, Carl; "African-American Smokejumpers Help Celebrate Smokey's 50th"; in *Fire Management News*, a publication of the U.S. Forest Service, Department of Agriculture

Hemingway, Al; "Brilliant Feat of Arms"; *World War II* magazine; September–October 1993

Hill, Adrian; "Where Pegasus Might Fly"; in *Journal of the Royal United Services Institute for Defence Studies*; June 1979; pages 45–52

Hughes, Les; "The Alamo Scouts"; in *Trading Post*; April–June 1986

—————; "Insignia of the OSS"; in *The Trading Post*; April–June 1993; pages 2–19

—————; "The Special Force Wing"; in *The Trading Post*; July–September 1988; pages 4–15

—————; "The Special Allied Airborne Reconnaissance Force"; in *Trading Post*; July–September 1991; pages 7–20

Hurwitt, David; Executive Secretary, Merrill's Marauders Association; letter to author; May 19, 1976

Johnson, Raymond and Alfred Hahn; "Alamo Scouts, U.S. 6th Army—1943–1945"; in *Company of Military Historians*; Plate 499

Johnson, Thomas M.; "The Most Dangerous Man in Europe"; *Reader's Digest*; March, 1949

Levins, Harry; "Merrill's Marauders Remember"; *St. Louis Post-Dispatch*; September 10, 1981

Lindsey, Beverly; "CSM Galen C. Kittelson Retires—Last of the Alamo Scouts"; in *Static Line*; probably September or October 1978

Margry, Karel; "Tragino 1941: Britain's First Paratroop Raid"; in *After The Battle*; unknown issue; pages 8–29

McCracken, W.W. and A. A. Littman; "The Alamo Scouts"; in *Trading Post*; April–June 1963

McGee, Deidra L.; "Triple Nickels Help Smokey Bear Celebrate 50th'; in *Pentagram*; August 12, 1994; page 12

McMichael, Scott R.; "Common Man, Uncommon Leadership: Colonel Charles N. Hunter with GALAHAD in Burma"; *Parameters*; Summer 1986

Mehle, Michael; "25 WWII Veterans Gather to Remember Their Alamo"; *Rocky Mountain News*; October 2, 1993

Morris, Boyd F.; 'Addendum to "The Triple Nickle [sic]"'; in *The Trading Post*, the publication of the American Society of Military Insignia Collectors; Winter (January–March 1993); page 72

Mucci, Henry A.; "We Swore We'd Die or Do It"; in *The Saturday Evening Post*; April 7, 1945

Nabbie, Eustace E. (pseud. Mayo S. Stuntz); "The Alamo Scouts"; in *Studies in Intelligence*; date unknown

Nakashima, Ellen; "'Triple Nickel' Adds Up To Respect—Black Paratroopers Recall WWII"; *The Washington Post*; August 17, 1995; pages B1 and B5

Pames, George; "The Great Cabanatuan Raid"; in *Air Classics;* two issues, date unknown but probably 1981–1984

Pitt, Barrie; "The Keyes Raid" in *War Monthly*; March 1980; pages 34–39

Pugh, Harry; Chute & Dagger Newsletter, Number 7

Ramirez, Roland J.; "British Airborne Forces"; in *World War II Journal*; Volume 2, Number 3; pages 50–51

Raymond, Allen; "Team of Heroes: The Alamo Scouts"; in *The Saturday Evening Post*; June 30, 1945

Reinhardt, Hellmuth; "Encirclement at Yukhnov: A Soviet Airborne Operation in World War II"; *Military Review*; May 1963

Ross, Daphne R.; "The 'Fu-Go' Project"; in Letters, *The Washington Post*; date unknown

Sa'adah, David M.; "Friendly Fire: Will We Get It Right This Time?"; Washington; Office of the Surgeon General, US Army; 1992

Sackton, Frank J.; "Southwest Pacific Alamo Scouts"; in *Armored Cavalry Journal*; January–February 1947

Shelton, George R.; "The Alamo Scouts"; in *Armor*; September–October 1982

Smith, Philip R., Jr.; "Jungle Fighters"; *Army Digest* magazine; May 1971

Spencer, Murlin; "Saga of the Alamo Scouts"; *The Detroit Free Press*; October 15, 1944

Stone, James, H.; "The Marauders and The Microbes"; *Infantry Journal* magazine; March 1949

Sutton, B.J.; "Merrill's Marauders"; *Infantry* magazine; November–December 1969

Taylor, Blaine; "Skorzeny—Germany's Classic Commando"; *Soldier of Fortune;* two-part series, June and July 1985

Turbiville, Graham H.; "Soviet Airborne Troops"; in *Military Review*; April 1943

—————; "Soviet Airborne Forces: Increasingly Powerful Factor in the Equation"; in *Army;* April 1976

Vail, Jason; "Raiders Clockwork Plan"; in *World War II* magazine; date unknown

Wellington, Mike; "The Australian Mounted Z-Force's Kayak Raid on Singapore was Totally Unexpected"; *World War II* magazine (volume 4, number 2)

Wells, Billy E, Jr.; "The Alamo Scouts—Lessons for LRSUs"; in *Infantry;* May–June 1989

Whyte, Pauline T.; "The Triple Nickel—An All-black Parachute Infantry"; in *Chicago Defender*, a six part series published in September 1981

Wukovits, John F.; "Marauders Trail of Fire"; *World War II* magazine; March 1989

Zedric, Lance Q.; "Prelude to Victory—The Alamo Scouts"; in *Army;* July 1994

————— and Michael F. Dilley; "Raid on Oransbari"; in *Behind The Lines*; November–December 1995

Numerous unsigned articles over the years appearing in "The Static Line," College Park, GA.

Interviews and letters with:

Calvin W. Byrd (interview on June 2, 1995; letters on July 9 and 26, August 23, and
    September 15, 1995)
R.J. Crawford in Scotland (letters)
R.D. Davidson in New Zealand (letters)
Peter G. de Lotz in London (letters)
Alva E. Gipe (interview on June 2, 1995; letter on August 9, 1995)
Rudolph A. Horak (interview on June 2, 1995; letters on July 12 and October 9,
    1995)
Philip D. Julian in England (letters)
Galen C. Kittleson (several interviews between 1992 and 1999)
William Nellist (several interviews in 1992 and 1995)
Doris Root (letter on Aug 3, 1995)
Tom J. Rounsaville (several interviews in 1992, 1995, and 1998)
Andy Smith (several interviews in 1992, 1995, and 1998)
Henry E. Staudt (interview on June 2, 1995; letter undated, received about July 18,
    1995 and letter dated November 13, 1995)
Robert S. Sumner (several letters and interviews between 1992 and 1999)
Mayo S. Stuntz (several interviews in 1992, 1995, and 1998)
Terry Santos (several interviews and letters between 1992 and 2001)

Other:

1967 Yearbook of the 173rd Airborne Brigade; publisher unknown; the introduction
    includes a brief history of the 503rd

The author is greatly indebted for the loan of interview material provided by George
F. Cholewczynski, which included interviews between Mr. Cholewczynski and Akira
Takizawa; this material provided much of the detail of the Palembang operation.

Portions of this book were previously published in slightly different versions:

The Tragino Aqueduct Mission, published under the same title in *Behind The Lines*,
    Online Issue #2, 1999
The Raid to Kill Rommel, published under the same title in *Behind The Lines*, May–
    June 1997
Stealing Henry, first published in a shorter version as "British Raid German Radar
    Site" in *Impact*, November 1978 and as "OPSEC for Stealing Henry" in *OPS
    News*, March 1995; later in longer versions as "OPSEC for Stealing Henry" in
    The OPSEC Journal, Second Edition, 1995 and as "Stealing Henry" in *Behind
    The Lines*, January–February 1996

The Great Jeep Raid, first published in a shorter version as "Desert Operation Nets Big Payoff" in *Impact*, December 1978; later in a longer version as "The Great Jeep Raid" in *Behind The Lines*, November–December 1992

Popski's Private Army: Spreading Alarm and Despondency, published as "Popski's Private Army" in *Behind The Lines*, March–April 1993

Popski's Private Army: Hide and Seek, published as "Popski's Private Army, Part II: Hide and Seek" in *Behind The Lines*, January–February 1994

The Amphibious Scouts, published under the same title in *Behind The Lines*, May–June 1996

Operation Jaywick, published under the same title in *Behind The Lines*, March–April 1996

Alamo Scouts: Alamo Scouts Training Center, published as "Training the Alamo Scouts" in *Behind The Lines*, March–April 1995 and as "The Alamo Scouts: World War II's LURPs" in *Patrolling*, June 1997

Alamo Scouts: Sumner Team at Pegun Island, published as "Sumner Team at Pegun Island" in *Behind The Lines*, May–June 1997

Alamo Scouts: Nellist and Rounsaville Teams at Cabanatuan first published in a shorter version as "Rescue at Cabanatuan" in *Behind The Lines*, September–October 1993

The Jedburgh Project, published under the same title in *Behind The Lines*, March–April 1997

Battle at Merville Battery, first published in a shorter version as "The Battle for Merville Battery" in *Impact*, January 1979

OSS Operations Groups published under the same title in *Behind The Lines*, Online Issue #1, 1999

Breaking and Entering, published under the same title in *Behind The Lines*, September–October 1996 and in *The OPSEC Journal*, Fourth Edition, 1998

Rescue at Gran Sasso, published under the same title in *Behind The Lines*, July–August 1993

The Triple Nickel, published under the same title in *Behind The Lines*, November–December 1996

INDEX